The Genealogy of National Socialism

Philosophical Foundations and Intellectual Precursors

Jake Leone

Copyright © 2025 by Jake Leone

All rights reserved.

No portion of this book may be reproduced in any form without written permission from the publisher or author, except as permitted by U.S. copyright law.

Contents

Introduction	1
1. Johann Gottlieb Fichte	4
2. Ernst Moritz Arndt	86
3. Johann Gottfried Herder	130
4. Friedrich List	172
5. Richard Wagner	203
6. Friedrich Wilhelm Joseph Schelling	243
7. The Völkisch Movement	254

Introduction

National Socialism did not randomly form in an intellectual vacuum outside of longstanding philosophical tradition, nor can its philosophical structure be adequately represented through an examination of history or political circumstance alone. There is no shortage of scholars who have researched the NSDAP as a historical entity, but the philosophical structure that formed its worldview remains insufficiently researched. This work intends to address this major gap through tracing the primary philosophical drivers as they developed over more than a century, culminating in their formal synthesization with Rudolf Jung in 1922.

It is for this reason that this book is not a political history of the National Socialist state, nor is it a moral indictment of its ideology, but rather a philosophical genealogy that examines the development, transformation, and systematization of thought within the specific intellectual tradition of National Socialism. Through a focus on the evolution of concepts such as nationhood, statecraft, moral duty, organic community, culture, freedom, and destiny, it can be seen how these ideas were gradually reorganized and recontextualized into a complete and coherent worldview.

Many concepts could be argued to have originated more immediately from diverse sources, but that speaks little to the development of the philosophy itself, which is the objective of this publication.

My previous publication on the subject, titled *National Socialism: A Comprehensive Examination*, extensively analyzes the primary sources that outline National Socialist doctrine itself, illuminating a consistent and logically interdependent worldview that clearly amounts to more than a reactionary political system. Through the examination of figures such as Johann Gottlieb Fichte and Johann Gottfried Herder, the core essence and moral idealism inherent to National Socialism can be seen originating in the philosophical rejection of the Kantian perspective, as well as in the historical circumstances, such as the Napoleonic conquest, that led to the formation of such ideas. From these foundations emerged a new stream of Romantic and nationalist thought, shaped by thinkers such as Ernst Moritz Arndt, Friedrich List, Richard Wagner, and Friedrich Wilhelm Joseph Schelling, who all contributed unique but overlapping elements to the nationally oriented worldview that would later become National Socialism.

The purpose of this research is therefore not to collapse all of these diverse streams of thought into a single worldview, but instead to emphasize the points of deviation, transformation, and synthesis, identifying the distinction between philosophical influence and the realization of such in practice. Additionally, due to the intended scope of this publication, extended treatments of certain subjects, such as racial science and theology, must be set aside for further investigation, so as to examine the primary philosophical structure on its own terms, without the inclusion of later advancements in biological sciences. This is important because even the NSDAP themselves recognized the developing nature of biological sciences and sought those elements that would uphold the core philosophical tradition as outlined in this book. Each chapter examines a philosopher or movement on its own terms and further situates it within the broader development of the environment from which National Socialism would emerge. It cannot be said that National Socialism is constrained to historical precedent or that it fails to live up to the title of a true philosophy, as it is clearly intentionally composed from longstanding European philosophical tradition and seeks to adhere to reason, thereby structuring a coherent system that defines and systematizes the nation and the organic world around it as an integrated totality of life.

Chapter 1
Johann Gottlieb Fichte

Johann Fichte(1762-1814) was once claimed by Rudolf Jung, a key early National Socialist ideologue, in 1919 to be a primary forerunner of National Socialism, where he was developing and teaching "nothing other than National Socialism". This statement, made in Jung's work *Der Nationale Sozialismus*, retroactively places Fichte within the intellectual genealogy of a movement that would not fully form until decades after Fichte's death. There is little doubt that Fichte stands as one of the most closely aligned philosophers with what would later develop into National Socialism, with much of his ideological underpinnings feeding into the spirit and logic of the later movement.

Despite this glowing commendation by Jung, Fichte's philosophy fails to match National Socialism in depth, stopping shy of directly recognizing the biological underpinnings which precede individual behavior and interpersonal communication. This is a rather significant difference because of the extreme emphasis National Socialist philosophy places on the racial construct of the nation. Besides this important differentiation, and a few more minor ones mostly resulting from Fichte's drastic idealism, it can be easily understood why the two would be connected in both spirit and ideal, as Fichte did recognize the importance of the nation, albeit in a more indirect way, laying the proto-nationalistic foundation for National Socialism to later develop upon.

Some scholars have gone as far as to deem it to be "preposterous" to regard Fichte as any sort of precursor to National Socialism, instead placing him alongside other thinkers who are claimed to be irrelevant to the question, like Plato and Thomas More.[1] This claim collapses once confronted with the primary evidence, with Jung directly citing Fichte as an integral part of National Socialism's intellectual lineage.

While Jung's invocation of Fichte was selective and strategically rearranged, the fact that he used Fichte at all demonstrates that Fichte was received as part of the intellectual genealogy of National Socialist thought, regardless of whether such readings were philosophically justified or not.

Moreover, Fichte's early vision of a moral state tasked with shaping virtuous citizens, and his rejection of Enlightenment cosmopolitanism in favor of national renewal, mirror themes that would later be adopted by National Socialist thinkers. While it could be argued that much of National Socialist philosophy can be traced to Fichte, his writings are relatively diverse, which some researchers suggest allowed for the theoretical isolation and adoption by those who resonated with some of the ideological objectives.[2] It is due to this massive impact that Fichte had on the development of National Socialism that his ideas and contributions will be examined first and to the greatest extent.

"We are accused of not having a doctrinal system such as that possessed by Marxism. But is that necessary? What our forebears forged and created, what Fichte, Friedrich List, and Adolf Wagner taught, was nothing other than National Socialism. We could also call it German Socialism, because the ideas and emotions which live within it are tied to no other Volk so intimately as they are to ours."[3]

Johann Gottlieb Fichte (1762–1814) was born into a modest family in Upper Lusatia, Saxony, which is now modern-day Germany, and showed great academic promise early on, studying theology at the University of Jena and Leipzig University. Initially drawn to the clergy, Fichte's early theological interests were later supplanted by his early engagement with Enlightenment rationalism, along with the critical philosophy of Immanuel Kant. He rose to prominence in German academia through his thoughtful reformulation of Kantian idealism.

Recent scholarship points toward works such as *The Contribution of the Correction of the Public's Judgement on the French Revolution*, along with his lectures on the scholars vocation, where scholars claim that he took up an Enlightenment-humanist and vaguely minarchist position. According to this early position of Fichte, the state exists only as a means to establish a perfect society, after which it withers due to the growing lack of necessity.[4] Additionally, in his article "The Paradox of Fichte's Nationalism," Hans Kohn points to Fichte's early inclination toward political cosmopolitanism, using Fichte's self-identification as a young man who had "abandoned his fatherland" and felt to be bound to no state.[5] The stark contrast between these early examples of Fichte's work and that which surfaced during his most fervently nationalistic years demonstrates the fault in claims that it was the totality of Fichte that developed into National Socialist thought. Despite his ideological shifts across his lifetime, Fichte maintained that the state exists to serve personal freedom, along with the right of popular revolution against an unjust state, demonstrating that his 1794 addresses did not simply erase his prior logical commitments.[6]

As he grew older, his approach developed into a form of philosophical nationalism that blended civic duty with spiritual unity and the development of the moral population. German Idealists of Fichte's generation thought that Immanuel Kant had clung too close to the strict scientific methods of system building and universal rationalism, and instead worked to merge German thought and German national destiny, even in ways that could be seen as intangible.[7] In 1794, Fichte was appointed a position as a professor of philosophy at the University of Jena, where he completed one of his most well known works, *Wissenschaftslehre (Science of Knowledge)*, ushering in the era of German idealism. During this earlier period, Fichte was focused on developing students into morally responsible citizens, delivering lectures that marked the beginning of his shift away from pure individualism toward a philosophy grounded in the community.[8] This is recognized as a turning point toward a model which contends that the moral structure of society precedes the formal authority of the state, developing alongside his ideological trend toward a socially embedded position.[9]

The philosophical method that he presented, which is rooted in the self and its interaction with all that exists outside of the self, would eventually influence other thinkers such as Hegel, some of which would also come to contribute to the development of National Socialist philosophy, although none as notably as Fichte. His emphasis on autonomy, moral law, and national unity laid a foundation for the collective idealism that National Socialism would later appropriate, though with different premises and ends.

During the Napoleonic occupation of German lands, Fichte shifted his focus from the more abstract epistemology to the practical, emerging as a clear national moralist. His famous *Reden an die deutsche Nation (Addresses to the German Nation)*, delivered at the

Academy of Sciences Berlin between 1807 and 1808 under French rule, called for a spiritual and cultural rebirth of the German people. In these addresses, Fichte articulated the essential elements of what would later be understood as German idealist nationalism, where he primarily considered the nation to be bound by language, culture, shared education, and a common guiding morality. These lectures became foundational to later conceptions of German identity, especially during the 19th-century rise of romantic nationalism.

The vague notion of Germanness is a common point that is attacked by some scholars who assert that it fails to adequately explain the reasoning behind why such a linguistic quality should belong to Germans alone, amounting to a baseless assertion instead of a demonstrated piece of logic.[10] Patriotic thought is hardly new, even in Fichte's age, and was even carried into the NSDAP, despite the focus on the nation in principle under National Socialism. Certainly, Jung also carried over this patriotic, rather than nationalistic, vocabulary on occasion as well as many other prominent National Socialist authors which convoluted the distinction between the two.

Politically speaking, Fichte was neither a liberal nor a reactionary in the conventional sense, as he overwhelmingly rejected individualism and the liberal conception of natural rights, envisioning the state as a moral institution whose purpose is not merely administrative or protective, but also educational and transformative, tasked with shaping the character of its citizens through educational systems and moral cultivation. Simultaneously, he opposed feudalism and, in his later economic works, specifically *Der geschlossene Handelsstaat* (*The Closed Commercial State*), continued to advocate for a strictly regulated, self-sufficient economy guided by ethical and national interests, asserting that only a closed economy could fully allow for moral development, social cohesion, and national independence. This position blatantly stands in contrast to the doctrines of free trade and laissez-faire capitalist practices.

Fichte considered *The Closed Commercial State* one of his best works, where a fully regulated national economy was proposed, whose prices, currency, and means of exchange were placed under state authority. The grain-based monetary model, national currency system, and deliberate commercial isolation reflected aspects of the economic practices at play throughout Revolutionary France, demonstrating that the French influence on Fichte was notable and not simply a catalyst for reaction as many assert.[11]

The philosophy of Fichte is heavily anchored in his reformulation of Kantian idealism, where the self-positing "I" (Ich) functions as the creative center of all experience and moral action. In his *Wissenschaftslehre*, it is asserted that the ego posits not only itself, but also that which composes the non-ego, functioning as a form of dialectical self-conscious limitation. Through this act of self-positing, the individual constitutes both the subject and the object, internally constructing moral laws based on the natural stance of the self. Due to the I positing itself, Fichte recognized it to be free, and thus responsible for that freedom, requiring self imposed limitations and an intersubjective sense of duty that are necessary conditions of existence. For Fichte, individual freedom is not a license to act arbitrarily, but instead imposes the heavy burden of a standard of behavior that is in accordance with reason and a self-recognized duty.

"But if a rational individual, or a person, is to find himself as free, then something more is required, namely, that the object in experience that is thought of through the concept of the person's efficacy actually correspond to that concept; what is required, therefore, is that something in the world outside the rational individual follow from the thought of his activity. Now if, as is certainly the case, the effects of rational beings are to belong within the same world, and thus be capable of influencing, mutually disturbing, and impeding one another, then freedom in this sense would be possible for persons who stand with one another in this state of mutual influence only on the condition that all their efficacy be contained within certain limits, and the world, as the sphere of their freedom, be, as it were, divided among them. But since these beings are posited as free, such a limit could not lie outside freedom, for freedom would thereby be nullified rather than limited as freedom; rather, all would have to posit this limit for themselves through freedom itself, i.e. all would have to have made it a law for themselves not to disturb the freedom of those with whom they stand in mutual interaction."[12]

This concept of an autonomous moral obligation that is inherent to freedom is clearly carried over into National Socialism, where the concept of freedom is nearly directly taken from Fichte's assertions and weighed almost immediately against its utility to the Volksgemeinschaft, the greater national-racial community. Unless one lives entirely alone with no other human contact, even indirect contact, there will be forms of community interaction and engagement that a person must entertain to a certain extent. Fichte recognized that this community is populated not by inanimate objects without will, but rather by other rational beings with their own sense of self, and an equal longing for freedom. Through this realization, it becomes clear that the freedom of others can be limited by our actions, just as our freedom can be limited by the actions of others.

Fichte argued that a collective agreement amongst the community is needed to maximize individual freedom through self imposed standards of conduct. Through the individual's application of free will as applied to self imposed limitations, the community can "stand in mutual interaction" where greater freedom is permitted through collaboration. Through the recognition of personal freedom by another and the reciprocation of that recognition, a person can become a full legal and moral individual according to Fichte. He urged that all members of the nation must "take pains first of all to better yourself and then better your neighbor," reconciling national cosmopolitanism with an inwardly focused ethic of communal improvement.[13]

"But the postulated coexistence of the freedom of several beings — and this obviously means enduring coexistence in accordance with a rule, not merely coexistence here and there by chance — is possible only insofar as each free being makes it a law for himself to limit his freedom through the concept of the freedom of all others."[14]

This concept was clearly carried over into National Socialism, as in 1934 Jacob Otto Dietrich, a German SS officer and Press Chief of the NSDAP, made the following statement in a lecture delivered at the University of Köln:

"So-called individual freedom is not something that would in any way be given to man from nature. From nature is given to man community-consciousness, consciousness of duty toward the community in which he is born. The individualistic concept of freedom however wants to liberate the individual from this duty toward the community."[15]

Within National Socialism, freedom is no longer an intersubjective recognition of moral autonomy, but rather a construct grounded in biological determinism. The collectivist spirit of Fichte is retained, but its basis shifts from a focus on idealist ethics to the immutable characteristics of race. This was not a single statement by a single officer either, but instead reflected a broader philosophical framework underpinning the community and the organization of the nation under National Socialism. The exact same concept was presented by Adolf Hitler in Berlin on May 1, 1939:

"Liberty? Insofar as the interests of the Volksgemeinschaft permit the exercise of liberty by the individual, he shall be granted this liberty. The liberty of the individual ends where it starts to harm the interests of the collective. In this case the liberty of the Volk takes precedence over the liberty of the individual."[16]

There was no notable development upon this base concept of an entangled web of individual freedoms encased within moral obligation by National Socialism, but the limits of the web itself were clarified through a more rigid and biologically defined interpretation of the construct of the nation, which will be examined later. It should be recognized that National Socialism seeks to safeguard the standing of the nation and guarantee its continuation, which is ultimately the protection of the freedoms inherent to the continued existence of the people. In this sense, National Socialism views freedom more in the light of collective survival rather than personal autonomy. For this reason, at the very core of National Socialism we find Fichte's concept of the self built upon the foundation of the natural human drive for self-preservation and genetic continuation. Reproduction and meaningful development absolutely require interpersonal contact, drawing the need for a stable societal order.

Below, Fichte recognizes the individual as subservient to the greater community, where both thought and action should be unified in a way that conforms to the limitations necessary for a positive interpersonal exchange. Additionally, it should be noted that he understood that it was more a natural unity, not mere circumstance, that binds individuals, demarcating a community. Here, Fichte's recognition of the developmental properties of the community lends fuel to the National Socialist development of the biological perspective, although in many instances it is relatively unclear how much of the nation he believed to be bound by descent, rather than by language, culture, and morality.

"I must think of myself as necessarily in community with other human beings with whom nature has united me, but I cannot do this without thinking of my freedom as limited through their freedom; now I must also act in accordance with this necessary thought, otherwise my acting stands in contradiction with my thinking, and thus I stand in contradiction with myself; I am bound in conscience, by my knowledge of how things ought to be, to limit my freedom."[17]

National Socialism recognizes the nature that unites the community as described by Fichte to be eternal laws rooted in blood. This is where we see the logical continuation of Fichte's philosophy, as National Socialism recognizes a need to clearly and unmistakably outline both the nation and the concept of freedom as it pertains to the natural inclinations of the population. National Socialism recognizes how intimately connected genetic composition and proclivities are, directly tying the community's concept of freedom to the natural state of the people.

"National Socialism serves eternal laws. This requires acceptance of the eternal laws to unselfishly serve the community and the welfare of the German nation and to live according to the eternal laws of our blood as they are expressed in the National Socialist Weltanschauung."[18]

It can be seen in the quote below, coming from Fichte's *Addresses to the German Nation*, a recognition of the need for state intervention within the field of culture, specifically in the protection of higher cultural expression. He asserted that this protection should be offered even if the state were to be inconvenienced throughout the process, positioning the development of national culture above the self-serving desires of the state. Fichte's organization of freedom, focusing on the development of the moral self through positive and self-limiting interactions, reveals a convergence of philosophy with National Socialism, where the state is emphasized to be a cultural and ethical agent.

"It is only the higher view of the human race and of peoples which extends this narrow calculation. Freedom, including freedom in the activities of external life, is the soil in which higher culture germinates; a legislation which keeps the higher culture in view will allow to freedom as wide a field as possible, even at the risk of securing a smaller degree of uniform peace and quietness, and of making the work of government a little harder and more troublesome."[19]

Freedom is thus understood in the context of the greater society, leading toward the development of what National Socialism frequently refers to as genuine socialism. This genuine socialism, as outlined by National Socialism, is simply the logical continuation of nationalism, where the best interests of the community are held to a higher regard than individual desire that is counterproductive to the greater community. This understanding of socialism forces the distinction between socially conscious action and antisocial action driven by selfish desire, and is precisely the tradeoff Fichte asserted in his formulation of individual freedom. He recognized that all people in a society seek to live as pleasantly as possible and that all people have an equal right to make the demand for such as human beings, as all are maintaining their own sense of self and equally must navigate the exchange of that which they are capable of doing and that which corresponds with the socially binding contract.

"The sphere of free acts, therefore, will be divided up among the individuals through a treaty of all with all, and this division will give rise to property. Yet how must this division be made if it is to accord with the law of Right? Or is it enough simply to divide things up, however this division may turn out? We shall see. The purpose of all human activity is to be able to live. All those whom nature has put to life have the same rightful claim to this possibility of life. Therefore, the division must first of all allow everyone to exist. Live and let live!

Everyone wishes to live as pleasantly as is possible. Since everyone demands this as a human being, and no one is more or less human than anyone else, everyone has an equal right in [making] this demand. In accordance with this equality of their rights, the division must be made in such a way that one and all can live as pleasantly as is possible when so many men as they are exist next to one another in the given sphere of efficacy."[20]

Hermann Göring presented this concept in his 1934 book *Germany Reborn* where personal sacrifice is expected to be an integral component of the societal fabric if the society hopes to employ socialism. Fichte may have understood the autonomous regulation of one's actions to be carried out through the implementation of free will, resulting in no observable limitation of freedom, but National Socialism recognizes this as more of a biologically defined social obligation to be fulfilled. This is a point that demonstrates a clear shift from Kantian autonomy to collectivist biological utility. Physical potential is constrained, and outlying components are to be sacrificed to fall within the agreed range of conduct. This does not mean that National Socialism fails to recognize that the development of the moral individual only comes through positive and self-limiting interactions, but rather chooses to emphasize the physical potential that is possible and yet nonetheless passed up by the individual out of an egalitarian sense of duty.

"The result was National Socialism, which is the unique and indissoluble union of the two ideas at their deepest and finest. He explained to the workers that there can be no socialism, no socialist justice, unless one is prepared to recognize the good of the whole nation. He who would better the lot of the individual must be ready to better the lot of the whole nation."[21]

Above, Göring's articulation of socialism emphasizes unity and shared destiny, echoing Fichte's economic moralism, as Göring worked with the exact same concept as presented in Fichte's book *The Closed Commercial State*, published 134 years prior. This can be seen below, where Fichte argues that nobody should do without while others hoard excess or continue on in luxurious fashion. This entails that some must accept material sacrifices so that all of those who exist within the community may live a life free of complete destitution.

"Let all be sated and dwell securely before someone decorates his dwelling. Let all be comfortably and warmly clothed before anyone dresses himself sumptuously."[22]

This presents two immediate questions:

Who is included in the community?

This is a central question for both Fichtean and National Socialist thought. It must be considered due to the practical impossibility of elevating the entirety of the world to the commonly accepted European standards of living and organization. Fichte, like National Socialism, did not seek universalist humanitarianism in his most developed position, but instead envisioned a cohesive community bound to moral obligations. Due to these constraining factors, a boundary must be set that stops the moral and economic obligations of a people from exceeding their material capacity. Otherwise, such a structure would result in the collapse of the community's well-being, with the collective dipping below the ideal standards required for meaningful cultural and physical growth. The philosophical circumstances must also be evaluated in the area of culture, as the inclusion into a community or a nation, especially in the way it solidified under National

Socialism, exists outside the realm of solely practical considerations, within deeper concepts of organic unity.

What is the standard quality of life that is to be provided?

The answer to this question for both Fichte and National Socialism aligns in principle. Each proposes a base level of dignity, not a ceiling of indulgence. The expected standard comes down to the capability of the age and the productive output of the national economy, but never dipping below that which is necessary for physical and moral survival. Neither Fichte, nor National Socialism offers up dreams of state-funded opulence for the masses. Instead, both assert the moral centrality of necessity, along with a collective reorientation away from material excess toward spiritual and communal values. This can be seen in the National Socialist rejection of capitalist materialism under the name of "Mammonism," which was regarded as a corrosive element to the soul of the nation.

"I am bound, as a matter of right, to protect you, only under the condition that you protect me. One should carefully consider what the latter clause means. It does not mean: "if you merely have the good will to protect me."[23]

Fichte recognized that these same social bonds that create this aforementioned obligation of duty carry over into every corner of life, even to instances that could be detrimental to the obligated individual beyond slight financial inconvenience. He rejected hollow promises of good will, in favor of active and tangible responsibility, carried out by the individual without outside coercion, fueled by a reciprocal social agreement and upheld by personal ethics.

It is important to emphasize that National Socialism does not seek to subject unwilling participants to its Weltanschauung, with citizenship to the state being limited to those who recognize this inherent communal duty, and who agree to follow the laws of the state which protect the natural will of the nation. In this way, the National Socialist state functions as an external and secondary method of self-limitation, still following the logical map laid out by Fichte on the matter.

Fichte did not initially recognize the state as capable of impeding an individual's actions without simultaneously limiting their freedom, hesitating to ascribe moral legitimacy to state coercion. What he failed to fully articulate was that just as an individual can limit their own actions and still be considered free, so too can an individual voluntarily submit themselves to the state which enforces the social contract and the ethical order of the nation. In both instances, conduct is limited on a voluntary basis for the well-being of the greater society.

Would waking up to an alarm clock that was intentionally set the night prior be any less of an expression of personal freedom than jolting awake by instinct at the perfect moment? Of course, the alarm clock is an outside entity, but I nonetheless agree to the limitations in action that it imposes knowingly and willingly. In this analogy, the state becomes the alarm: a facilitator of order agreed upon beforehand.

This idealistic and internally focused aspect of Fichte's philosophy appears finely polished on paper, where individuals operate as self-regulating moral machines, upholding the well-being of the community simply because they seek an ethical life. This moral vision was later intentionally brought back down to earth under National Socialist philosophy, offering more practicality in the process. The evolution of the concept is grounded in the realities of managing a large body of people, where a strong and authoritative entity is needed to enforce the standards of the nation. In Fichte's later works, some of these necessary state impositions were more recognized than his earlier works, demonstrating movement toward something that would more closely resemble the National Socialist position. This shift can be seen in other areas as well, such as his growing recognition of biological and generational attributes as integral to national development.

"What man of noble mind is there who does not earnestly wish to relive his own life in a new and better way in his children and his children's children, and to continue to live on this earth, ennobled and perfected in their lives, long after he is dead?"[24]

In the quote above, Fichte introduces the concept of the persistence of spirit through genetic continuation, along with the aforementioned obligations extending to generations that the individual will never personally interact with. This is the construct of the transgenerational ethical community, where the younger generation is assisted by those who came before in order to improve their ethical and tangible standing in the world. This principle was similarly adopted by National Socialist philosophy, although with a much more direct treatment of race compared to Fichte.

Georg Usadel emphasized this in his 1935 book titled *Discipline and Order: Foundations of National Socialist Ethics,* stating that the youth had the potential to achieve a "higher form" of National Socialism than their predecessors. This comes not just from the youth standing upon the shoulders of the aging generation, but also from the aging generation supporting them and creating the environment necessary for the emergence of a new ethos. In this way, both National Socialism and Fichte highlight the developmental process of an ethical individual as a process that cannot be separated from the intergenerational construction of the ethical community. Duty is thus not limited in a temporal context to those in your immediate surroundings, but rather an element that spans through time and space.

"Offspring will be born who achieve a better and higher form of National Socialist German than we."[25]

Fichte articulates the value of the natural impulses of man in *Reden an die deutsche Nation (Addresses to the German Nation)*, where he warns against abandoning them except in cases of genuine necessity. Through the acceptance of and subservience to the natural order, he argued that it was possible to participate in the eternal structure of existence, tapping into the greater stream of consciousness to transcend the temporal limitations placed on the self. It is clear that a prerequisite for acceptance into this elevated state of being comes from the ethical evolution of the individual into a more community minded and social person.

"The natural impulse of man, which should be abandoned only in case of real necessity, is to find heaven on this earth, and to endow his daily work on earth with permanence and eternity; to plant and to cultivate the eternal in the temporal—not merely in an incomprehensible fashion or in a connection with the eternal that seems to mortal eye an impenetrable gulf, but in a fashion visible to the mortal eye itself."[26]

According to Fichte, it is only through adherence to the natural order that true freedom becomes possible. Below, a description of an analogy regarding the growth of a tree and the manifestation of freedom can be found, coming from his book *Die Bestimmung des Menschen (The Vocation of Man)*. It is only through the tree growing along the blueprint of its specific biology, producing the fruit it was intended by nature to grow and doing so without outside hindrance that the tree can grow truly free.

"Bestow consciousness on a tree, and let it grow, spread out its branches, and bring forth leaves and buds, blossoms and fruits, after its kind, without hindrance or obstruction: it will perceive no limitation to its existence in being only a tree, a tree of this particular species, and this particular individual of the species; it will feel itself perfectly free, because, in all those manifestations, it will do nothing but what its nature requires; and it will desire to do nothing else, because it can only desire what that nature requires. But let its growth be hindered by unfavourable weather, want of nourishment, or other causes, and it will feel itself limited and restrained, because an impulse which actually belongs to its nature is not satisfied."[27]

This raises two important points:

First, Fichte's reference to the tree growing "after its kind" could signal a recognition of the role of biological design, understood today as genetics, in shaping one's natural obligations and capacities. This offers an interesting counterpoint to the notion that National Socialism has inappropriately applied Fichte's conceptualization of the nation, with many claiming that it was purely cultural, linguistic and ethical, with no biological implications. National Socialism understands the cultural and ethical nature of the nation to spring from the genetic body of the people, a point which in this instance clearly overlaps with Fichte's assertion.

Second, the introduction of foreign elements that hinder, obstruct, or detract from the tree's potential to follow the pattern of growth laid out by nature was clearly a primary concern of Fichte, as half of the analogy is focused on just that. Of course, this is also consistent with the social negotiation of independent self-positing I's who must collaborate enough to determine the boundaries of the social contract to be followed. That which is foreign to the nature of the individual is understood as detrimental to one's freedom and health by both Fichte and National Socialism for the same fundamental reason, offering further support that Fichte's system was, at least, to some degree, entangled with elements of biological metaphor and logic.

"It should be free of all foreign influences, whether they originate inside or outside of its borders, and it should be social, i.e., imbued with equal love and equal justice for all of its children."[28]

The above assertion, made by Rudolf Jung, shows two concepts heavily steeped in Fichte's philosophy: the rejection of influences that are foreign to the nature and spirit of the nation, along with the call for equal justice amongst all members of the community. Fichte recognized that not all that arises from the nation is genuinely national in spirit and that the corruption of truly national elements could lead to the development of something that is unrecognizable, introducing an unsavory spirit that disrupts the adherence to the proper life path of the people, preventing them from the circumstances that permit significant ethical development.

National Socialist philosophy has not sought to focus on the philosophical system of ethics to the extent that Fichte did, instead settling for the adoption of his concluded positions and relying on the common sense of the community to recognize their validity without a need for pedantic philosophical explanations. Of course, the topic of ethics did appear within National Socialist contexts, but was explored nowhere close to the extent found in Fichte, and was most expressed within the terminology of honor especially in literature directed at the public. The communally reciprocated claim to equal love and equal justice has clear origins in Fichte's recognition of the self-positing I, which exists in others to an equal extent as in the examiner, resulting in an equal claim to individual rights. As such, the moral obligations one places on others must be equally placed upon oneself, creating the basis for collective life.

"Whatever has lost its independence has at the same time lost its power to influence the course of events and to determine these events by its own will. If it remain in this state its age, and itself with the age, are conditioned in their development by that alien power which governs its fate."[29]

THE GENEALOGY OF NATIONAL SOCIALISM 23

Above, Fichte touches on a point that is a major focus under National Socialism: national self-determination. When a nation is stripped of its ability to command its own future, it becomes a slave, as it must answer to foreign commands which originate from outside of the spirit of the nation, culminating in a self-destructive cycle of cultural loss and further reduction of freedom. National Socialism clearly recognizes the danger of competing power structures existing within the same sphere of influence, as is the case with the elements presented by Fichte. Such things as a dishonest press or foreign capital could easily lead citizens astray from the true nature of the nation, subtly stripping them of their self-determination.

What is a slave if not an individual who is involuntarily subservient to a dominating influence?

Adolf Hitler said at the Bürgerbräukeller in Munich on November 8, 1938:

"I did not eliminate two democracies this year, rather, I destroyed, as the epitome of a true democrat, two dictatorships! Namely, the dictatorship of Herr Schuschnigg and the dictatorship of Herr Beneš. It was by peaceful means that I attempted to persuade these two dictators to open up a path toward democracy for their peoples by permitting them to exercise their right to self determination."[30]

This statement by Hitler closely overlaps with the aspects of voluntary self-limitation that were previously discussed in relation to Fichte's interpersonal negotiation of freedom among a community. The will of the nation forms through and in the shape of the average citizen's will, passing on the ethical obligation of adherence to the individual. An external mechanism and its composition, as in the state, that is purely directed toward the fulfillment of the demands of the nation cannot be judged as a negative system based on its composition alone if one wishes to remain logically consistent and recognizes the ethical implications of national enslavement. From this perspective, no amount of ethnocentrism can logically justify the attack on a system called for by the nation, simply because it is viewed as "authoritarian" relative to the political façade at play in their own homelands.

In 1799, Fichte claimed that even if political independence was stripped from the nation, literature and language must be preserved in order to "remain a nation". First, it should be noted that this comes eight years prior to the previously mentioned analogy involving the tree growing according to its specific nature, showing a development within Fichte's ideology, where a refinement of the composition of the nation was made that seemingly moved toward the more concrete foundations of National Socialism. It could be argued that Fichte's earlier analogy concerning the tree was of an ideological nature instead of a biological one, which is a fair point to be made given the frequency with which Fichte overlooks the biological foundations of culture and societal norms in favor of focusing on the linguistic, moral, and cultural nature of the nation. It is on this basis that National Socialism is accused of bastardizing Fichte's concept of the nation, reducing it down to little more than a racial matter.

Was Fichte's philosophy simply a misappropriation of Kant's philosophy? Of course not; the alterations made to Kant's philosophical framework were done with purpose through logical deliberation just as the development of National Socialism drew from the philosophy of Fichte and others. Otherwise, we must proclaim that all Western philosophy is simply a misappropriation of Ancient Greek philosophy!

"For example, long before the most recent events, we had to hear, in advance as it were, a saying which since then has frequently been repeated in our ears: that even if our political independence were lost we should still keep our language and our literature, and thereby always remain a nation; so we could easily console ourselves for the loss of everything else."[31]

Below, it seems that Fichte is asserting that the life-form of the race must conform to the development of the race and the circumstances in which it exists, further connecting biological concepts with the limits of conduct, albeit significantly less directly than National Socialism. This means that to Fichte, the death of a racial identity can only be corrected through the rebirth of a new identity that sees to the spirit of both the race and the age. Speaking to the ever-developing nature of higher life, National Socialism similarly recognizes the necessity of moving forward in a healthy manner, specifically advising against excessive rumination of past circumstances which only clouds the current path that is being navigated.

"Now if, for a race which has lost its former self, its former age and world, such a world should be created as the means of producing a new self and a new age, a thorough interpretation of such a possible age would have to give an account of the world thus created."[32]

In *Mein Kampf*, Hitler disregards a linguistic boundary within the nation as irrelevant, directly stating that National Socialism understands race to be determined through blood alone. Nationalism, in the context of National Socialism can be simply summarized as the doctrine of race, offering a much more stable foundation to the concept of the nation than Fichte ever offered.

"It is not however by the tie of language, but exclusively by the tie of blood that the members of a race are bound together."[33]

Fichte's close embrace with German nationalism was made very clear by 1808 as can be seen throughout *Addresses to the German Nation*:

"But, in regard to space, we believe that it is first of all the Germans who are called upon to begin the new era as pioneers and models for the rest of mankind."[34]

Who exactly were the "Germans" that Fichte believed to be the model for the rest of mankind? Below we can see that Fichte's concept of the nation was not just something that could be corrupted, but also something that would fundamentally change in nature with the addition of outside elements. This alone would suggest that the concept of the German nation was limited by Fichte, beyond even "European," as he expressed concern about French influence on the German nation and its culture. National Socialism bypasses this more idealistic concept of nation by grounding its definition in the biological foundations of race. This admixture Fichte references could be taken to mean that of a cultural variety, just as the preservation of a kind's natural state could be argued to hold cultural, not racial, foundations. National Socialism fully recognizes cultural corruption as a threat but seeks to stop it primarily through racial means, directly recognizing the growth of culture as a tangible manifestation of the unique genetic composition of the nation.

"Only in the invisible qualities of nations, which are hidden from their own eyes—qualities as the means whereby these nations remain in touch with the source of original life—only therein is to be found the guarantee of their present and future worth, virtue, and merit.. If these qualities are dulled by admixture and worn away by friction, the flatness that results will bring about a separation from spiritual nature, and this in its turn will cause all men to be fused together to their uniform and conjoint destruction."[35]

Clearly both Fichte and National Socialism recognize the nation as a unique expression of a particular German spirit, regardless of whether Fichte believed that it could exist outside of German descent or not. He names nature as the driving force behind one's capacity for self regulation, further asserting that an individual's innate composition dictates their potential in different realms, including intelligence and morality. Logic would have it that if an individual's potential and perspective is dictated through their "natural" composition as Fichte claimed in *The Vocation of Man* below, and this inward sense of self is what posits the not-self, the ideal community that allows for the greatest moral growth of the people would be one composed of individuals with similar perspectives, and thus similar natural endowments. The logical extension of this aspect of Fichte's philosophy can be seen in the manner in which National Socialism recognizes the blood community which composes the nation.

"I cannot indeed make use of this discovery in the regulation of my actions, for I do not truly act at all, but Nature acts in me; and to make myself anything else than that for which Nature has intended me, is what I cannot even propose to myself, for I am not the author of my own being, but Nature has made me myself, and all that I am. I may repent, and rejoice, and form good resolutions; although, strictly speaking, I cannot even do this, for all these things come to me of themselves, when it is appointed for them to come; but most certainly I cannot, by all my repentance, and by all my resolutions produce the smallest change in that which I must once for all inevitably become. I stand under the inexorable power of rigid Necessity: should she have destined me to become a fool and a profligate, a fool and a profligate without doubt I shall become; should she have destined me to be wise and good, wise and good I shall doubtless be."[36]

Both Fichte and National Socialism do not offer solutions in the way of overcoming the natural order, but instead seek to understand its point of origin to better grasp the proper composition of the nation and the most effective organization of the community within.

In this way, they both set a limit to who can be included in the nation, demonstrating an exclusionary and voluntary approach to societal organization. Below, Adolf Hitler explained in *Mein Kampf* that the natural in-group preferences of a race protect this common inward characteristic that composes the interconnecting social fabric of the nation. Altering the genetic foundations for these characteristics would also alter their expression, necessitating the need for a new common standard of conduct and organization. This position that National Socialism holds comes from both a philosophical continuation of Fichte's understanding of the self in relation to others and the emergence of biological sciences that began taking shape mostly after Fichte's death.

"This urge for the maintenance of the unmixed breed, which is a phenomenon that prevails throughout the whole of the natural world, results not only in the sharply defined outward distinction between one species and another but also in the internal similarity of characteristic qualities which are peculiar to each breed or species. The fox remains always a fox, the goose remains a goose, and the tiger will retain the character of a tiger."[37]

As can be seen below in *Die Bestimmung des Menschen (The Vocation of Man)*, Fichte explained that he thought the "savages" to be capable of development according to their own nature where they would reach a recognizable standard of civility in time. He could not fathom why they would continue to exist if this weren't the case, as nature, and thus the world, is arranged through logic and reason. However, this optimistic claim overlooks the overwhelming savagery of the natural order, where animals exist outside of European moral confines, driven purely by biological necessity.

The wild boar will never develop beyond its savage nature, taking on the traits that the European would recognize as ethically evolved and virtuous. How absurd it is to think that a wild boar would recognize that digging up a farmer's crop for food is unethical and cease its actions! Shall we also expect orangutans to refrain from forceful copulation? Such actions are fitting for the nature of the beast and do not necessarily need to be aligned with European ethical standards, or even recognized as acceptable by the European, for it to be perfectly in line with the nature of the "kind" in question.

"It cannot be not so, unless the idle game, intended that those savage tribes should always remain savage; no race can be born with all the capacities of perfect humanity, and yet be destined never to develop these capacities, never to become more than that which a sagacious animal by its own proper nature might become. Those savages must be destined to be the progenitors of more powerful, cultivated, and virtuous generations; otherwise it is impossible to conceive of a purpose in their existence, or even of the possibility of their existence in a world ordered and arranged by reason. Savage races may become civilized, for this has already occurred; the most cultivated nations of modern times are the descendants of savages."[38]

In *Addresses to the German Nation*, Fichte introduces the concept of divinity and its relation to the natural law of a people. The strictly religious aspect of this concept will be examined later on in this chapter but it should be noted that the fundamental racial position of National Socialism is ideologically consistent with Fichte's later works, where the rejection of foreign nature becomes a moral imperative due to the Holy nature of that which is to be preserved. His early focus on the cultural, ethical and linguistic aspects of the nation seem to gradually soften in the face of the biological realities of nature, notably around the same time that he began adopting antisemitic positions.

"So long as this people exists, every further revelation of the divine will appear and take shape in that people in accordance with the same natural law. But this law itself is further determined by the fact that this man existed and worked as he did, and his influence has become a permanent part of this law. Hence, everything that follows will be bound to submit itself to, and connect itself with, that law. So he is sure that the improvement achieved by him remains in his people so long as the people itself remains, and that it becomes a permanent determining factor in the evolution of his people."[39]

Fichte certainly offers more credit to environmental factors in the development of the individual and their attributes than National Socialism, which sees this development as almost completely a result of genetic composition. In the NSDAP publication *The Nazi Primer*, which was geared toward orienting the youth into National Socialism, it says the following:

"The foundation of the National Socialist outlook on life is the perception of the unlikeness of men."[40]

This is the philosophical anchor that National Socialism relies on to ground the entire worldview. On this matter, National Socialism operates under the following logic:

- Man must communicate.

- Man should live according to the nature that is organic to him.

- Man must conform to the expectations of a mutual and reasonable social contract, prioritizing the needs of the community over himself so as to carry on within the healthy, positive and commonly accepted limitations of the community. This is how freedom is achieved under National Socialism.

- The mutually understood social contract arises from a unique mix of traits such as intelligence, proclivities, and disposition that determine societal norms, individual expectations, and ultimately the organic arrangement of the community.

- These traits are primarily a product of genetics.
- Races show different manifestations of culture, governance, and societal contracts due to the genetic differences that separate them.

The tangible relevance of genetic contribution is the keystone of National Socialist philosophy, and without it, the entirety of the philosophy unravels, starting with the concept of the nation and ending with the abandonment of the initiative to safeguard unique cultural identities. In the following passage by Fichte, he directly deals with race in the context of passing on the spirit of the nation, where a noble status is even granted by him to those who seek to pass on this spirit through "action or thought". This is a critical point to be made, in that he explicitly recognizes that there are more elements to the continuation of a nation than simply passing on a language or literature, again trending toward the deeper roots of the biological perspective that National Socialism would later adopt.

"Does he not wish to deposit these qualities, as his best legacy to posterity, in the souls of those he leaves behind, so that they too, in their turn, may some day hand them on again, increased and made more beautiful? What man of noble mind is there who does not want to scatter, by action or thought, a grain of seed for the unending progress in perfection of his race, to fling something new and unprecedented into time, that it may remain there and become the inexhaustible source of new creations?"[41]

Again, the divine appears to Fichte as the hand that guides the nation's connection and growth. It is only through obedience to this divine path that the individual can refine oneself, becoming a more ethical and properly oriented person. This has obvious implications for a society of similarly natured people who can congregate along their organic path, allowing for the highest level of collaboration possible. How can a group congregate when all involved walk along different natural paths separated by dense treelines? National Socialism resolves this starting point, only permitting those who can freely walk the same path to partake in the society.

"This, then, is a people in the higher meaning of the word, when viewed from the standpoint of a spiritual world: the totality of men continuing to live in society with each other and continually creating themselves naturally and spiritually out of themselves, a totality that arises together out of the divine under a certain special law of divine development."[42]

It's difficult to see Fichte's assertion below, found in *The Vocation of Man*, as not being at least parallel to the aforementioned position of National Socialism, where all things are bound to their nature. Additionally, the recognition of these natural laws as unalterable is yet another aspect of direct philosophical overlap with National Socialism, who recognizes these same laws as eternal.

"Nature proceeds throughout the whole infinite series of her possible determinations without outward incentive; and the succession of these changes is not arbitrary, but follows strict and unalterable laws. Whatever exists in Nature, necessarily exists as it does exist, and it is absolutely impossible that it should be otherwise."[43]

It can also be reasonably inferred that Fichte sought a unified Germany where a singular nation would be formed culturally, morally, and possibly racially, from the fragmented territories of the decaying

Holy Roman Empire, which had been dissolved by Napoleon in 1806, just two years prior to these addresses. As with much of his philosophy, this aspect can be seen as trending toward the National Socialist position as time progressed, where he recognized the importance of overcoming political, regional, dynastic, religious, and linguistic divisions that were inhibiting a cohesive German nation from forming out of the rubble. This straightforward assertion certainly cuts through many of the softer descriptors of the nation and its binding that he was adamant about in his earlier works, although it still lacks a stable descriptive foundation.

"I speak for Germans simply, of Germans simply, not recognizing, but setting aside completely and rejecting, all the dissociating distinctions which for centuries unhappy events have caused in this single nation."[44]

The same spirit of unity was carried directly over to National Socialism in the following ways:

Politics are to function as a tool leading to the betterment of the racially defined nation. All politicians in a National Socialist state exist to serve the nation, as they must themselves be National Socialists who have accepted the fundamental objectives of the state. This creates a total political unity on the side of the government, which is essential for the productive and effective management of state affairs. Below, it can be seen how Dr. Goebbels understood the purpose of politics in a society, in a way that clearly aligns with both the unity that Fichte envisioned and the role of the state itself, which functions to better the standing of the nation, though with more practical grounding than the idealistic moral development sought by Fichte.

"Politics is responsible action that serves people. Its goal is to create the conditions that will enable this people to build a life from this hard earth, to maintain and defend its life, to increase in number, and to assure freedom and prosperity for its descendants."[45]

One of the reasons why the NSDAP sought to reclaim the regions that had been stripped from Germany due to the Treaty of Versailles was because these areas contained members of the nation, namely racially "German" volk, who were facing starvation, abuse and abandonment. Because National Socialism recognizes the racial boundaries of the nation, it must also recognize that these racial connections exist outside of the physical limitations of the country or reach of the state, resulting in a unity despite physical or geographical separation. In *You and Your People*, Kurt Schrey places a great deal of importance on the poem below to demonstrate that the confines of the nation are genetic, unified through both time and space:

"A people is not time, a people is not space,

A people is not day, a people is not a dream —

A people is a love that flows within

A holy stream of which we are a part.

— Lex Schloss[46]

Through the unification of blood, which is understood to house the biological precursors to culture, morality, religion, and the social expression of the race, coupled with the unification of state and its associated political objectives and processes, unity is achieved under National Socialism in a way that permeates every level of the society. From this genetic unity grows the fruits that Fichte had planted, even if it was planted with slightly different intentions, which remains debatable especially given the development of his later philosophy as previously outlined.

"He who has once undertaken to interpret his own age must make his interpretation keep pace with the progress of that age, if progress there be. It is, therefore, my duty to acknowledge as past what has ceased to be the present, before the same audience to whom I characterized it as the present."[47]

The role of history and the advancement of societal standards based on modern circumstances is also treated similarly by Fichte and National Socialism, both recognizing that circumstances will inevitably alter the implementation of the new system. This is directly supported by Gottfried Feder in *The German State on a National Socialist Foundation*:

"People and state are not mummies and constructions, but living entities; the clothes cut once do not suit forever."[48]

Society and all of its components must progress with time and circumstance, or it will quickly find itself unfit and face the negative reinforcement of nature. National Socialism recognizes that the changes that must occur operate outside the eternal racial laws that directly compose the nation, where progress is to be had while still remaining anchored in biological reality. This allows for the greatest possible alignment with the race's natural order, while offering the flexibility needed to adapt to changing circumstances, ultimately drawing a hard line between the temporary and the everlasting. Failure to adhere to the natural order of the race means the destruction of the nation's unique cultural identity, as well as an overall decline in efficiency caused by an improperly arranged society interacting in a way foreign to its nature.

Below, in *Reden an die deutsche Nation (Addresses to the German Nation)*, Fichte touches on the subject of rebellion against a foreign system, even if the system is marked by the flag of one's own people. This was also clearly adopted by National Socialism with the notion that when the state reaches the point of no longer representing the nation, it ceases to be the lawful state governing the nation and is to be rejected for the good of the people. Fichte raises this in the context of self-serving officials who lead the nation astray for selfish desires. This is the rejection of what National Socialism labels individualism, where the desires of the individual are placed over the needs of the many. This sort of conduct represents the complete antithesis of true socialism.

"Later on, the rulers, abandoned and betrayed on all sides, are compelled to purchase their further existence by submission and obedience to foreign schemes; and so those, who in battle for their country threw away their arms, now learn to wield those same arms bravely under foreign colours against their mother - country. Thus it comes about that self-seeking is destroyed by its own complete development; and upon those who would not voluntarily set themselves any other aim but self, another aim is imposed by alien power."[49]

Fichte raises a very interesting point in that if an individual's primary objective is to serve the self, he ultimately becomes the servant to outside forces, as he must rely on others to achieve the ends he is seeking out of selfishness. This could be put into a modern context where someone, for example, seeks only personal wealth and comfort, rejecting all higher obligations to their nation, community, or principles. In doing so, he may become dependent on foreign corporate interests, ideological trends, or political actors that appear to promise personal gain; and through this process, he forfeits his own cultural agency and autonomy in favor of the one he traded for. In the end, he becomes an instrument of forces he neither controls nor fully understands. For instance, a government official who acts only to preserve his own career by appeasing foreign powers or multinational institutions may find himself implementing policies that directly undermine the sovereignty or moral structure of the very state he was obligated to serve. Fichte succinctly warned that what may appear at first as self-interest will inevitably develop into a new form of servitude.

"When it masters the rulers too, I said. A people can be completely corrupted, i.e., self-seeking —for selfseeking is the root of all other corruption—and yet at the same time not only endure, but even outwardly accomplish splendid deeds, provided only that its government be not also corrupt."[50]

Similar to Fichte, National Socialism sees an individual as a piece of a larger body, wherein interaction is necessary and ethical duties exist alongside these interactions, including indirect interactions that can be equally impactful on another's ability to live according to their own nature. In *The Philosophical Foundations of National-Socialism: A Call to Arms of the German Mind*, Otto Dietrich paints the community in a way that is reminiscent of an eternal flame; where generations are united through a single ever-burning lineage of blood, all of which carry the same raw material that fuels the organization of the society and the bounds of interaction.

"Underlying individualistic thought is the premise, taken to be self-evident, that man is an individual essence (Einzelwesen). This premise—however firmly it may even be rooted in the universal conception—is false and based on a catastrophic error in thinking. Man confronts us in the world not as an individual essence but as a member of a community. Man is in all his actions a collective essence (Kollektivwesen), and is utterly unthinkable except in this way. Man by definition therefore lives in community with others; his life actualizes itself only in the community. Community is a concept to which the whole history of humanity is subordinate; it is the form in which human life runs its course from cradle to grave, without which it would be unthinkable.

The actual givens that we find in the world are not individual men but races, peoples, and nations."[51]

It cannot be expected that all people will genuinely sacrifice their selfish desires to join a greater effort, even if it more closely corresponds to their nature and offers a deeper set of benefits, just as some people simply cannot shake the vices that significantly limit them in daily life. Fichte argues that someone who decides not to properly engage in the development of the nation should remove himself from it, reintroducing the aspect of voluntary submission that is crucial to both Fichte's and National Socialism's philosophical basis. In this way, both seek to liberate the individual from the shackles of outside imposition, not to enslave him under a system that was thrust onto them.

"Now in the doctrine of right there is no talk of moral obligation; each is bound only by the free, arbitrary [willkürlichen] decision to live in community with others, and if someone does not at all want to limit his free choice [Willkiir], then within the field of the doctrine of right, one can say nothing further against him, other than that he must then remove himself from all human community."[52]

The previous quote from Fichte is perfectly contrasted with the following, written by Gottfried Feder in *The German State on a National Socialist Foundation*:

"One who wishes to exercise state-citizenship rights must have also served the state, he must also have proved himself duty-conscious and loyal to his state through deed and indeed without remuneration, that is, possibility of enrichment, exactly as the soldier serves his fatherland."[53]

Similar to how National Socialism expects unity within governmental systems, so too does it expect unity within the population. Without unity, no coherent social contract can be outlined, and would remain a disjointed nation suffering from an immature societal posture. In addition to the ideological basis for voluntary involvement in the nation, there is also a practical one: it is disadvantageous to have segments of the population who draw on the safety, advancement and resources of the nation without assisting in its maintenance or development, becoming a net negative impact on the community. This is exactly why National Socialism does not simply ask for a claim of loyalty to the nation, but also a display of loyalty which could take the form of obligatory work programs or military service. Citizenship is predicated on one's commitment to joining and upholding the very same stable societal order that was discussed by Fichte over a century prior.

As mentioned previously, the proper state is not a force capable of enslaving the citizenry. If the state stops representing the interests of the nation yet continues to rule it under the threat or application of force, it can be said that the state is operating through a foreign spirit and has enslaved the nation, ceasing to hold the title of a proper state. Either the nation is free and supported in this freedom by the state that acts as an ideological exoskeleton, or it is enslaved to a foreign power. The state receives the power to regulate those who live within its bounds and to protect the interests of the nation from the nation itself through this voluntary transaction, binding citizens to the same moral and behavioral obligations. Fichte makes it clear below in *Foundations of Natural Right* that a man cannot simply divorce himself of these obligations when it comes time to be judged for his actions, as he has already subordinated himself to the laws of the state in order to join the nation.

"Applied to the civil contract, this means it is originally up to the free and arbitrary choice of every individual to determine whether he wants to live in this particular state or not, although if he wants to live among other human beings at all, then it is not up to his arbitrary choice to determine whether he enters into a state, or whether he wants to remain his own judge; but, just as he expresses his will to enter into a particular state and just as he is accepted into such a state, so he is, by virtue of this simple, reciprocal declaration, subjected without further ado to all the limitations that the law of right requires for this group of human beings; by virtue of the words, "I want to live in this state," he has accepted all the laws of that state."[54]

Fichte believed that all who exist within the community hold an identical moral obligation toward the nation, where they are determined to be equal despite possible differences in education, occupation or otherwise. This obligation does not arise from a position of egalitarian liberalism, but rather from ethical self-determination within a culturally and spiritually unified national community. Fichte played a crucial role in the development of Idealism and Romanticism in Germany, centered on this positioning of the individual through duty, ultimately positing that true self-consciousness can flourish only within morally structured interpersonal relations.[55] This equality is subordinate to the recognition of a population that shares similar attributes and natural ethics, along with the voluntary submission to the fabric of the community, upheld by the state and national pressure. Even with the removal of the somewhat controversial interpretation of Fichte's nation as a racially bound body, we still are left with this framework that bears a strong resemblance to the overarching framework of National Socialism. Initially, Fichte was not represented in scholarship as a nationalist, but rather through the traditional socialist lens until after the First World War, where his reputation shifted toward that of a nationalistic figure.[56]

"He is to expect neither reward for it, for under this system of government all are quite equal in regard to work and pleasure, nor even praise, for the attitude of mind prevailing in the community is that it is just everyone's duty to act thus; but he alone enjoys the pleasure of acting and working for the community, and of succeeding, if that should fall to his lot."[57]

This was a very important point for the NSDAP as it was positioned very early on in *The Program of the National Socialist German Workers Party* (commonly referred to as the 25 Points). This Program isn't necessarily pure National Socialist ideological doctrine in the strictest sense because it mainly focuses on the political platform and objectives of the NSDAP at the time, which do not always speak to the doctrinal aspects that are devoid of physical and temporal limitations. Nonetheless, outside of the handful of points that speak directly to National Socialism, a coherent spirit emerges, along with insight regarding the structure and intention of the different national elements. Below, point number nine is clearly one of these examples that speaks more to the nature of National Socialism than the needs of the day, where citizens are equal in rights and duties no matter what that may entail, directly aligning with Fichte's position.

"9. All citizens must be equal in rights and duties."[58]

This is also backed by Rudolf Jung, who tied Fichte's concepts of freedom and societal obligation to the nature of a socialist society, representing socialism as the highest order of communal participation.

"In socialist society:

1. All able-bodied people shall be called upon to work.

2. A harmony of interests shall prevail.

3. Labor will be organized.

4. Productivity will expand.

5. Consuming power will increase.

6. The contrast between mental and manual labor shall disappear.

7. There shall exist an equal duty to work for all."[59]

National Socialism understands the nation and the state to be two separate entities, where the state is composed of the nation and always serves the nation, yet nonetheless exists as an outside structure that is secondary to the nation. Fichte similarly asserted that if the distinction between the nation and the state is made clear, it becomes evident that no true conflict between them can exist. For Fichte, the state is the instrument through which the moral and spiritual destiny of the nation is secured; its legitimacy derives solely from its service to the ethical development of the people.

Despite being frequently recognized as a foundational thinker of German national Romanticism, some scholars focus on Fichte's early work that features universal cultural principles, and as late as 1804, he speaks of the homeland of Christian Europe as wherever provides the highest level of culture.[60] This demonstrates that the underpinnings of his early view were rooted in religious and cultural narratives instead of a simple commitment to German exclusivity. Hans Sluga suggests that despite Fichte's early universalism and his later shift toward more stringent nationalism, the portrayal of a continuous ideology from Fichte to National Socialism is artificial and neglects Fichte's ideological grounding in Enlightenment moral universalism.[61] While no such direct unadulterated line exists from Fichte to National Socialism, Sluga's position rules out the possibility of being judged as a thinker by your matured philosophy, always being chained to the philosophies of youth which would seemingly contradict the underlying purpose of scholarship itself. Due to the overflow of moral condemnation in much of the "scholarship" surrounding this subject, many "scholars" seek to discredit the philosophical concepts presented by National Socialism and in doing so, neglect the blatant connections that would not be ignored if they were as truly illogical as some insist.

"If only we keep in mind the distinction that has been drawn between State and nation, it is clear that even in the past it was not possible for their interests ever to come into conflict."[62]

Additionally, both philosophies recognize that the nation is second only to God, not in the sense of being subservient to church hierarchies, but rather to the divine order and natural law that gives structure and meaning to existence. Further, both are in agreement that the removal of a foreign and illegitimate state by the will of the nation is to be a just cause and an act of natural restoration. Under this framework that Fichte proposed, only the people, acting as the highest earthly authority under God can carry out a restructuring of state in a way that is morally valid if the interests of the nation no longer align with the actions of the state. The legitimacy of these actions thus lies outside the bounds of legal formalities, clearly encouraging revolutionary activity if necessary.

"But what on earth is superior to the people! The people can rebel only against themselves, which is absurd. Only God is above the people; therefore, one can say: if the people have rebelled against their ruler, then one must presume that the ruler is a god, which just might be difficult to prove.

Therefore, two scenarios are possible: either in such a case the people themselves rise up unanimously, perhaps provoked by violence too terrible to ignore, and pass judgment on the ephors and the executive officials. By its very nature, their uprising is always just — not only formally, but also materially — for so long as the insecurity and the poor administration of the state do not oppress them all and do not become universally harmful, every individual will look out only for himself and try to get by as best he can."[63]

On September 16, 1930, Adolf Hitler made a speech in Munich where he said the following:

"Today our whole official political outlook is rooted in the view that the State must be maintained because the State in itself is the essential thing; we, on the other hand, maintain that the State in its form has a definite purpose to fulfill and the moment that it fails to fulfill its purpose the form stands condemned. Above everything stands the purpose to maintain the nation's life - that is the essential thing and one should not speak of a law for the protection of the State but for the protection of the nation: it is of this protection that one must think...."[64]

Fichte would have likely viewed the dilapidated country that was the Weimar Republic and its governing body in a similarly critical light as Adolf Hitler, due to the incongruence between the needs of the nation and the actions of the state. He would have almost certainly interpreted the behavior of the foreign few who refused to conform to the nation, yet gained significant control over the majority, as actions satisfy many of his points of concern regarding national governance. Kohn points out in a 1949 paper that National Socialist writers such as Adolf Baeumler had taken hold of the voluntarist, anti-materialist Fichtean framework, subsequently casting him as a prophet of German struggle against foreign power.[65] The retention of Jewish tradition, language, religion and internal hierarchy directly inflicted with the way Fichte envisioned a properly developed nation, as it appeared to him to supplant and displace native German conduct and organization.

The broader German Romantic nationalist position held, similarly to some of the claims made by Fichte, that the nation produces its own standards which cannot be judged in comparison to external principles and systems.[66] This concept provides the foundation for Fichte's specific critique of foreign peoples who had continued to maintain their foreign language and customs despite emigration, crafting a central component of the exclusionary model that would later be adopted by National Socialism under a biological pretense.

Fichte famously remarked in his early work on the French revolution that the only way to properly integrate a Jew would be to "cut off their heads at night" and to replace them with heads that lacked "Jewish ideas". This offers an interesting insight in that the problem and solution which Fichte outlined seems less biological in nature and more concerned with the cognitive or spiritual attributes of the Jew.

"People and fatherland in this sense, as a support and guarantee of eternity on earth and as that which can be eternal here below, far transcend the State in the ordinary sense of the word, viz., the social order as comprehended by mere intellectual conception and as established and maintained under the guidance of this conception. The aim of the State is positive law, internal peace, and a condition of affairs in which everyone may by diligence earn his daily bread and satisfy the needs of his material existence, so long as God permits him to live. All this is only a means, a condition, and a framework for what love of fatherland really wants, viz., that the eternal and the divine may blossom in the world and never cease to become more and more pure, perfect, and excellent. That is why this love of fatherland must itself govern the State and be the supreme, final, and absolute authority. Its first exercise of this authority will be to limit the State's choice of means to secure its immediate object —internal peace."[67]

While Fichte saw the nation as transcending the state in many capacities, he also acknowledged that the state must sometimes act contrary to the opinion of the screaming masses, seemingly contradicting the earlier points that he made where the state would be dissolved if the nation so chooses. While it may seem contradictory, it is logically consistent in its approach to serve the nation. If the state were to restructure every time someone protested, then the state would be extremely unstable and would certainly fail to function as intended, creating a logical necessity for the state to ignore the pleas of its citizens to some extent.

Fichte argued that there is a "firm and certain course" that arises from the common interests of the people, with demands made outside of this scope falling outside of the state's ethical obligations. This is the path of the nation that he is describing, constructed and planned based on the shared ethical perception that springs from the individual conception of freedom and the form of interaction that is common for the community. According to this same logic and moral grounding, Fichte argued that the "right to work" does not bind others if the person who is impoverished had failed to make reasonable attempts to sustain himself, and further, that those who fall to such a state through "dishonorable" conduct maintain no right to claim public support.[68]

"It was just because we ourselves, individually and collectively, were never of one opinion, but wanted one thing to-day and something different tomorrow, and because each one made the clamour more confused by shouting something different—it was for this reason that our governments, who to be sure listened to us, and often listened more attentively than was advisable, became confused and swayed to and fro just like our own opinion. If our common affairs are at last to pursue a firm and certain course, what is there to prevent us from beginning at once with ourselves and setting the example of firmness and decision?"[69]

In a 1933 New Year's Proclamation, Adolf Hitler recognized this in the following way:

"Our demand for strengthening the basic racial principles of our Volk, which this term signifies and which at the same time includes safeguarding the existence of our Volk in general, is also the determining factor in all of the aims of National Socialist domestic and foreign policy."[70]

Under National Socialism, all state actions are measured by their alignment with the racial interests of the nation. Both Fichte and National Socialism thus seek to walk the path of the nation, though one does so with greater biological, or at least, more direct biological implications. It may be argued that National Socialism offers a more adaptable set of solutions for the state than the model Fichte proposed through the introduction of an eternal biological element. National Socialism posits that it is racial composition that stands unchanged over time in a way that would allow for an external comparison to ensure that the conduct of the state and the population progress appropriately. Fichte on the other hand sees the nation as much more transitory in nature, where the nation itself functions as the state's anchor, not being explicitly tethered to racial composition. It could be argued that Fichte tethers the state to the nation and the nation to race, but this would still be an indirect relationship in comparison to the approach that National Socialism takes on the matter.

"It follows, too, that the vision and the love of this eternal development, and nothing else, should have the higher supervision of State administration at all times, not excluding periods of peace, and that this alone is able to save the people's independence when it is endangered."[71]

Fichte proposes a state of ongoing national and personal refinement, including the reform of the state itself. An area where this is readily apparent is in the refinement of racial policy under the NSDAP, where the state can be seen developing and transitioning between racial theories, refining their approach over time. This is an example of the humble National Socialist spirit that would readily grow from inadequacy so as to best serve the nation, even if that means altering a plan of action, provided such alterations fall within the previously discussed scope of permissible conduct.

"The state has the right to make this into a condition of the civil contract; and so the upbringing of children becomes an external duty that one can be coerced to fulfill; it is not a duty owed directly to the child, but to the state. It is the state that, as part of the civil contract, acquires the right to impose this duty."[72]

In both Fichte's philosophy and National Socialism, the state even plays a role in what many would consider to be the private affairs of marital couples, on account of the preservation of the nation. The nation will cease to exist if the dying population is not continually replaced with a new generation. It is a simple exchange that is absolutely vital to the nation, and as such offers a moral and ethical basis to the state to intervene in such affairs. Fichte argues that the state acquires this right to enforce these things through the agreement to the civil contract required of citizenship, with this duty being owed to the state itself. National Socialism departs from this stance as the duty to further the nation is owed to the nation itself, where the state is merely acting in an enforcement capacity in this instance. In this way, even when a duty is said to be owed "to the state," it truly is owed to the nation as the state simply arranges for the interests of the nation.

"The question of having many children is not a private business of individuals but a duty to his ancestors and our nation."[73]

The very same book that we had previously extrapolated biological reasoning from also offers evidence that Fichte's stance toward the management aspects of the nation ultimately leans more toward cultural refinement than the much more biologically focused National Socialist doctrine. Fichte proposed a mandatory system of education for the youth of the nation, with the educational process being refined over time to offer the greatest possible development for the individual.

"In a word, it is a total change of the existing system of education that I propose as the sole means of preserving the existence of the

German nation. That children must be given a good education has been said often enough, and has been repeated too often even in our age; and it would be a paltry thing if we, too, for our part wished to do nothing but say it once again. Rather will it be our duty, in so far as we think we can accomplish something new, to investigate carefully and definitely what education hitherto has really lacked, and to suggest what completely new element a reformed system must add to the training that has hitherto existed."[74]

National Socialism recognizes education as a crucial component for national progress, but does not consider it the "sole means of preserving the existence of the German nation," as Fichte put it. This difference arises because National Socialism views the nation in terms of racial composition, and as such logically prioritizes the protection of the genetic pool first and foremost. Educating an individual who shares linguistic or even cultural similarities with the German nation is not enough to preserve the nation, as the raw material for its development and continuation is not being tended to. Both Fichte and National Socialism agree that the foundation for national education originates in healthy social interactions, allowing for the collaboration needed to enact real educational and national advancement.

"The question of the national progress of a people is largely a question of creating a healthy social atmosphere, that will make it possible to provide each individual with the right kind of education."[75]

Fichte's contribution to the National Socialist educational structure can truly be seen below in the following quote from *Reden an die deutsche Nation (Addresses to the German Nation)*:

"They propose that you establish deeply and indelibly in the hearts of all, by means of education, the true and all-powerful love of fatherland, the conception of our people as an eternal people and as the security for our own eternity."[76]

Fichte encouraged the state to take on the task of refining the individual early on through education, molding the student into a duty-conscious adult who has the tools necessary to live according to the standards of the nation. This starts by educating the individual on their place within the greater community, teaching them to confront their comparative insignificance while offering a more impactful existence through union with the eternal nation. National Socialism also frequently looks toward the youth as an opportunity to improve upon the previous generation, growing the nation ethically, intellectually and culturally over time to initiate and maintain an upward societal trend.

"The very first image of a social order which the pupil's mind should be stimulated to create will be that of the community in which he himself lives. He will be inwardly compelled, therefore, to fashion this order for himself bit for bit, just as it is actually sketched out for him, and to conceive it in all its parts as absolutely inevitable because of its elements."[77]

All aspects of engagement with the nation and its surrounding structures were understood by Fichte to be carried out on a voluntary basis, which makes perfect sense when we track this concept back to the foundations of communal formation that he presented.

"Anyone who discovers an improvement, or understands most clearly, and before the others, an improvement proposed by a teacher, is expected to work it out by his own efforts, without being set free for this purpose from his other personal tasks of learning and working which are understood. Everyone is supposed to fulfil this expectation voluntarily, not compulsorily; for anyone who is unwilling is free to refuse."[78]

In the popular NSDAP pamphlet *Little ABC of National Socialism*, Joseph Goebbels touches on this same notion of voluntary duty that must be agreed upon by all members of the community. It is expected that individuals will work according to their capabilities, a process which cannot be externally regulated to any meaningful degree, thus requiring individual cooperation along with the willingness to sacrifice and persevere.

"True socialism is that form of political, cultural, and economic attitude which, instead of seeking an inwardly false liberalism, strives instead for the voluntary, socialist binding of every folk-comrade to the state, with their rights and duties corresponding to their nature, their character, and their abilities."[79]

Fichte clearly places a greater emphasis on education than National Socialism does, which makes sense given that Fichte did not rely as heavily on inherited biological differences to explain conduct, leaving more blame for poor behavior to be placed elsewhere in the development of the individual. National Socialism nonetheless shares the understanding that education is of significant concern as the philosophy of National Socialism needs to be taught, even though it is understood to align with the natural conduct of the people. There are many possible arrangements for a nation that would fall within this natural scope, and only one of them conforms to the philosophy of National Socialism: National Socialism itself. Therefore, it cannot be expected that National Socialism will randomly emerge in an entire population without systematic educational efforts aimed at outlining the philosophy.

"In the last address this new education, as distinguished from the old, was described thus: the existing education has at most only exhorted to good order and morality, but these exhortations have been unfruitful in real life, which has been moulded on principles that are quite different and completely beyond the influence of that education; in contrast to this, the new education must be able surely and infallibly to mould and determine according to rules the real vital impulses and actions of its pupils."[80]

Below in *Addresses to the German Nation*, Fichte emphasizes the overwhelming impact of education on the resulting conduct, seemingly with a lack of regard for other formative factors that may have impacted the development of the individual beyond simply educational methods.

"It is for the present, then, quite sufficient to describe this education by these its results, and for our purpose we can spare ourselves the wearisome task of analysing the inner sap and fibre of a tree whose fruit is now fully ripe and lies fallen before the eyes of all, proclaiming most clearly and distinctly the inner nature of its creator."[81]

Fichte recognized education as a system that should be required for all members of the German nation, mainly due to the ethical development that results from this guidance. This widespread educational project was intended to create a "new self" at both the individual and national level, ultimately accelerating the moral progress of the people.[82] While Fichte did not suggest that all members of the nation should be subject to the exact same line or level of study, he placed a strong emphasis on the development of a core curriculum that was focused on developing the individual into a fully ethical member of the nation.

"So there is nothing left for us but just to apply the new system to every German without exception, so that it is not the education of a single class, but the education of the nation, simply as such and without excepting any of its individual members. In this, that is to say in the training of man to take real pleasure in what is right, all distinction of classes, which may in the future find a place in other branches of development, will be completely removed and vanish."[83]

Joachim von Ribbentrop conveyed this exact same idea in *Germany Speaks*:

"It is the purpose of all education to prepare the rising generation for its functions in after-life as the true representatives of the nation and the State, both in a political and a cultural sense."[84]

National Socialism and Fichte both seek to recognize the world and the logic it presents through its organic processes in an unflinching way, fully dedicated to the adherence to the observable natural order. Due to this connection, a 1941 German anthology, *Thus Spake Germany*, made good use of four excerpts from Fichte's work, two from *On Machiavelli* and two from his famous Addresses, demonstrating direct interaction with his work by National Socialist thinkers beyond Jung.[85] To truly search for clarity means to face the realities of life head-on, which is why Fichte demands that ignorance be confronted and destroyed through education.

"Why, then, should we be afraid of this clear perception? Evil does not become less through ignorance, nor increase through knowledge; indeed it is only by the latter that it can be cured."[86]

The ethics that Fichte sees as education's responsibility to develop can be seen within every aspect of life, perfectly encapsulated through the example of the individual's role in the national economy. The vast majority of Fichte's commentary on the proper functioning of an economy comes from his work titled *The Closed Commercial State*, published in 1800. Despite many of his economic theories being successfully implemented later under the NSDAP, scholars have maintained that *The Closed Commercial State* was less an exercise in practical economic planning, and more of a theoretical exercise to determine its ideal configuration.[87] The first thing that becomes clear in this publication is that the economy and economic profitability are secondary to the ethical duty to the community and its citizens. This offers a clear separation from capitalist principles in the exact same way as it appears under National Socialism.

"Whatever a citizen needs and should have, a fellow citizen of his, who has taken his needs into account, will certainly have, and the former can receive it as soon as he wants. If someone has anything left over, then another citizen, whose needs take the other's surplus into account, will surely need it, and the former can deliver it to him as soon as he wants. Every piece of money that someone earns for himself will quite certainly remain forever worth these specific goods—e.g., this measure of grain—for him and his grandchildren and great-grandchildren, and he will be able to exchange it for these goods at any time. The value of this money against these goods may indeed rise, but it can never fall.—Everyone can be sure that, as long as he continues to work, he will continue to enjoy the state of existence to which he is accustomed. Nobody can grow poor and suffer want, nor could this happen to his children and grandchildren—as long as they work as much as the common custom of the country demands of them."[88]

Gottfried Feder summed up the state's responsibility in economic concerns succinctly in *The Programme of the N.S.D.A.P. and its General Conceptions,* where he recognized the economy as a means to provide for the needs of the nation. The National Socialist position certainly rejects capitalism in a much more outright manner than Fichte, but Fichte was nonetheless against a runaway economy that pulled the nation in tow through the promise of speculative returns. For Fichte, the economy functioned primarily as an instrument to develop the moral standing and cohesion of the nation, rather than as a sphere for individual profit-seeking.

"It is the duty of the National Government to provide the necessaries of life and not to secure the highest possible profits for Capital."[89]

Fichte argued that it is in the best interest of the people to close off the national economy from foreign trade, protecting the nation's sovereignty from foreign money powers. It has been noted in scholarship that this nationalism presented here is radically different from Fichte's earlier universalism, which is readily apparent when considering his early outlines of an international Christian society that exists at the far end of the universalism spectrum.[90] National Socialism recognizes this same threat to national self-determination and seeks to limit these foreign influences through a focus on domestic production, looking to reduce imports and increase exports wherever possible. In this way, the nation's economy is closed off, but not to such an extent as proposed by Fichte. Fichte argued that a state holds the responsibility of economic management, along with a duty to use it to serve the nation which would simply not be possible if the strings were being pulled by foreign forces who have no regard for the wellbeing of the nation or state. Due to this, he takes a more hardline stance than National Socialism where he suggested that all trade with foreigners should be made not only practically impossible, but also outright forbidden. National Socialism ultimately seeks to make the nation self-sufficient but also recognizes the potential in strategic trade with outside nations, appearing as a softer approach than what Fichte had suggested.

"The state is obliged to guarantee for all its citizens, through law and compulsion [Zwang], the state of affairs that results from this balance of commerce. Yet it cannot do this if there is any person able to influence this balance who does not stand under the state's law and command. Thus, it must cut the very possibility of such influence off at the root.—All commerce with foreigners must be forbidden to its subjects and rendered impossible."[91]

Fichte saw the ideal economic model as one where all would engage in both a moral and logical way, taking only what was needed and ensuring others were being equally compensated after expenses. Scholars, such as Richard Gray have noted that Fichte's exclusive economic theories resemble the planned systems of the twentieth-century, which included state pricing, regulated consumption and redistribution, undertaken to improve the health of the nation.[92] Another point of deviation can be found here as National Socialism expects economic actors to maintain their honor and national dedication while also seeking to employ state measures to provide definitive external boundaries on the individual, limiting the damage that a single individual or business could cause to the nation. In several areas, Fichte articulated a much more utopian ideal that offers the perfect equation of conduct and circumstance, which unfortunately rarely exist in any decently sized populations, but nonetheless offered a spirit of ethical economic interactions that contributed inspiration to National Socialism. Some National Socialist scholars, such as Emmanuel Hirsch and August Faust attempted to place Fichte as the direct precursor to National Socialism which can only be done through the oversimplification and isolation of Fichte's ideas as there were many other crucial elements such as is the case with racial theory.[93] Others like Ernst Krieck argued that Fichte's universalist philosophical framework was fundamentally contradictory to the racial anthropology of National Socialism.[94] The truth, however, lies between, in that depending on what period of Fichte's work you're engaging with, and the specific question being considered, one could reasonably support either interpretation. Of course, this does not detract from the very real logical frameworks that he constructed which would later be pieced together into National Socialism, of which there are many.

"Then a positive treaty: both estates promise to deliver to the merchant whatever produce and manufactured goods are superfluous for their own needs, and to take from him in return what they require, following the standard rule that, beyond the basic price that we determined above, the merchant will be left with enough produce and manufactured goods to allow him to live as pleasantly as the producer and artisan while he is taking care of the trade. The merchant, in return, promises both to supply at all times the customary needs of the people, determined by the standard rule we just discussed, and obliges himself to accept at all times all the customary articles of exchange at the basic price that was previously determined."[95]

Fichte argued that the stability of the national currency is of utmost importance, focusing less on state controls over individual market exchanges in favor of leveraging state power to seal off the economic bounds of the nation and to protect the legitimacy of the currency itself. This leaves the remaining aspects of the economic system to function according to the ethically self-regulating nature of the morally educated population.

"Such a state need only be sure that its national currency cannot be counterfeited, and that absolutely no man or power other than itself is able to manufacture it. This is the sole limiting condition, the reason for which we will see further down."[96]

Gottfried Feder conveyed an almost identical sentiment, without the more extreme aspects imposed by Fichte, in *The German State on a National Socialist Foundation*:

"The right to issue notes will thereby be exercised exclusively by the state. Such an issue of notes can occur only after an ordinance of the Ministry of Finance and only against complete coverage. Here in this connection is to be resolved the great task of the stabilization of our currency."[97]

It would be entirely illogical to close off the national economy to a great extent and guide markets so that they are managed along ethical lines, just to allow the nation's currency to be debased through private printing. This would lead to the growth of a power that exists outside the moral and practical confines of the nation and state, defeating the purpose of closing off the economy and regulating it in the first place

"In all public areas - and any area outside the house, e.g. an open field, is a public area (the garden is usually counted as part of the house and falls under its rights) - I am always under the protection and guarantee of the state."[98]

Fichte's stance on ownership was also maintained by National Socialism, even down to the garden falling under private ownership, something explicitly supported later by Rudolf Jung, Helmut Stellrecht, Gottfried Feder and many more. It is important to note that at the time of the emergence of the NSDAP in Germany, a significant portion of the population was starving due to previous naval blockades, along with the agricultural and economic impacts of the Treaty of Versailles, which helps explain why it was so pressing that individuals were given the means to feed themselves and their families. Fichte saw the land and resources of the nation as belonging to the nation itself, which National Socialism later reaffirmed, leading to restrictions in ground rent along with other forms of individual profit derived from the nation's collective property. Scholars note that Fichte's framework of basic rights maintains compatibility with both common property and private property, as his economic model did not require exclusive ownership in any direction.[99]

"National Socialism recognises private ownership of property as a principle and protects it by law, — given that it is acquired and employed honourably. We cannot discuss it here, but any one who rightly comprehends the term 'work' will quickly see that the product of 'work' must be the property of him who works. A producer will fail to understand why his work, or its value, should be the property of a vague 'community', nor will he readily admit that the fruits of his labour should go to an individual, the capitalist.

Hence a right understanding of the meaning of 'work' leads naturally to recognition of private ownership. There is finally a further subject — the conception of the home. The Home is not a reality unless it really is a man's own property, and his own home shelters his own family. A man's own fruit and vegetables out of his own garden taste better than a meal eaten in a crowded eating house. Any one who does not know the longing for possessions nor the joy of possession, will fail to understand the importance of recognising private ownership."[100]

Fichte often approached the topic of religion from an individual philosophical perspective rather than directly weighing the roles of religion in different facets of national life. Some historians, such as Kohn, place a greater emphasis on Fichte's political vision for Christianity than others, suggesting that Fichte positioned Christianity itself as the constitutional principle of humanity, and sought to replace all political rule with ethical unity.[101] Despite official accusations, Fichte was not an atheist in the strict sense, as his understanding of God was directly tied to the moral law and the continual striving toward the development of the rational self. He understood the structure of moral reality to be that of a natural order which can be revealed through duty, allowing for direct interaction with the divine. In this way he asserted God not to be a personal being and offered a philosophical interpretation of the divine in the context of the ethical foundations of freedom and purpose. This logically subordinates religious practice to the ethical scope of the people, which carried directly over into the logic that can be examined with National Socialism. It truly is an unavoidable stance from the determination of the social ideal as understood by National Socialism, where the wellbeing of the entire nation is the priority. Actions that negatively affect this objective must be disallowed regardless of who carries them out or for what purpose as they all are equally illegitimate in the face of national wellbeing. This brings us back to the same circular and fundamental argument that was initially asserted where voluntary submission to the nation entails abiding by the conduct and priority as established by national interest.

"Thus the apostles, for example, and the primitive Christians in general, because of their belief in heaven had their hearts entirely set on things above the earth even in their lifetime; and earthly affairs—the State, their earthly fatherland, and nation—were abandoned by them so entirely that they no longer deemed them worthy of attention. Possible though this is, and to faith not difficult, and joyfully though one must resign one's self, once it is the unalterable will of God, to having an earthly fatherland no longer and to being serfs and exiles here below, nevertheless it is not the natural condition nor the rule of the universe; on the contrary, it is a rare exception. It is a gross misuse of religion, a misuse of which Christianity among other religions has frequently been guilty, to make a point of recommending, on principle and without regard to existing circumstances, such a withdrawal from the affairs of the State and the nation as the mark of a true religious disposition."[102]

Both Fichte and National Socialism demand that man not put off the necessary struggles of life in favor of a subpar existence, remaining entirely focused on the promised afterlife, as such a focus is certain to result in communal neglect. These two philosophies demand action, not excessive deliberation. Similarly, action taken on behalf of the best interests of the nation cannot be retarded or impeded by any influence including religion, as this would then allow for a system that is permitted to actively oppose national interests.

"Strict proof can, and in due course will, be given that no man and no god and not one of all the events that are within the bounds of possibility can help us, but that we alone must help ourselves if help is to come to us. Rather shall I try to lift you above that pain by clear perception of our position, of our yet remaining strength, and of the means of our salvation."[103]

In both philosophies it is clear that such an influence cannot be permitted regardless of the faith or denomination; otherwise, a logical hole is created that leads to the collapse of the philosophy in its entirety. If a religion or a religious doctrine has the potential to take a position above the nation, then it can be reasonably understood that either:

    1. The nation is always subordinate to religion or religious doctrine.

If the nation is always of secondary importance behind religion, that means that there is a primary duty to uphold religious conviction, not the protection of the nation which is contradictory to both Fichte and National Socialism, both of whom directly posit religion to be permitted only to the extent that it is limited by national interest. This limitation is logical as both philosophies recognize the necessity of interpersonal contact and the intrinsic obligation which arises from it as the foundation of the social contract. This is where the obligations of the individual who wishes to live within the society must be upheld through service to communal interests, not to a personal God before all else.

2. The nation can be temporarily subordinated to religion or religious doctrine.

The exact same problems exist if the nation can be temporarily or sporadically subordinated to religion as if it is constantly subordinated, as in both cases the nation fails to take priority, directly contradicting both the philosophies of Fichte and National Socialism. This sporadic shifting of national priority is even more detrimental to the nation than if the primary reference for conduct was of a steadily religious nature, as it would be inherently wavering and unsteady, thus also disjointed.

"For the freedom for which we strive does not consist of us renouncing our own folk's essence, rather of fulfilling it. We want to finally be, and be allowed to become, those who we actually already always were, and we want the freedom to act accordingly."[104]

Fichte viewed religion, specifically Christianity as the moral seed of modern civilization both in ethical and spiritual terms. He understood the essence of Christianity to exist beyond doctrine, instead acting as a living force that elevates the remnants of antiquity through the internal recognition of moral duty which can be seen as grounded in the development of the rational self. There are countless prominent National Socialists who agree with this position, and others who would not, but such matters exist outside the scope of this publication, as the focus here is on the philosophical structure and growth of National Socialism, not the religious sentiment held by individuals in 1930s Germany.

"True religion, in the form of Christianity, was the germ of the modern world; and the task of the latter may be summed up as follows: to make this religion permeate the previous culture of antiquity and thereby to spiritualize and hallow it. The first step on this path was to rid this religion of the external respect of form which robbed it of freedom, and to introduce into it also the freethinking of antiquity. Foreign countries provided the stimulus to this step; which is really the continuation and completion of the first; namely, to discover in our own selves this religion, and with it all wisdom—this, too, was prepared by foreign countries and completed by the German."[105]

Below, Adolf Hitler describes the NSDAP's position on the church, where no actions would be taken to prevent the continuation of religious practice provided that it falls within the allowable scope of conduct expected by the nation. This passage carries Fichte's concerns about the misuse of religious systems, along with his general acceptance of religious pursuits within the aforementioned confines. It clearly confirms that religious practice under National Socialism is limited by the nation, not the other way around, which is perfectly consistent with the development of Fichte's interconnected nation and its mandatory priorities, placing national interest at the forefront of concern. In this way, Fichte would have considered the abandonment of the nation in favor of an outside element to be highly unethical, and those who choose to do so would be deemed as unfit for existence within the community. In this address to the Reichstag in early 1939, Hitler conformed closely to Fichte's earlier religious conclusions, specifically in regard to the interaction between the state and religious practice, thereby avoiding the logical contradiction that was previously explored in this chapter. For both Fichte and National Socialism, it does not matter what a person is wearing or what clerical role you hold if they are acting against the interests of the nation. There is no secondary consideration by either philosophy that allows for destructive individuals to be redeemed through adherence to a specific faith.

"The National Socialist State has not closed even one single church, neither prevented church services nor infringed on the conduct of Mass. It has not imposed its views on any confession's church doctrine and faith. In the National Socialist State, man is free to seek absolution in the fashion desired.

However, the National Socialist State will relentlessly deal with those priests who, instead of serving the Lord, see their mission in propagating derisive comments on our present Reich, its institutions, or its leading men. It will bring to their attention the fact that the destruction of this State will not be tolerated.

The law will prosecute a priest who implicates himself in illegal activities and he will be held accountable for these in the same manner as any other, ordinary German citizen. It must, however, be stated at this point that there are thousands upon thousands of priests of all Christian beliefs who attend to their clerical duties in a manner infinitely superior to these clerical warmongers and without entering into conflict with the established law and order. To protect these is the mission of the State. To destroy the enemies of the State is the duty of the State."[106]

Despite the limits which he asserted, Fichte was not anti-Christian; rather, he opposed religious overreach and external formalism in his later work, which does contrast sharply with some of the theocratic themes he had presented in his earlier writings. This is evident in *Addresses to the German Nation*, where he recognized the Protestant Reformation as a genuine cultural advancement because the German people themselves took the leading role in its development, purifying inherited structures through an inward moral filter.

"We have still to throw more light upon an observation, which has already been made twice, as to the natural course of development which events have taken with our nation, viz., that in Germany all culture has proceeded from the people. That the reformation of the Church was first brought before the people, and that it succeeded only because it became their affair, we have already seen."[107]

It can be confidently asserted that both Fichte and National Socialism:

1, Did not predicate their philosophies on religious doctrine; if either had done so, there would be no need for the national constraint on religious practice as the religious practice would be the core comparative factor of behavioral obligation, rather than the standards of the nation.

2. Allowed for varying forms of truly held religious expression that has grown according to national, rather than foreign, spirit, provided that it conforms to the needs and standards of the nation.

Albert Hartl, among many other National Socialist thinkers further confirmed this position, pushing it into popular thought and supporting Fichte's stance in his book titled *Eternal Front*:

"Nordic man knows that all folks and eras have a different concept of God according to their blood and level of culture. Hence he will always have the deepest reverence for all genuine religious expressions, because he knows that every honest religion bearing is directed at the one divine power." 108

Fichte saw the operations of the state as guided fundamentally by national interest, in a manner comparable to National Socialism. However, a rather significant difference can be seen in his downplaying of the importance of national militaristic structures. The following passage illustrates his idealistic interpretation of conflict, where Fichte asserted that the political seclusion of the nation would be enough to prevent the actions of outside forces from behaving opportunistically and imposing their will on the relatively undefended country. Fichte recognized that such a plan could fail in which case the citizenry, who have received basic weapon training would reinforce the standing military that had previously existed to enforce internal conduct. This stops short of the militaristic nature that National Socialism instills, where military service to the nation is seen as highly honorable and something that is to be particularly sought after,

"This state, moreover, will require no more standing troops than are necessary to maintain internal peace and order, since it does not wish to conduct wars of conquest and, having renounced all participation in the political relations of other states, hardly has to fear an attack. To be ready for this latter, extremely improbable case, the state will provide weapons training for every citizen fit to bear arms."109

The average National Socialist man is expected to trend closer to a martial order than what is suggested here by Fichte, and likewise the state is expected to take preventive actions that contribute to the protection of the nation. These preventive measures must include a formidable military, or it cannot be said that the nation can be secure from foreign threats that may have the physical means to enslave or destroy it. Clearly, Fichte recognized the military duty that the individual owes to the nation, as seen in the suggestion to train and arm the population, but stops short of the logical conclusion of National Socialism, as demonstrated by Adolf Hitler in a 1923 Munich speech:

"THEREFORE WE NATIONAL SOCIALISTS STAND FOR COMPULSORY MILITARY SERVICE FOR EVERY MAN. If a State is not worth that - then away with it! Then you must not complain if you are enslaved. But if you believe that you must be free, then you must learn to recognize that no one gives you freedom save only your own sword.110

In *Grundlage des Naturrechts (Foundations of Natural Right)*, Fichte further cements interpersonal relationships as the foundation of moral right, where the adherence to the order that one has submitted himself to is what offers an honorable lifestyle. There are two components that must be present in order to logically support this conceptualization of honor: the recognition of the natural organization and communication of the nation, and the willingness to voluntarily engage through the means that national interests dictate. Without the recognition of the scope of conduct organic to the nation, national directives will find it difficult to remain within the naturally prescribed bounds, leading to the adoption of foreign or inconsistent systems. Likewise, without the individual's voluntary submission to the specific path that the nation chooses to take within the wider natural scope of conduct, there will be no ethical development along the lines which Fichte recognized. Put simply, this is because ethical development for Fichte does not originate directly from the self, but rather from its relationship to the not self and similarly, the individual develops ethically through the continuous act of conforming to national expectations.

"Now a person could not give his word as something he intends to keep, nor could he actually keep it in the future, unless he has willed that there be a relation of right between himself and the other, i.e. unless he has subjected himself to the law of right."111

This is directly echoed in National Socialist philosophy, mainly under the banner of "honor," which is heavily emphasized across all literature, be it directed toward the youth or to the soldiers at the front. Of course, the recognition of a greater communal obligation that outweighs the selfish desires of the individual must be deemed worthy of developing in a population that operates on voluntary circumstances to perpetuate desired conduct. Below, Georg Usadel describes the exact same moral circumstances that originate in national interaction as Fichte did previously:

"Certainly, honor is the virtue within us that is most closely related to the eternal, to the "spark in the soul". From it develop all those other values that move our life:

duty, justice, truthfulness and heroism. For if we want to conceptually define honor, then we must find that this is hardly possible. Honor has this in common with the concepts sacredness, eternity and omnipotence. The honor of the individual can only receive its basis from the folk, because it, as we have seen, is divine will and mission."112

Fichte recognized a society that operates under individually self-imposed limitations without the need for a looming threat of punishment to be of a higher stage of civilization than one that requires governmental enforcement. Even if the individual is reformed and begins to abide by the standards of the nation, how can it possibly be known if he has truly bound his will to that of the nation voluntarily, or if it has been accomplished under duress?

"Moreover, the instruction concerning the constitution must make it quite clear that anyone who still needs the idea of punishment, or even indeed to revive that idea by suffering punishment, is at a very low stage of civilization. Yet, in spite of all this, it is clear that in these circumstances the pupil will be unable to show his good will outwardly, and education will be unable to estimate it, since no one can ever know whether obedience results from love of order or from fear of punishment.."113

National Socialism repurposes Fichte's approach outside of the idealistic framework it was originally presented, recognizing a greater need for governmental intervention and rehabilitation of criminals. As with all else, National Socialism weighs the correct course of actions taken in regard to specific criminal conduct according to the interests of the community and the greater nation. This could certainly mean expulsion as Fichte initially proposed, but not necessarily, and in this regard National Socialism could be asserted as the less extreme of the two, as the pathways to rehabilitation and reentry into the nation are still entertained to some extent.

"The Government desires to give effective protection to the community as well as to the individual against the activities of the criminal element and has taken suitable steps to ensure that chief attention shall be paid to the interests of the community when the penalties to be inflicted are fixed."114

To Fichte, excuses such as a loss of control only speak to the lower order that the individual belongs to and does not offer a reasonable excuse or any redemption for their poor conduct. Again we can see Fichte call for the expulsion of those who fail to conform to the standards of the nation in *Foundations of Natural Right*, where these individuals of a lower order are directly categorized with animals, as the two have an equal lack of self-restraint. Fichte and National Socialism both agree that existence within a community requires adherence and alignment with the greater nation, offering no place for those who do not intend on doing so.

"Intensity of passion does not excuse the crime but makes it more serious. Anyone who cannot control himself is a raging animal; since society has no means of taming him, it cannot tolerate him in its midst."115

Is Fichte's philosophy the same as National Socialism?

No.

The first critical difference can be seen in how National Socialism explicitly defines the nation in racial terms, wherein the foundational attributes and behavior of the population are held to originate in biological inheritance, specifically race. For Fichte, the nation was initially defined primarily in linguistic, cultural, moral, and educational terms, offering a more transitory and less rigid conceptualization of the nation. In his later works, Fichte increasingly moved away from this position, alluding to genetic continuity through bloodlines, along with a natural duty to future generations, ultimately stopping short of National Socialism's firm biological determinism.

Another philosophical divergence can be seen in their approaches to state power. Fichte recognized the state to function mainly as a moral institution, obligated to shape ethical citizens through systemic education and voluntary self-limitation of action. Fichte stood apart from later Romantic nationalists because his idea of nationhood was grounded in the Enlightenment ideal of moral reason shaped by the French Revolution, rather than in historical myth as was common.116

National Socialism does embrace many of Fichte's ethical and civic expectations but grounds those ideals in the concrete biological reality of the Volk, while emphasizing a practical need for state control in areas that Fichte often idealized. This is most evident in the way that National Socialism treats crime, military service, religious confession and economic stability, thereby demonstrating a significantly more pragmatic stance. Instead of relying on expulsion or the hope of voluntary conformity resulting from moral development as Fichte did, National Socialism instead recognizes the necessity of punishment and state enforcement, compulsory military service, and realistic crime control measures. National Socialism does not reject Fichte's ethics but instead grounds them in observable biological and societal necessity.

Despite these differences, substantial philosophical overlap exists. Fichte's insistence that moral growth only occurs through interpersonal interactions finds a close parallel in National Socialism's emphasis on social duty and communal identity. Both recognize the value of duty, especially toward future generations, and the position of the individual as a member of a greater moral community, where life as a self-contained entity is rejected in favor of voluntary submission to national interest. The mechanism of continuity remains similar as well because the nation stands as an ongoing project, where each generation must act as its steward and contribute to its development.

On economic theory, the two align considerably in concept, but differ in application. This can be seen in Fichte's *Closed Commercial*

State where he proposed a complete ban on foreign trade and strict moral constraints on all internal economic conduct. National Socialism, while also skeptical of international trade and foreign influence, opts for a more flexible approach, aiming for national self-sufficiency but offering a more flexible and soft approach than Fichte through the acceptance of strategic trade. Nonetheless, both philosophies reject international capitalism, Mammonism, and unregulated profit-seeking at the expense of others in favor of an ethically ordered economy that functions to fulfill the needs of the community.

Regarding religion, both directly reject dogmatic interference in national life. Fichte and National Socialism both consider the ethical duty that is held toward the nation to be of greater importance than ritual observance or theological authority. This can be seen in how National Socialism permits religious practice only to the extent that it does not interfere with the priorities of the state or nation, and in how Fichte rejected those who act unethically toward the nation from within the church hierarchy. Both recognize that a nation divided by religious dogmas exists in a weakened state, and therefore rectify the concern through the subordination of religious conviction to national survival.

In conclusion, National Socialism does not merely adopt Fichte, but rather takes on a portion of the idealistic framework that Fichte provided and anchors it in race, biology, and pragmatic governance. Due to these differences it can be asserted with confidence that Fichte is not the sole architect of National Socialism, nor was he a National Socialist, as Rudolf Jung had claimed. Rather, he was an essential precursor, whose philosophy, when biologically interpreted, proved to be a prominent ideological cornerstone of the National Socialist worldview.

Endnotes

1. Hoselitz, Bert F. "Professor Hayek on German Socialism." *The American Economic Review* 35, no. 5 (1945): 929-34.

2. Rory Lawrence Phillips, "Was Fichte a Proto-Fascist?" *The European Legacy* 30, no. 5 (2025): 539-58.

3. Rudolf Jung, *National Socialism: Its Foundations, Development, and Goals*, 2nd fully revised ed. (Munich: Deutscher Volksverlag, Dr. E. Boepple, 1922), 54.

4. Rory Lawrence Phillips, "Was Fichte a Proto-Fascist?" *The European Legacy* 30, no. 5 (2025): 539-58.

5. Hans Kohn, "The Paradox of Fichte's Nationalism," *Journal of the History of Ideas* 10, no. 3 (1949): 319-43.

6. H. C. Engelbrecht, "IV. Socialism and the Dawn of Nationalism 1794-1806," in *Johann Gottlieb Fichte: A Study of His Political Writings With Special Reference to His Nationalism* (New York and Chichester, West Sussex: Columbia University Press, 1933), 65-94.

7. M. R. Adams, *Behold the Kingdom of God: The Intellectual and Theological Origins of National Socialism* (PhD diss., 2014).

8. H. C. Engelbrecht, "IV. Socialism and the Dawn of Nationalism 1794-1806," in *Johann Gottlieb Fichte: A Study of His Political Writings With Special Reference to His Nationalism* (New York and Chichester, West Sussex: Columbia University Press, 1933), 65-94.

9. H. C. Engelbrecht, "IV. Socialism and the Dawn of Na-

tionalism 1794-1806," in *Johann Gottlieb Fichte: A Study of His Political Writings With Special Reference to His Nationalism* (New York and Chichester, West Sussex: Columbia University Press, 1933), 65-94.

10. Mariano Gaudio, 2021. "People, Nation, State: The Ground in Fichte's *Addresses.*" *Comparative and Continental Philosophy* 13 (1): 75-87.

11. H. C. Engelbrecht, "IV. Socialism and the Dawn of Nationalism 1794-1806," in *Johann Gottlieb Fichte: A Study of His Political Writings With Special Reference to His Nationalism* (New York and Chichester, West Sussex: Columbia University Press, 1933), 65-94.

12. Johann Gottlieb Fichte, *Foundations of Natural Right: According to the Principles of the Wissenschaftslehre*, ed. Frederick Neuhouser and trans. Michael Baur (Cambridge: Cambridge University Press, 2000), 9.

13. H. C. Engelbrecht, "IV. Socialism and the Dawn of Nationalism 1794-1806," in *Johann Gottlieb Fichte: A Study of His Political Writings With Special Reference to His Nationalism* (New York and Chichester, West Sussex: Columbia University Press, 1933), 65-94.

14. Johann Gottlieb Fichte, *Foundations of Natural Right: According to the Principles of the Wissenschaftslehre*, ed. Frederick Neuhouser and trans. Michael Baur (Cambridge: Cambridge University Press, 2000), 85.

15. Otto Dietrich, *The Philosophical Foundations of Nation-*

al-Socialism: A Call to Arms of the German Mind, lecture delivered at the University of Köln, 16 November 1934, trans. Hadding Scott (2015), 9.

16. Adolf Hitler, *Speech at the Lustgarten*, Berlin, May 1, 1939.

17. Johann Gottlieb Fichte, *Foundations of Natural Right: According to the Principles of the Wissenschaftslehre*, ed. Frederick Neuhouser and trans. Michael Baur (Cambridge: Cambridge University Press, 2000), 11.

18. Nationalsozialistische Deutsche Arbeiterpartei, *Ich Kämpfe (I Fight): The Responsibilities of Party Comrades*, trans. Rad Cowdery, 99.

19. Johann Gottlieb Fichte, *Addresses to the German Nation*, trans. R. F. Jones and G. H. Turnbull (Chicago and London: The Open Court Publishing Company, 1922), 139.

20. Johann Gottlieb Fichte, *The Closed Commercial State*, trans. and with an interpretive essay by Anthony Curtis Adler (Albany: State University of New York Press, 2016), 93.

21. Hermann Göring, *Germany Reborn* (Neues Europa Verlag, 2009), 20.

22. Johann Gottlieb Fichte, *The Closed Commercial State*, trans. and with an interpretive essay by Anthony Curtis Adler (Albany: State University of New York Press, 2016), 98.

23. Johann Gottlieb Fichte, *Foundations of Natural Right: According to the Principles of the Wissenschaftslehre*, ed. Frederick Neuhouser and trans. Michael Baur (Cambridge: Cam-

bridge University Press, 2000), 172.

24. Johann Gottlieb Fichte, *Addresses to the German Nation*, trans. R. F. Jones and G. H. Turnbull (Chicago and London: The Open Court Publishing Company, 1922), 133.

25. Georg Usadel, *Zucht und Ordnung: Grundlagen nationalsozialistischer Ethik* (Berlin: Zentralverlag der NSDAP, 1935), 7.

26. Johann Gottlieb Fichte, *Addresses to the German Nation*, trans. R. F. Jones and G. H. Turnbull (Chicago and London: The Open Court Publishing Company, 1922), 133.

27. Johann Gottlieb Fichte, *The Vocation of Man*, trans. William Smith, with introduction by E. Ritchie (Chicago: The Open Court Publishing Company, 1931), 19.

28. Rudolf Jung, *National Socialism: Its Foundations, Development, and Goals*, 2nd fully revised ed. (Munich: Deutscher Volksverlag, Dr. E. Boepple, 1922), 63.

29. Johann Gottlieb Fichte, *Addresses to the German Nation*, trans. R. F. Jones and G. H. Turnbull (Chicago and London: The Open Court Publishing Company, 1922), 2.

30. Adolf Hitler, *Speech at the Bürgerbräukeller,* Munich, November 8, 1938.

31. Johann Gottlieb Fichte, *Addresses to the German Nation*, trans. R. F. Jones and G. H. Turnbull (Chicago and London: The Open Court Publishing Company, 1922), 213.

32. Johann Gottlieb Fichte, *Addresses to the German Nation*, trans. R. F. Jones and G. H. Turnbull (Chicago and London: The Open Court Publishing Company, 1922), 3.

33. Adolf Hitler, *Mein Kampf*, (London: Hurst and Blackett Ltd., 1939), 244.

34. Johann Gottlieb Fichte, *Addresses to the German Nation*, trans. R. F. Jones and G. H. Turnbull (Chicago and London: The Open Court Publishing Company, 1922), 47.

35. Johann Gottlieb Fichte, *Addresses to the German Nation*, trans. R. F. Jones and G. H. Turnbull (Chicago and London: The Open Court Publishing Company, 1922), 232.

36. Johann Gottlieb Fichte, *The Vocation of Man*, trans. William Smith, with introduction by E. Ritchie (Chicago: The Open Court Publishing Company, 1931), 25.

37. Adolf Hitler, *Mein Kampf*, (London: Hurst and Blackett Ltd., 1939), 223.

38. Johann Gottlieb Fichte, *The Vocation of Man*, trans. William Smith, with introduction by E. Ritchie (Chicago: The Open Court Publishing Company, 1931), 120.

39. Johann Gottlieb Fichte, *Addresses to the German Nation*, trans. R. F. Jones and G. H. Turnbull (Chicago and London: The Open Court Publishing Company, 1922), 134.

40. Fritz Brennecke, *The Nazi Primer: Official Handbook for Schooling the Hitler Youth*, 9.

41. Johann Gottlieb Fichte, *Addresses to the German Nation*, trans. R. F. Jones and G. H. Turnbull (Chicago and London: The Open Court Publishing Company, 1922), 133.

42. Johann Gottlieb Fichte, *Addresses to the German Nation*, trans. R. F. Jones and G. H. Turnbull (Chicago and London: The Open Court Publishing Company, 1922), 135.

43. Johann Gottlieb Fichte, *The Vocation of Man*, trans. William Smith, with introduction by E. Ritchie (Chicago: The Open Court Publishing Company, 1931), 7.

44. Johann Gottlieb Fichte, *Addresses to the German Nation*, trans. R. F. Jones and G. H. Turnbull (Chicago and London: The Open Court Publishing Company, 1922), 3.

45. Johann Gottlieb Fichte, *Addresses to the German Nation*, trans. R. F. Jones and G. H. Turnbull (Chicago and London: The Open Court Publishing Company, 1922), 5.

46. Kurt Schrey, *You and Your People: An English Translation of Du und dein Volk (München, 1936)*, trans. and ed. Nathan R. Lawrence, 32.

47. Johann Gottlieb Fichte, *Addresses to the German Nation*, trans. R. F. Jones and G. H. Turnbull (Chicago and London: The Open Court Publishing Company, 1922), 2.

48. Feder, Gottfried. *Der deutsche Staat auf nationaler und sozialer Grundlage.* (Munich: Verlag Franz Eher Nachfolger, 1923), 49.

49. Johann Gottlieb Fichte, *Addresses to the German Nation*,

trans. R. F. Jones and G. H. Turnbull (Chicago and London: The Open Court Publishing Company, 1922), 9.

50. Johann Gottlieb Fichte, *Addresses to the German Nation*, trans. R. F. Jones and G. H. Turnbull (Chicago and London: The Open Court Publishing Company, 1922), 9.

51. Otto Dietrich, *The Philosophical Foundations of National-Socialism: A Call to Arms of the German Mind*, lecture delivered at the University of Köln, 16 November 1934, trans. Hadding Scott (2015), 5.

52. Johann Gottlieb Fichte, *Foundations of Natural Right: According to the Principles of the Wissenschaftslehre*, ed. Frederick Neuhouser and trans. Michael Baur (Cambridge: Cambridge University Press, 2000), 12.

53. Feder, Gottfried. *Der deutsche Staat auf nationaler und sozialer Grundlage.* (Munich: Verlag Franz Eher Nachfolger, 1923), 75.

54. Johann Gottlieb Fichte, *Foundations of Natural Right: According to the Principles of the Wissenschaftslehre*, ed. Frederick Neuhouser and trans. Michael Baur (Cambridge: Cambridge University Press, 2000), 15.

55. Nedim Nomer, "Fichte and the Idea of Liberal Socialism," n.d.

56. Tom Rockmore, "Fichte, Heidegger and the Nazis," in *Rights, Bodies and Recognition*, ed. A. Timothy Justus (London and New York: Routledge, 2006), chapter 16.

57. Johann Gottlieb Fichte, *Addresses to the German Nation*, trans. R. F. Jones and G. H. Turnbull (Chicago and London: The Open Court Publishing Company, 1922), 35.

58. Nationalsozialistische Deutsche Arbeiterpartei, *Ich Kämpfe (I Fight): The Responsibilities of Party Comrades*, trans. Rad Cowdery, 20.

59. Rudolf Jung, *National Socialism: Its Foundations, Development, and Goals*, 2nd fully revised ed. (Munich: Deutscher Volksverlag, Dr. E. Boepple, 1922), 90.

60. Zoltan Michael Szaz, "The Ideological Precursors of National Socialism," *The Western Political Quarterly* 16, no. 4 (1963): 924-45.

61. Hans Sluga, *Heidegger's Crisis: Philosophy and Politics in Nazi Germany* (Cambridge, MA: Harvard University Press, 1993), 40-41.

62. Johann Gottlieb Fichte, *Addresses to the German Nation*, trans. R. F. Jones and G. H. Turnbull (Chicago and London: The Open Court Publishing Company, 1922), 152.

63. Johann Gottlieb Fichte, *Foundations of Natural Right: According to the Principles of the Wissenschaftslehre*, ed. Frederick Neuhouser and trans. Michael Baur (Cambridge: Cambridge University Press, 2000), 160.

64. Adolf Hitler, *Speech in Munich*, September 16, 1930.

65. Hans Kohn, "The Paradox of Fichte's Nationalism," *Journal of the History of Ideas* 10, no. 3 (1949): 319-43.

66. Carl Mayer, "On the Intellectual Origin of National Socialism," *Social Research* 9, no. 2 (1942): 225-47.

67. Johann Gottlieb Fichte, *Addresses to the German Nation*, trans. R. F. Jones and G. H. Turnbull (Chicago and London: The Open Court Publishing Company, 1922), 138.

68. Nedim Nomer, "Fichte and the Idea of Liberal Socialism," n.d.

69. Johann Gottlieb Fichte, *Addresses to the German Nation*, trans. R. F. Jones and G. H. Turnbull (Chicago and London: The Open Court Publishing Company, 1922), 212.

70. Adolf Hitler, *"New Year's Proclamation to the National Socialists and Party Comrades"* January 1, 1933.

71. Johann Gottlieb Fichte, *Addresses to the German Nation*, trans. R. F. Jones and G. H. Turnbull (Chicago and London: The Open Court Publishing Company, 1922), 147.

72. Johann Gottlieb Fichte, *Foundations of Natural Right: According to the Principles of the Wissenschaftslehre*, ed. Frederick Neuhouser and trans. Michael Baur (Cambridge: Cambridge University Press, 2000), 312.

73. Heinrich Himmler, *The Laws of the SS Order*, (SS Main Office internal regulation, 1937).

74. Johann Gottlieb Fichte, *Addresses to the German Nation*, trans. R. F. Jones and G. H. Turnbull (Chicago and London: The Open Court Publishing Company, 1922), 13.

75. Joachim von Ribbentrop, *Germany Speaks: By 21 Leading Members of Party and State*, pref. by Joachim von Ribbentrop (London: T. Butterworth Ltd., 1938), 212.

76. Johann Gottlieb Fichte, *Addresses to the German Nation*, trans. R. F. Jones and G. H. Turnbull (Chicago and London: The Open Court Publishing Company, 1922), 151.

77. Johann Gottlieb Fichte, *Addresses to the German Nation*, trans. R. F. Jones and G. H. Turnbull (Chicago and London: The Open Court Publishing Company, 1922), 33.

78. Johann Gottlieb Fichte, *Addresses to the German Nation*, trans. R. F. Jones and G. H. Turnbull (Chicago and London: The Open Court Publishing Company, 1922), 34.

79. Joseph Goebbels, *Kleines ABC des Nationalsozialismus* (Berlin: Reichspropagandaleitung der NSDAP, 1932).

80. Johann Gottlieb Fichte, *Addresses to the German Nation*, trans. R. F. Jones and G. H. Turnbull (Chicago and London: The Open Court Publishing Company, 1922), 20.

81. Johann Gottlieb Fichte, *Addresses to the German Nation*, trans. R. F. Jones and G. H. Turnbull (Chicago and London: The Open Court Publishing Company, 1922), 14.

82. Rory Lawrence Phillips, "Was Fichte a Proto-Fascist?" *The European Legacy* 30, no. 5 (2025): 539-58.

83. Johann Gottlieb Fichte, *Addresses to the German Nation*, trans. R. F. Jones and G. H. Turnbull (Chicago and London: The Open Court Publishing Company, 1922), 15.

84. Joahim von Ribbentrop, *Germany Speaks: By 21 Leading Members of Party and State*, pref. by Joachim von Ribbentrop (London: T. Butterworth Ltd., 1938), 99.

85. Rory Lawrence Phillips, "Was Fichte a Proto-Fascist?" *The European Legacy* 30, no. 5 (2025): 539-58.

86. Johann Gottlieb Fichte, *Addresses to the German Nation*, trans. R. F. Jones and G. H. Turnbull (Chicago and London: The Open Court Publishing Company, 1922), 7.

87. Rory Lawrence Phillips, "Was Fichte a Proto-Fascist?" *The European Legacy* 30, no. 5 (2025): 539-58.

88. Johann Gottlieb Fichte, *The Closed Commercial State*, trans. and with an interpretive essay by Anthony Curtis Adler (Albany: State University of New York Press, 2016), 191.

89. Gottfried Feder, *The Programme of the N.S.D.A.P. and Its General Conceptions* (Munich: Franz Eher Nachfolger, 1927), 37.

90. Hans Kohn, "The Paradox of Fichte's Nationalism," *Journal of the History of Ideas* 10, no. 3 (1949): 319-43.

91. Johann Gottlieb Fichte, *The Closed Commercial State*, trans. and with an interpretive essay by Anthony Curtis Adler (Albany: State University of New York Press, 2016), 107.

92. Richard T. Gray, "Economic Romanticism: Monetary Nationalism in Johann Gottlieb Fichte and Adam Müller," *Eighteenth-Century Studies* 36, no. 4 (2003): 535-57.

93. Rory Lawrence Phillips, "Was Fichte a Proto-Fascist?" *The European Legacy* 30, no. 5 (2025): 539-58.

94. Rory Lawrence Phillips, "Was Fichte a Proto-Fascist?" *The European Legacy* 30, no. 5 (2025): 539-58.

95. Johann Gottlieb Fichte, *The Closed Commercial State*, trans. and with an interpretive essay by Anthony Curtis Adler (Albany: State University of New York Press, 2016), 97.

96. Johann Gottlieb Fichte, *The Closed Commercial State*, trans. and with an interpretive essay by Anthony Curtis Adler (Albany: State University of New York Press, 2016), 123.

97. Feder, Gottfried. *Der deutsche Staat auf nationaler und sozialer Grundlage*. (Munich: Verlag Franz Eher Nachfolger, 1923), 121.

98. Johann Gottlieb Fichte, *Foundations of Natural Right: According to the Principles of the Wissenschaftslehre*, ed. Frederick Neuhouser and trans. Michael Baur (Cambridge: Cambridge University Press, 2000), 215.

99. Nedim Nomer, "Fichte and the Idea of Liberal Socialism," n.d.

100. Gottfried Feder, *The Programme of the N.S.D.A.P. and Its General Conceptions* (Munich: Franz Eher Nachfolger, 1927), 39.

101. Hans Kohn, "The Paradox of Fichte's Nationalism," *Journal of the History of Ideas* 10, no. 3 (1949): 319-43.

102. Johann Gottlieb Fichte, *Addresses to the German Nation*, trans. R. F. Jones and G. H. Turnbull (Chicago and London: The Open Court Publishing Company, 1922), 133.

103. Johann Gottlieb Fichte, *Addresses to the German Nation*, trans. R. F. Jones and G. H. Turnbull (Chicago and London: The Open Court Publishing Company, 1922), 5.

104. Wolfgang Schultz, *Basic Ideas of National Socialist Cultural Policy* (Munich: Zentralverlag der NSDAP, 1939), 45.

105. Johann Gottlieb Fichte, *Addresses to the German Nation*, trans. R. F. Jones and G. H. Turnbull (Chicago and London: The Open Court Publishing Company, 1922), 103.

106. Adolf Hitler, *Address to the Reichstag*, Berlin, January 30, 1939.

107. Johann Gottlieb Fichte, *Addresses to the German Nation*, trans. R. F. Jones and G. H. Turnbull (Chicago and London: The Open Court Publishing Company, 1922), 103.

108. Albert Hartl, *Eternal Front: A Book for the Nordic Youth*, trans. (Munich: Zentralverlag der NSDAP, ca. 1937), 27.

109. Johann Gottlieb Fichte, *The Closed Commercial State*, trans. and with an interpretive essay by Anthony Curtis Adler (Albany: State University of New York Press, 2016), 194.

110. Adolf Hitler, *Speech in Munich*, April 27, 1923.

111. Johann Gottlieb Fichte, *Foundations of Natural Right: According to the Principles of the Wissenschaftslehre*, ed. Freder-

ick Neuhouser and trans. Michael Baur (Cambridge: Cambridge University Press, 2000), 124.

112. Georg Usadel, *Zucht und Ordnung: Grundlagen nationalsozialistischer Ethik* (Berlin: Zentralverlag der NSDAP, 1935), 19.

113. Johann Gottlieb Fichte, *Addresses to the German Nation*, trans. R. F. Jones and G. H. Turnbull (Chicago and London: The Open Court Publishing Company, 1922), 34.

114. Joahim von Ribbentrop, *Germany Speaks: By 21 Leading Members of Party and State*, pref. by Joachim von Ribbentrop (London: T. Butterworth Ltd., 1938), 85.

115. Johann Gottlieb Fichte, *Foundations of Natural Right: According to the Principles of the Wissenschaftslehre*, ed. Frederick Neuhouser and trans. Michael Baur (Cambridge: Cambridge University Press, 2000), 276.

116. Hans Kohn, "The Paradox of Fichte's Nationalism," *Journal of the History of Ideas* 10, no. 3 (1949): 319-43.

Chapter 2
Ernst Moritz Arndt

Ernst Moritz Arndt (1769–1860) was born toward the end of the Holy Roman Empire, where he witnessed and contributed to the development of modern German nationalism through his writings and teachings. Despite being born into an impoverished family in Swedish Pomerania, Arndt came to be a well-known figure in German academic and literary circles primarily for his writings on history and poetry. He studied theology and history at the University of Greifswald and later at Jena, where he encountered German Idealism and Romanticism. His early academic writings focused on legal history and ethics, but they gradually shifted toward pro-German activism as the Napoleonic Wars progressed.

Throughout this formative stage Arndt admired Goethe and Schiller, and was deeply impressed by Fichte while at Jena, and as such, naturally gravitated toward Romanticism. It has been asserted that Arndt inherited a significant portion of Herder's philosophy, likely from his studies at Stralsund and Jena.[1] It was during the period of French occupation of German lands that Arndt stepped out of academic obscurity into the role of a public intellectual and nationalist agitator, becoming a critical voice for the shaping of a moralized nationhood grounded in language, culture, blood and spiritual mission. During this period his pamphlets, poetry and songs proved to be valuable propaganda against Napoleon, so incendiary that he was forced into exile in Sweden from 1812 to 1815. Contemporary scholars note that Arndt's early reactions to the French Revolution and to Napoleon were rather typical of his intellectual circle. Initially, Arndt viewed Napoleon enthusiastically in the ode *Der Mächtige*, where he envisioned a German and French alignment that would bring about a new European order. By 1801, however, his view had shifted against Napoleon, painting him as Germany's archenemy and marking his transition to a conscious rejection of cosmopolitanism.[2]

Arndt was certainly no philosopher in the formal sense, but he was nonetheless a potent cultural ideologue who seamlessly blended Romantic and Lutheran ideas into militant German nationalism. Like the NSDAP and Fichte, Arndt understood the German Volk to be grounded in the divine order of nature, which dictated the acceptable range of behaviors and lifestyles. He explored these subjects mostly through exclusionary and sometimes mystical prose that portrayed the peasantry and the nation's soldiers as embodiments of national purity, standing against the cosmopolitanism and Enlightenment rationalism that characterized the invading hegemony. He took great care to portray the German Volk as a sacred organism inseparable from the land, guided by moral destiny to remain a pure, unified and sovereign entity. His writings infused German identity with a quasi-religious nature, allowing for a visceral portrayal of national unity being a moral calling and a duty grounded in the spirit.[3] Much of the comparatively limited scholarship on Arndt touches on his synthesis of Christian devotion and older Germanic symbology, insisting on a Christian society anchored in national tradition and myth.[4]

Over time, Arndt's publications began taking on increasingly pessimistic and proto-völkisch tones, but they never strayed from the recognition of divine providence and moral order, regularly invoking religious themes and language in the framing of political problems. While he certainly did not take up the biologically focused stance that National Socialism would later take up, his cultural essentialism and moral dualism between what is German and foreign laid the groundwork for the spiritual and racial positions later embedded in National Socialist philosophy. This national vision influenced many of the later nationalist and völkisch thinkers, including Paul de Lagarde and Rudolf Jung.

Underlying Arndt's vision was the conviction that God had formed diverse organisms and that the destruction of the divinely ordained should be avoided. Despite not forming a complete racial theory comparable to that of National Socialism, he nonetheless recognized a racially connected Volksgeist and condemned the blending of peoples and cultures.[5]

In the genealogy of National Socialism, Arndt functions not as an architect of ideology, but as a cultural prophet, sharpening the moral boundaries between the Volk and that which is foreign. His fusion of a Romanticized national rebirth and religion certainly played a part in shaping the emotional and spiritual vocabulary that would later define National Socialism, alongside other Pan-German thinkers such as Görres, and the Grimms.[6]

To understand the role of Ernst Moritz Arndt within the ideological trajectory that culminated in the development of National Socialism, it is necessary to view him as a critical bridge between the likes of Johann Gottlieb Fichte, who presented a more philosophically grounded nationalism, and the racial essentialism of the later völkisch movement. Fichte offered a relatively abstract framework of national unity within a larger philosophical system, seeking to invoke rationalism and ethical individual action, whereas Arndt worked with many of these same themes, presenting them in emotionally arousing and poetic form. Arndt's indirect role in the development of National Socialist philosophy is not as a system-builder, but rather that of a translator of rational sentiment into collective feeling. It is in this respect that Arndt additionally bridged the gap between Herder's nationalism and the more militant and politically driven nationalism of later thinkers such as Häusser and Treitschke.[7]

Through the rejection of a universal union, Arndt argued that both individual nations and the whole world would be better off, as each people must cultivate their own particular national character. Further, he recognized the proper legal systems and constitution of the people must grow out of their unique character, instead of abstract and universal principles. As the reader will note, the striving toward an organic whole within the nation's particular natural scope is not a novel concept introduced to National Socialist thought by Arndt alone, yet it became a primary component of Arndt's work after he shifted his views on Napoleon and the French.[8]

Arndt was significantly influenced by some of the same factors that influenced Fichte, most notably the occupation of German lands by Napoleon's forces. Fichte reacted to this by emphasizing the shared ethical principles and spiritualized self-discipline, contrasting the nature he perceived of the French, while Arndt offered a more exclusionary and visceral perspective. They were ultimately both exclusionary perspectives to some extent, but the composition and relevance of the nation itself varied from Fichte's more idealistic and dynamic portrayal to what Arndt presented in a more essentialist and romantic light.

One of Arndt's most famous works was a poem called *Was ist des Deutschen Vaterland? (What is the German Fatherland?)*, which was published in 1813 at a pivotal point in German history as the German Wars of Liberation were in full swing against Napoleon's forces. This period marked the start of a German awakening, where the idea of a united and self-determining German people gained momentum, crafting a cultural kernel that would later fully expand under the NSDAP. Due to the significant cultural impact and central role that this poem-turned-song had in shaping the nationalist imagination, it will be presented in full to allow for a thorough examination.

"The German Fatherland" (1813)

Which is the German's fatherland?
Is't Prussia's or Swabia's land?
Is't where the Rhine's rich vintage streams?
Or where the Northern sea-gull screams?—
Ah, no, no, no!
His fatherland's not bounded so!
Which is the German's fatherland?
Bavaria's or Styria's land?
Is't where the Marsian ox unbends?
Or where the Marksman iron rends?—
Ah, no, no, no!
His fatherland's not bounded so.
Which is the German's fatherland?
Pomerania's, or Westphalia's land?
Is it where sweep the Dunian waves?
Or where the thundering Danube raves?—
Ah, no, no, no!
His fatherland's not bounded so!
Which is the German's fatherland?

O, tell me now the famous land!
Is't Tyrol, or the land of Tell?
Such lands and people please me well.—
Ah, no, no, no!
His fatherland's not bounded so!
Which is the German's fatherland?
Come, tell me now the famous land.
Doubtless, it is the Austrian state,
In honors and in triumphs great.—
Ah, no, no, no!
His fatherland's not bounded so!
Which is the German's fatherland?
So tell me now the famous land!
Is't what the Princes won by sleight
From the Emperor's and Empire's right?—
Ah, no, no, no!
His fatherland's not bounded so!
Which is the German's fatherland?
So tell me now at last the land!—
As far's the Germans accent rings
And hymns to God in heaven sings,—
That is the land,—
There, brother, is thy fatherland!
There is the German's fatherland,
Where oaths attest the grasped hand,—
Where truth beams from the sparkling eyes,
And in the heart love warmly lies;—
That is the land,—
There, brother, is thy fatherland!
That is the German's fatherland,

Where wrath pursues the foreign band,—
Where every Frank is held a foe,
And Germans all as brothers glow;—
That is the Land,—
All Germany's thy fatherland!"[9]

The question: "Which is the German's fatherland?" might seem, on the surface, to be a straightforward inquiry in the modern world, but in 1813 Germany was a shattered nation, divided into dozens of sovereign principalities, free cities and duchies. This lack of political unity following the collapse of the Holy Roman Empire, combined with the impact of the Napoleonic Wars, intensified this sense of national fragmentation, which Arndt addressed directly. All of the regional, political and dynastic answers that immediately follow this opening question are emphatically rejected with the refrain: "Ah, no, no, no! His fatherland's not bounded so!" This is Arndt's poetic and systematic deconstruction of the prevailing idea that a fatherland is defined by political boundary or dynastic rule. In this way, he rejected feudal loyalty and geographic provincialism, insisting that a nation could not be determined by such superficial elements.

According to Arndt, the German fatherland can be seen wherever the German language is spoken, and where people sing hymns to the Christian God in that tongue, intertwining language and religion as core elements of a national identity. For Arndt, the nation is something more than a stationary feature of the land it occupies, not merely a legal or political entity, but a cultural, linguistic, and racial community. This constitutes one of the many proto-ethnonationalist themes that would later feed into the ideological development of National Socialism. The concept of a sacred nature and unique character within the Volk is central to National Socialism and is clearly demonstrated here with the hymns that directly connect spiritual unity and nationhood.

Arndt further reinforced this vision of German uniqueness by asserting, in a manner similar to Fichte, that it was solely the Germans who had managed to preserve an original Ursprache, an unmixed primordial language, which was deeply tied to both the national spirit and its racial purity. There are many examples of this almost mystical portrayal of the German language within Arndt's intellectual milieu, as well as later in National Socialist thought, as will be discussed in subsequent chapters.[10]

Additionally, Arndt places heavy emphasis on the rejection of the "foreign spirit," revealing the exclusionary character of his form of nationalism, specifically directed toward the French at this point. The lines in which he referred to every Frank as a "foe" demonstrate a call for a clear moral and cultural boundary for the German nation. In this way, the poem outlined both who was to be included and who was to be excluded from the national community, thereby articulating a unified resistance against elements that worked contrary to the wellbeing of the nation. This poem became one of the most recited nationalistic texts of nineteenth-century Germany, eventually being revived under the Third Reich, who saw Arndt's rejection of cosmopolitanism and his portrayal of German moral purity as among the many precursors that culminated in the development of National Socialism.

In *Mein Kampf*, Adolf Hitler made the boundaries of the National Socialist nation perfectly clear:

"It is not however by the tie of language, but exclusively by the tie of blood that the members of a race are bound together."[11]

Clearly Arndt stops short of the strict biological determinism that would later come to define National Socialist doctrine, but his work nonetheless internalized aspects of Fichte's belief that the nation must resist foreign influence to preserve its spirit, including foreign spirit that originates within the nation itself. Those whom Arndt believed were corrosive to the natural order and cultural continuity of the volk, such as the cosmopolitans, Jews, and liberals, became internal enemies equivalent in threat to the invading French. In this way, Arndt helped transform idealistic nationalism into an emotionally charged perspective revolving around betrayal, struggle, and purification.

Whereas Fichte chose to operate within the ethical bounds of Enlightenment thought, grounding his concept of nationalism in moral duty, reason and rational autonomy, Arndt emphasized more emotional and visceral themes, approaching the conception of the nation by means of ethno-cultural determinism. This vision of the nation became central to the völkisch movement and, eventually, serve as the emotional and symbolic foundation for a number of themes within National Socialism.

In Arndt's 1808 publication, *Geist der Zeit (Spirit of the Times)*, his position on the nation becomes clear as that of a consistent and organically developing entity that must be preserved through the prevention of unnatural disruptions. For Ardnt, the vitality of the nation was not tied to political institutions, but rather the moral, spiritual, and cultural characteristics of the people. In his work, he presents the Swedes as possessing a fixed and enduring national character, where the degeneration of such through cultural and spiritual erosion is equivalent to a moral failure. Arndt portrayed national identity as inherent and organic rather than constructed, resulting in his ideas falling closer to the organic-nationalist outlook later adopted by völkisch and National Socialist perspectives than Fichte's educational idealism. Fichte held that national belonging could be cultivated through individual ethical development and state-implemented patriotic education, while Arndt suggested that national character is an innate trait that remains resistant to transformation.

"There was a period, when the Swedes were in possession of all the strength and energy of the north, and we may expect that they will recover their ancient tenure. Their national character is still what it formerly was, and their climate and country do not permit them to degenerate."[12]

This passage asserts a climatic determinism, where the environment and national heredity function to preserve the nation's essence. National Socialism recognizes this national character to ultimately be a product of race, where its expression is tied to the unique genetic composition of the people. The idea that character and culture exist downstream from racial composition is absolutely central to National Socialist philosophy, extending far beyond Arndt's relatively non-biological, essentialist thinking. One literary movement that indirectly influenced National Socialism is known as the Heimatkunstbewegun, which transformed the earlier Romantic regional sentiment into a collective focus on the return of the Volk to the native land in order to achieve an organic wholeness. Scholars have noted the significant role that the writings of Arndt had on the developments of this ecological-national concept, alongside such men as Wilhelm Heinrich Riehl, both of whom emphasize the bond between people and soil, with Riehl being much closer to the later explicit concepts of "blood and soil."[13]

Despite commonly being remembered for what some may deem militant nationalism, Arndt spoke on the betterment of the peasant class, and when this is combined with the drive toward organic life rooted in native soil, the influence on men such as Walther Darré becomes readily apparent. It is held that Arndt was one of the first

German writers to reposition ecological stewardship in modern terms, though always steeped in demands for national exclusivity.[14]

"The racial composition of a folk is unique. Its alteration always has a transformation of its nature and culture as a consequence."[15]

Whereas Arndt viewed the problem of national degeneration through a moral and cultural perspective, National Socialism, as can be seen above, is grounded in racial science, which identified the source of national degeneration to be racial mixing. Nonetheless, both hold the same stance: the nation must protect its own spirit from corrupting external forces or face death.

Arndt continues this line of reasoning in *Geist der Zeit* when referring to Russia, which he saw as a country composed of many nations that failed to achieve national cohesion, rejecting the idea that a shared language alone could overcome innate national differences. He recognized that it wasn't simply language, but rather shared manners, religion, and national propensities that serve as the true markers of an organic unity. In this regard, Arndt and National Socialism align in their understanding that meaningful nations are formed through ethnic and spiritual unification, leaving those who fail to overlap in such a way to face instability and inorganic activity. The two diverge at a point just shy of the biological racial theory that sits as the keystone of National Socialism because while Arndt did recognize the ancestral and hereditary aspects of the nation, he did so with the inclusion of other elements such as spiritual inheritance, outside of a strictly biological sense, making his model less exclusionary than National Socialism's.

"The number of original Russian tribes is stated differently, from twelve to fifteen millions, the remaining subjects being composed of a great variety of nations, obeying one sceptre, but essentially differing from each other in manners, habits, religion, and national propensities. The majority of this heterogeneous mass do indeed speak the Russian language, but very few have as yet become Russians."[16]

In *The Life and Adventures of Ernst Moritz Arndt,* Arndt presents the nation and its honor as something worthy of fighting, and if need be, dying for. This is a common sentiment among patriotic and nationalist minded individuals so it cannot be reasonably asserted that this is the origin of National Socialism's similar position, yet such themes certainly contributed to the wider emotional vocabulary that later bolstered this stance.

"I was sitting in cheerful conversation over our wine, in a public garden, with some of my dearest friends, when the Swede let fall a contemptuous expression about the German people, just when I had been praising the Swedes. I was moved like Moses in Egypt, we fell out, and three days after met with pistols about a mile and a half from Stralsund, on the sea-shore, at a distance of fifteen paces."[17]

Dr. Joseph Goebbels considered the defense of national honor so essential that he included it as commandment number six in the *Ten Commandments for Each National Socialist*, included in one of the NSDAP's most referenced pamphlet on National Socialist doctrine, *Der Nazi-Sozi*. Dr. Goebbels framed the defense of the nation as a sacred obligation to the ancestors, closely mirroring Arndt's view of the nation as a transgenerational living entity.

"He who insults Germany insults you and your dead. Punch him."[18]

In *Geist der Zeit*, Arndt asserted that even within a single ethno-linguistic nation like Germany, regional variations in history, climate, and culture could lead to distinct sub-national characteristics. He acknowledged in the passage below that foreigners and regionally distinct Germans were capable of assimilating into Germandom over centuries, thereby offering justification for cultural conquest as a legitimate nation-building process. It was due to these regional differences that Arndt cautioned against assuming the character of the nation from a single region; to avoid misrepresentations, he insisted that a fuller picture must be gathered that factors in these subtle regional differences. This aspect of national unity through limited diversity is a position that was later echoed by NSDAP ideologues who saw Germans as a racially unified people but who should nonetheless retain their regional nuances.

"German settlers and masters introduced German manners and the German language, and the remains of the oppressed nation were, after the lapse of some centuries. waited, into one nation. But this produced in the north quite a different spirit and disposition, contrasting not only climatically, but nationally with that in the south of Germany, so much so that no one having seen only the north of Germany as far as Magdeburg or Dresden,. can form a just idea of the real character of the Germans."[19]

Arndt sought to define the moral and temperamental essence of the German people through ancient and enduring values that he believed reflected their national character. He conceptualized nationhood as rooted in ancestry, history, and the environment, attributing inconsistent regional characteristics mostly to environmental differences, thus presenting a partially deterministic view of nationhood.

"Industry, economy, soberness of mind, forbearance without pusillanimity, honesty blended with some portion of climatic heaviness, are ancient virtues by which the nation is generally allowed to be distinguished."[20]

All of these traits were later echoed under National Socialism, which also upheld such values as integral components of the German Volk's character. This parallel should not be surprising, given how much Arndt contributed to the ideological soil from which the völkisch movement, and later National Socialism, emerged. Moreover, these values are recognized by both Arndt and National Socialism as ancient and unchanging, serving as the ideal attributes for members of the nation.

"In the National Socialist state therefore selection and state help are not based on rank or social classes, but solely and limited to ability and accomplishment, industriousness and bearing."[21]

Arndt's writings frequently feature a sort of Romantic nationalist anxiety concerned with the deterioration of the spiritual foundation of the volk. He recognized national virtue as an organic, but nonetheless vulnerable, entity that, once corrupted, leads not merely to a cultural decline but to a deeper moral and civilizational collapse. Below, Arndt points out the deterioration of modesty, which he believed had slowly been replaced by a foreign, egotistic, and theatrical spirit, especially in the period preceding publication of *Geist der Zeit* in 1808.

"Modesty too was once a prominent feature in the German character; but boasting has of late stepped in its place-a proof that the national spirit is degenerating, though it would not be surprising, were it still more glaringly corrupted than it actually is."[22]

Ultimately, Arndt recognized this erosion of national spirit as leading to indifference, where common interest had been supplanted by material goods and convenience, culminating in a clearly heard national death rattle picked up by Arndt and his Romantic contemporaries. Not only does he place blame on external forces for Germans deterioration, but he also condemns the princes of Germany, accusing them of cowardice, greed and manipulation. This position would later grow into a foundational sentiment of the völkisch movement, emphasizing the betrayal of the people by both corrupt elites and conspiring foreign influences.

"We have now reached the extremity; the people, having lost all political confidence, all sense of common interest, and all hopes, are at last, become indifferent, and struck dumb. The miseries of war, the disgrace of peace, the spoilations of gold and silver, the violations of wives and virgins, the demolition of fortresses, the scorn of strangers, and the timidity, artifice, and covetousness of their princes: These must finally produce important effects, and must produce them to our ruin."[23]

Arndt adamantly renounced cosmopolitanism, specifically in its Enlightenment form, which held that the universal interests of "mankind" justly override the unique identities of individual nations. This was a common idea circulating throughout the revolutionary French and Enlightenment circles, which amounted to a national sacrifice of identity, one Arndt refused to accept. National and cultural sovereignty, he believed, must remain paramount. This critique of cosmopolitanism became a central theme in the völkisch tradition due to the work of Arndt and others, eventually embedding itself into the philosophy of National Socialism.

"They add, that this was the only means of producing cosmopolitism, that this was much superior to nationalism, inasmuch as the human race was of greater consequence than any individual nation, and that it therefore was not to be regretted if a nation lost its individuality, whilst mankind in general was benefited by it."[24]

Rudolf Jung echoed these same statements just over a century later, expanding and clarifying the sentiments of Arndt and other Romantic thinkers by rejecting internationalism and cosmopolitanism in favor of a racially defined folkdom that lives according to its specific nature. It can be plainly seen through the works of Rudolf Jung that National Socialist thought had anchored itself in a biological conception of the nation by 1919, allowing for greater clarity regarding the confines of the nation and the constitution of that which is foreign.

"This characteristic is what distinguishes us from other races; we should not concern ourselves with seeking to emulate or to understand them. We will never penetrate their spiritual and intellectual world, and they will never penetrate ours. That is why we hold the opinion that it is folkdom which defines the natural limits of our abilities; for this reason we reject internationalism (cosmopolitanism, pan-folkdom), no matter what motives it may arise from and no matter what guise it may be garbed in."[25]

Through the recognition of the critical role that nature and identity play, Arndt emphasized the necessity to function within and according to the organic way of the community. From this premise follows the belief that forced submission or adherence to a way of life that falls outside of the natural scope for the people is simply servitude. In this way, it is not simply a matter of political subjugation, but instead a form of cultural and spiritual degeneration.

"Without the people there can be no human race, and without free citizens there cannot be free men. In a nation of slaves, every thing assumes a slavish cast: you will rarely meet with a person whose sentiments are so exalted, that he could endure a state of servitude and contempt, without degenerating, and never a whole nation."[26]

National Socialism similarly recognizes national strength and unity to be the primary defensive barriers against cultural collapse and national enslavement. Arndt offered an emotional and moral framework rooted in Romanticism and Lutheran ethics, elements of which National Socialism partially incorporated into its more complete worldview. Below, Rudolf Jung again channels this völkisch inheritance, where he equated the loss of national sovereignty, along with the lack of adherence to an organic range of conduct, to be equivalent to national and individual slavery.

"And yet: National Socialism strives for more than one or the other partial reform; it goes all out. Its goal is, purely and simply, the reform of life itself; it fights against everything which arises out of foreign thinking, which binds our Volk in the fetters of slavery."[27]

Arndt condemned the priestly nature of the Holy Roman Empire, instead asserting a need for absolute political and spiritual unity in the hopes of avoiding self-interested rulers that may work counter to the wellbeing of the population. In the following passage, originally presented in *Germanien und Europa* in 1803, he calls for the formation of a society where individual interests are subordinated to the collective good of the nation, prefiguring what would later be referred to as the Volksgemeinschaft (people's community).

"A nation that has a hundred lords can never be happy or great, because it lacks the consciousness of strength, the love of a great totality, [the love] of self-sacrifice for this totality. It lacks the idea of community and of the fatherland; the lasting, greatest idea for a people."[28]

Arndt's framing mirrors the National Socialist demand for unity across class, party, and region in pursuit of a unified racial and national destiny. In *Germany's Hitler*, Heinz A. Heinz offers one out of a seemingly endless supply of quotes on unity within National Socialism. This is a perfectly logical position as a unified group operating together toward a singular objective offers the greatest amplification of efficiency, along with the greatest amount of focused energy possible within the nation. National Socialist doctrine repeatedly emphasizes this unity as both a moral and functional necessity. It would be foolish to assert that a divided nation rife with infighting would collaborate well enough to match the efforts of the fanatically unified, a point suggesting that this aspect of National Socialist thought had already reached considerable ideological depth even during Arndt's lifetime. This does not mean that Arndt and National Socialism overlap perfectly in terms of the nation's construct, but rather that they share a commitment to internal unity and the subordination of individual will to the needs of the nation. This is the concept that National Socialism presents as genuine socialism. Fichte interpreted this in terms of ethical development and reciprocal obligation, whereas Arndt framed the duty to the nation in a more romantic light.

"The National Socialist must be convinced, enthusiastic, energetic: he must be ready and eager to do his utmost without any necessary wage or return. He must be fanatic for the unity which means strength."[29]

In *The life and adventures of Ernst Moritz Arndt,* Arndt asserted that even after years of foreign rule, the German people of French-occupied regions retained their unique Germanic customs, demonstrating nationhood to be a matter of blood, language, and custom, not something that could be easily erased by occupation or political boundaries.

"The rest of the Rhine-provinces, though they were only held by the French for twelve or fifteen years, yet have had in some degree to accustom themselves again to Germany and their German brothers. The greater part of Alsace has been united to France for from one hundred and fifty to two hundred years, but still the Teutonic language and Teutonic manners prevail among the inhabitants, though few of them feel what they have lost in not being united to the great German nation. And here is a great perversion of nature; for when a people is governed by a greater foreign nation, the elements of its own nature grow feeble and are little developed, while it can with difficulty adopt the elements of its foreign neighbour."[30]

Arndt uses explicitly moral and metaphysical language when interpreting foreign domination, seeing it as a violation of the natural order, wherein each people possesses a unique internal character and destiny. This perspective highlights Arndt's skepticism toward the possibility of assimilation as ethnic and cultural origins constrain the individual's potential. In this regard, he anticipated the racial essentialism of the 20th century in terms still oriented toward cultural and spiritual qualities rather than a fully biological theory.

"And here is a great perversion of nature; for when a people is governed by a greater foreign nation, the elements of its own nature grow feeble and are little developed, while it can with difficulty adopt the elements of its foreign neighbour. Will, or can, a German Alsatian, brought up under French influence and in French habits of thought, ever become a man of the first rank in the French kingdom.? I doubt it."[31]

Below, Arndt warns of the intermingling with the French population, as it would result in the corruption of the racial stock of the Germans, which, although not grounded in biological race science, nonetheless suggests an essentialist view of race as tied to cultural and moral decline.

"In fact, it is not only the ill-treatment of these poor people which vexes me, but also the tolerably certain prospect that the Rhine, of which Germany was once so proud, will be shared with the Franks, that this fine race will be reduced to a hybrid set; that Germany, the unconquered, will become the scorn of all nations."[32]

Napoleon could be argued to hold a rather substantial, albeit indirect, role in the development of National Socialism as he set the locomotive in motion that would lead to philosophers and poets alike rejecting foreign rule while looking inward towards the nation. Interestingly enough, despite despising Napoleon in his mature works,

Arndt places the blame on the entirety of the French nation, marking a shift toward a pattern of collectivized moral judgments directed at the people as a whole, not just their leader.

"It was not Napoleon only; not the cunning, taciturn, sneering Corsican, born in the land where honey is poison, who has been made a scapegoat on which the anger of Europe should be heaped, whom I hated most; it was the French-the deceitful, the insolent, covetous French-for centuries the cunning and faithless enemies of the empire. I hated them with entire hatred, and recognised my Fatherland, and loved it with entire love."[33]

In *Germanien und Europa*, Arndt maintains his opposition against Kantian-style cosmopolitanism and the unification of Europe, a recurring theme which proves to be integral to Arndt's worldview. Additionally, his use of the term "Völker," meaning nations or peoples, implies ethnically and culturally distinct groups, not just political or geographic entities, which is an important distinction. He viewed the mixing of these distinct groups as equivalent to the destruction of both, and thus an existential threat to the nation, through his brilliant metaphor of confluence turning into diffluence: the mixing of waters (nations) leads not to unity, but to disintegration, loss of cultural and spiritual clarity, and national fragmentation. This is a central theme in Romantic and proto-völkisch worldviews, where the nations are understood to be sacred, organic entities whose unique characteristics and composition must be preserved.

"I have said more than once what I think about the universality of peoples [Völker], and how ill-pleased I am by what others hope and dream for from a universal empire and from a union of all peoples accompanied by progressive humanization and ennoblement. I hate any type of confluence on earth, because it will turn into diffluence, that is, into the political and moral death of the various nations."[34]

Despite the commonly held misunderstanding, National Socialism is not an ethnocentric philosophy, as its primary focus is not the denigration or domination of foreign races, but rather the preservation and cultivation of the nation. Like Arndt, National Socialism recognizes a dysgenic threat posed by interbreeding between disparate peoples, though it is articulated more explicitly through a racial and biological lens. National Socialism is markedly more racially oriented than Arndt's position due to the development of modern racial sciences that were not available to Arndt in his time.

"In the second place, we believe that races receive their different natures in order to develop them and not to mix them. In this connection, we have already stated that we see in racial differences no real differences in quality, but rather differences in kind. Therefore, we will preserve the race of Germans in its true character and guard it against false mixing."[35]

Arndt's Romantic nationalist view that nations are defined by enduring racial, moral, and aesthetic characteristics is made clear in *Geist der Zeit*, where the Spaniards were used as an example of a pure nation. The physiognomy of a people was thus asserted by Arndt to be tied to their moral and cultural qualities, a perspective later absorbed into völkisch and, when pairing physiognomy and race, National Socialist thought. He recognized that the Spaniards have the potential to degenerate, but argued that they have withstood such, demonstrating a historical continuity of essence spanning back to the time of the ancient Iberians.

"Where the Spaniards are not degenerated, there you will discover tall, slender, and nervous bodies, agile and strong at the same time. Their free and serious physiognomy displays a broad and lofty forehead, large black and sparkling eyes, a beautiful nose, and manly lips, with a lion's chin. Their complexion is dark, but the women of the better classes in some parts are extremely beautiful. The Spaniards in general, in their character, exhibit a happy medium between levity and heaviness, which distinguishes the noblest race of men, to be produced only in climates as highly favoured as theirs: a most charming mixture of ardour and seriousness, of grandeur and amiableness. It is from this cause that Spain has produced the greatest excellencies which modern refinement could create. The nation could degenerate; but it has not become contemptible. All Europe must do justice to the honourable principles displayed by the Spaniards in social transactions, and in politics. They are still the ancient Iberians."[36]

Despite living before the period where race was used in a strictly biological context such as under the NSDAP, Arndt invoked racial premises through his use of physiognomy, as the phenotypic expression that constitutes physiognomy is bound to genetic composition, and thus too bound to race. Around a century later, National Socialism codified the ideas of the pre-biological nationalist thinkers like Arndt with the unmistakable recognition of the racial boundaries of the nation, eliminating the vague qualifiers that previously accompanied the construct of nationhood. There are many occasions where Ardnt walks the line of such later thought, which can be seen in how he viewed Russia as a mixed country that was "half Mongolian and half Oriental", demonstrating some extent of a racialized worldview, where the European spirit stands in opposition to Asiatic or Eastern traits.

"A man who could sabre the Streltzi, behead his son, immure his wives in cloisters, and raise his concubines upon the throne, could not but possess the energy required for making Europeans of the Russians, who in manners, arts, and mode of life were still half Mongolian and half Oriental. Even the little incidents occurring in his family and at his table, his gracious -executions, entirely characterize the barbarian; for, incipient culture as precipitately acquired as his, is very apt to assume a strong tinge of singularity and ridiculousness."[37]

With descriptions such as "gracious executions," Arndt expressed moral disdain through irony, contrasting the refined European way with the Eastern despotism that demonstrated a level of brutality indicative of the uncivilized. To Arndt, these mixed societies were culturally and racially alien to the European, leaving the barbarian king with unsuitable raw materials to sculpt a true European society no matter what level of savagery he employed in the process.

"Peter, that august barbarian, early comprehended that he ruled over an half- savage, despised, and politically insignificant nation; and he early formed in his great mind the design to effect a total reform, and to render the Russian name respected in Europe."[38]

This continues with Arndt asserting that Central Europe is the ultimate source of refined civilization, indicating the existence of a civilizational hierarchy, where certain peoples who are rooted in specific lands are more capable of obtaining the vital flame, representing the European spirit. The artifacts of Arndt's Romantic position, and others who hold similar positions, can be seen interacting with the emerging biological sciences for primacy within National Socialist philosophy and within the personal writings of NSDAP officials outside of official doctrinal publications. This point of interaction between the two concepts reveals a significant portion of the roots of National Socialism to be firmly planted in some elements of the völkisch movement, although this is hardly a novel conclusion.

"The dreadful seclusion from the polished part of society, the difficulty of communicating with it, will never admit of the vital flame being kindled as bright and instantaneously as in the centre of Europe; nor will the sacred life-blood of enthusiasm be capable of circulating as briskly there as here."[39]

In *Geist der Zeit*, Arndt references Spain multiple times in in a romantic-nationalist light, where intangible virtues such as spirited independence, fervent passion in love and religion, and dedication to the arts come together in such a way that they overshadow imperial conquest or simple political power.

"An aspiring mind, a spirit of independence, together with enthusiasm in love, in religion, and in the cultivation of the arts, exalted the nation, and rendered the Spanish name renowned among the nations of Europe."[40]

Arndt expressed his deep scorn for cultural subservience and the importation of foreign ideals, especially from France. The mocking imagery ridicules the Spaniards who abandoned their national character in favor of French refinement, which Arndt clearly views as superficial and corrupting. His rejection of this mimicry reflects a broader Romantic nationalist defense of cultural authenticity, where true refinement is seen as something organically grown within a people, not borrowed from others. For Arndt, the idea that Spain needed to be "improved" by the French is both offensive and unnatural, tying into the National Socialist themes on foreign influence that have already been covered in this chapter.

"Spaniards should become slaves of the French, and crow and skip like them, as many seem to wish, imagining that all higher refinement, of which the present generation stands in need, must be imported from, the banks of the Seine?"[41]

Below, Arndt asserted the formative power of culture, tradition, and historical continuity, suggesting that national character is not merely innate or biological. Through shared habits and values, Arndt argued that an individual is capable of joining with a distinct national spirit that they are not genetically bound to, a threat that the NSDAP would later directly recognize. National Socialism maintains that character, strength, and unity must be cultivated through education and national renewal in a way that is similar to Arndt, but recognizes the nation and the membership to such in strictly racial terms. In this way, Arndt becomes a precursor to the cultural-nationalist side of National Socialist thought: emphasizing not only blood, but the enduring power of national heritage and unity in shaping man into something greater than an individual.

"What was not originally in man, becomes innate by means of custom, continued from century to century, and a nation gradually, acquires a spirit which is not naturally in man."[42]

To Arndt, honor is inseparable from moral character for both individuals and entire nations, where truly great people are capable of upholding their principles even when facing adversity. He saw in France the opposite of true German values, a point that heavily influenced both the later völkisch and National Socialist spheres, which saw in France a symbol of cultural decline, materialism, and rootlessness that stood in clear contrast to the moral purity of the German volk. Arndt's words such as these helped to lay the foundation for the National Socialist conception of national honor as something rooted not in global domination but in ethnic authenticity, cultural continuity, and collective virtue.

"Frenchmen, you are the nation that has cheated Europe of its fairest hopes; and yet you presume to be the benefactors and masters of others-you, who have become the most wretched slaves of one man, who employs no nobler arts to lord over you than common cunning and imposing monkey-tricks! You call yourselves the great nation. If the despoliation of countries, the subversion of states, the subjugation of free nations, if bartering away for gold and silver all virtue and honour, can be called greatness, then few nations indeed have been greater than yourselves. But if incorruptible probity, good faith, justice and moderation are required to make individuals and nations great, you cannot but be sensible of your excessive littleness."[43]

Arndt saw honor not as an abstract or personal concept, but as something that is intrinsically linked to the collective sacrifice of one's ancestors and community. To waver in the moment where action is required is seen as nothing short of a betrayal of those who gave their lives for the preservation and dignity of the nation. This transforms honor into a binding moral obligation to the living, a sentiment frequently invoked under National Socialism, creating a mythos of a noble death which positions collective sacrifice as the highest moral act.

"Besides, how should any honourable fellow waver, when so many brave men have died for their fatherland?"[44]

Many National Socialist writers drew similar conclusions to Arndt, as seen in the 1940 publication *The Eternal Front*, where it was directly claimed that honor constitutes the deepest essence of the nation. According to the National Socialist framework, the spirit of true socialism can only be found through the adherence to a selfless lifestyle dedicated to the nation, as compelled by honor.

"In all times in Germany, loss of honor was always considered the greatest shame and humiliation, and the worst treason. The loss of honor is the loss of one's own deepest essence. There have been times and folks that had no understanding for the concept of honor, they only knew moral action under the whip or an action of pure selfishness. We Germans are happy and proud that the Creator has given us honor as the guidelines of our life and as the highest moral property at the same time. We are happy that National Socialism has again led us back to this moral basic value."[45]

In *Geist der Zeit*, Arndt passionately presents an ethical vision of freedom that is cultivated through communal virtue, not just through brute force or physical domination. He proposed a new universal standard of "love and charity" as the foundation of a free society, whose members would then voluntarily join together as one in labor and responsibility. In this way, Arndt asserted that a nation becomes free, not through mere resistance to tyranny, but rather through ethical self-restraint and a shared understanding of social responsibility. He thus reorients the concept of freedom from external opposition to internal moral order.

"The modern human race must submissively renounce the proud reliance on physical strength, the savage use of power, and the uncharitable treatment of free-born men as slaves, if they are to fulfil the precepts of the new universal law of love and charity. Virtues less boisterous-a gentler kind of enthusiasm, labour, and moderation, practised by the whole community, in order that no one may be necessitated to submit to the yoke of servitude-these are the moderate demands made upon a nation desirous of deserving the name of freemen."[46]

This concept of freedom may sound very similar to Fichte's conceptualization, and they do overlap in that both believed real freedom to be more than a simply external phenomenon. However, from this point, a significant deviation appears between the internalized moral reason presented by Fichte and the less philosophically systematized, more organically rooted national character as presented by Arndt. This is an extremely important theme throughout the development of National Socialism, where Romantic notions collide with philosophical systems, resulting in the formation of a philosophically sound, yet emotionally dense worldview. It was through the introduction of racial sciences that both the philosophical segment and the Romantic segment became anchored in more quantifiable terms, solidifying race as the central attribute from which all national functions, including morals and cultural production, originate.

Arndt's conception of liberty was based on disciplined civic tradition, which can be seen in his praises of the German people's "susceptibility for obedience to the laws," suggesting that to him liberty does not mean unchecked freedom, but rather self-governance rooted in communal ethics and individual moderation.

"If you search the history of German guilds and corporations, and examine the constitutions and transactions of the petty imperial towns, you will discover an astonishing susceptibility for obedience to the laws, and can it be denied that this is a disposition for genuine liberty? This reflecting, equal and good-natured spirit of the nation, which, as yet, lives only in recollection and slight remains, produced moderation and consideration, without which no real liberty can exist."[47]

Arndt frequently compared and contrasted northern and southern Europe, viewing the south as both a source of cultural greatness and political deterioration, while the north remained uncorrupted by decadence and thus the liberators of degraded worldviews. He framed the role of northern Europe in the avenging and restoration of the south as more than coincidental; it amounted to a spiritual and moral duty of the Nordic peoples to usher in a return to the European spirit for all Europeans.

"The improvers of the human race ever came from the south, but thence also issued its despoilers; whereas it was from the north that her avengers and deliverers proceeded. If all Europe should be ruined by weakness, cowardice, and despotism; if every part of it should be reduced under the control of cunning and tyranny; if in all Europe not a single voice should dare to defend the cause of liberty and truth, and not-one sword be drawn for their protection, yet the forests and mountains of Scandinavia will continue inhabited by a free race of men, who will chastise and deliver the afflicted and debased world."[48]

In *SS Mate Selection and Race*, an SS-issued pamphlet designed to expose soldiers to racial hygiene practices, the Germanic peoples are said to be predominantly Nordic, resulting in a unique predisposition that was to be protected. Arndt was one of the most influential early proponents of such ideas, which continued to evolve through sections of the völkisch movement, eventually merging with biological sciences to form the strains of Nordic heavy racial theory that reached its peak during the time of the NSDAP. While the complete dissection of racial theory ought to be left to subsequent publications that are focused solely on the matter, it should nonetheless be recognized here that not every thought and action taken by the NSDAP or its officers, along with their constantly evolving racial theories, speaks to the stance of National Socialism as a philosophy. The philosophy itself seeks to maintain the core nature of the people, through whatever means is most fitting and available in the moment. In this way, technology changes and scientific innovation continues but poses no threat to the logical standing of the worldview.

"The predominant race determines the folkish character and continues its influence in it as a hereditary factor. As in the Germanic peoples, the predominant Nordic race gives the German folk, too, the predisposition of our kind."[49]

Below, in *Spirit of the Times,* Arndt references the tale of Numantia, which was a city that resisted Roman rule by setting itself on fire in order to choose death over submission. This theme of national honor and the refusal to be enslaved, even at great personal cost, carried over into National Socialism as an extension of the socialist duty toward the nation. An individual's death for one's people or homeland was not viewed by Arndt as tragic, but rather as extremely honorable, giving rise to the völkisch and National Socialist conception of a heroic death. Arndt recognized that freedom requires a blood sacrifice, something that would be seen in the 1923 Beer Hall Putsch, where the death of the martyrs provided the necessary seed for national rebirth.

"But those vile wretches, who boasted of past victories, employed the dagger of the midnight assassin against their brave and dreaded foes-by this means fell Numantia, the heroine. Her conquered citizens rather chose to die than yield to the rapacious foe, and died the death of freemen beneath the ruins of their burning city, fired by the despairing hand of dying liberty."[50]

Arndt examined the moral and physical degeneration of Iberia's kings, concluding that their separation from the organic spirit of the nation and wavering morality ultimately stifled national greatness and weakens the civic body. The degeneration described below clearly relates to what is now understood as racial hygiene practices, and the lack thereof. This narrative prefigures völkisch, and later National Socialist, thought on hereditary corruption and the need for rebirth through new leadership rooted in the nation, rather than decaying systems that no longer represent the interests of the volk.

"But alas! Iberia's kings degenerated into despots, undermining the liberty of their own people, and threatening subjugation to other nations. In one place resistance prevailed, in another growing weakness; and after a century, celebrated by the most astonishing feats, the nation began to decline. After a succession of great sovereigns, of brave despots, weaklings, and devotees occupied the throne. The princes of the house of Habsburg degenerated through frequent intermarriages, and thenceforth no great man was produced by that family."[51]

In *Germanien und Europa*, Arndt painted governmental systems that lack a strong centralized power as inherently weak, facing predictable deterioration due to competing personal interests. He identified polyarchies as a considerable vulnerability that allowed foreign entities to gain power and subvert the nation.

"Germany can thank this polyarchy, just as Italy can thank hers, for the fact that it has been the theater of all wars for three-and-a-half centuries; wars that are often waged with its own blood and at its own expense. Have not virtually all the nations of Europe taken turns trampling Germany in wars every ten, twenty, thirty years? And has another country – with the exception of Italy and, in the last hundred years, Poland – suffered an equally harsh fate?"[52]

Arndt's quote above stands as both a historical diagnosis of eroding states and a proto-nationalist justification for the consolidation of governmental power that would later be leveraged by the NSDAP under National Socialism to form a cohesive governmental body focused on a unified objective. Centralized authority, unity of will and abolition of internal factionalism grew into hallmarks of National Socialism, where the state and the nation align in thought and action for the benefit of all. Adolf Hitler spoke about this inner unity of will and the alignment of the community in a speech at the Party Congress of the Gau of Thuringia in Gera on June 17, 1934:

"My Volksgenossen, I wish only to bid and remind you to perceive the strength of our Volk in our inner unity of will, in our unity of spirit and our common way of thinking. Rest assured that strength is expressed not so much in divisions, in cannons and in tanks, but that it is ultimately expressed in the community of a single Volkswille. And further, may you be imbued with the conviction that men must be taught this community and that safeguards must be created for this purpose."[53]

Arndt fully recognized the negative effects of a foreign entity holding power over the nation, but also focused his frustrations inward, arguing that it was primarily acts of internal betrayal that led to the involvement of foreign interests. It was the self-serving behavior of the princes and the political fragmentation of the nation that Arndt recognized as the precursors to foreign intervention and domestic deterioration. In this way, internal disunity becomes one of the greatest threats to the nation, a concept that was certainly furthered under National Socialism.

"But it is not only foreigners who have battered the fatherland, and do so to this day; it was the power hungry ambition of our princes that called in these foreigners, usually to ravage the land, and taught the Germans to fight them as well as their fellow countrymen."[54]

To Arndt, these degrading states, despite being terrible for the health of the nation at the time, still offered the silver lining of a better tomorrow through a greater opportunity for renewal. In a way that ties back into previously discussed themes, the nation is understood to retain a level of plasticity where it may degenerate or improve depending on the actions of both the leaders and the greater population.

"However, as good qualities may be gradually debased, so could their bad qualities have been gradually corrected. The revolution had designedly and accidentally produced much misery, much evil had been committed, and sanguinary coercion had rendered the people patient and ductile. This would have enabled a wise and good ruler greatly to improve the nation."[55]

Arndt suggested a strong central government composed of the nation's spirit, that is put to work for the benefit of the nation, to hold the necessary position to free the people from foreign occupation. Though he believed a monarchy to be ideal, the spirit of his writings aligns with National Socialist thought in this way. National Socialism does not require any specific arrangement of state, beyond a strong and unified central government, making Arndt's vision on the matter more narrow.

"Let them be roused from their lethargy-let them be governed by a king who knows how to rule, and how to break the chains in which they are held by foreigners, and you will see what they can achieve."⁵⁶

While glorious sacrifice for one's nation was always supported by Arndt, in *The life and adventures of Ernst Moritz Arndt* he took a sobering pause from his typical Romantic nationalistic fervor to express a disillusionment with war. This moment tempers some of his earlier works, demonstrating a fracture between the Romantic ideal and the lived horror of such circumstances.

"I meant to have added something about the Frankfort blockade, about the Landsturm of Spessart and Odenwald, and its wonderful marches, and so go on to Wurzburg. But there came over me such a disgust at the whole atrocious war that I shall be only too glad if too much gall has not already flowed from my pen."⁵⁷

Arndt didn't solely focus on the unity of the nation through the rejection of foreign influence, but also through the internal unification of the nation and the destruction of divisive class relationships. This stands in contrast to some of his more fiery calls for action against foreign oppression, instead urging a spiritual and moral connection in order to achieve societal cohesion, even ending in a prayer.

"But the saddest part of it is, that the old animosity between ranks and classes is being sharpened again, and they are becoming embittered towards one another. Against this one must arm oneself and pray: Lord, preserve me from that worst thing, hatred."⁵⁸

This is an area that has been expanded on by National Socialism to a considerably greater extent than by Arndt, which is almost certainly a byproduct of his work, which tended to appeal more to emotional rejection of that which is foreign than to an unconditional embrace of that which is internal. Arndt emphasized struggle and reaction, National Socialism emphasizes preemptive moral cohesion of the nation. National Socialism recognizes that through this focus on internal cohesion, the rejection of foreign spirit and power can be organically fulfilled by the nation, both frequently steeping these themes in Christianity, such as in *Germany's Hitler*:

"The future belongs to National Socialism since, like Christianity, it is founded on love, and reconciliation between high and low, rich and poor. Herein lies its special, creative, and effective power. Marxian Socialism, on the contrary, flourishes on class clash and hatred. It is anti-Christian and destructive."[59]

Of course this equality that Arndt recognized was only associated with European nations, and not simply all who may live within the borders of the country. Following nineteenth-century Romantic tradition, Arndt expresses a deep dislike for Jews, referring to them as "greasy" and invoking their presence in the same breath as he did dung heaps and burning garbage. Many scholars who took note of Jewish influence at this time did so in less artistic ways than that of Arndt, discussing the problem more directly with supporting figures or calling the population to logically evaluate their presence. This distinction is one element that gives Arndt a unique place in the ideological genealogy of National Socialism. His emotional portrayal of the Jew being an agent of deterioration offered support to the growing sentiment throughout the völkisch movement, leading into the development of National Socialism.

"Everywhere abominable filth and Paris after its capture, and afterwards was plenipotentiary of the King of Prussia at Neufchâtel. In 1847 he was Governor of Berlin, and the next year was employed in suppressing the insurrection in Posen. In the September of 1848 the King, in his extremity, entrusted him with the formation of a new Cabinet; but his incapacity becoming evident, he resigned in the next month. From that time he retired into private life until his death in

1866. fearful stenches; greasy Jews and a few unfortunate prisoners, chiefly wounded men or convalescents, creeping miserably about; all the streets darkened with dirty smoke, for in front of almost every house the inhabitants had gathered together heaps of everything that could be burnt- in some cases they were merely dung-heaps."[60]

The intersection of the calculated, philosophically grounded antisemitism with the developing racial sciences and the emotional appeals of figures like Arndt demonstrates a revealing microcosm of the greater National Socialist framework. In *Der Nazi Sozi*, Dr. Goebbels makes this clear through two points in response to a fictional question about the NSDAP's stance on antisemitism. The first point appeals more to calculated logic stemming from the philosophical roots of National Socialism where the stance is viewed as a pragmatic solution to the power held over the nation by the unintegrated Jewish population. The second draws more from figures like Arndt, where the Jew is recognized as human but compared to an unpleasant flea that must be shaken from the hide of the nation. The alignment of both natural emotional reaction and logic fortifies National Socialism into a complete worldview that offers multiple points of entry for the populace.

"1. If we were only anti-Semites, we would be out-of-place in the twentieth century. However, we are also socialists. For us the two go together. Socialism, the freedom of the German proletariat and thereby of the German nation, can only be achieved against the Jews. Since we want Germany's freedom, or socialism, we are anti-Semites.

2. Sure, the Jew is also a human being. None of us has ever doubted that. But a flea is also an animal, — albeit an unpleasant one. Since a flea is not a pleasant animal, we have no duty to defend and protect it, to be of service to it so that it can bite and torment and torture us. Rather, our duty is to make it harmless."[61]

In *Geist der Zeit*, Arndt called for a system of governance rooted in moral responsibility as defined by Christian ethical principles. Despite appearing similar to Enlightenment secular universalism on the surface due to the invocation of "all living beings," it is specifically rooted in Christian tradition, adding cultural context that implies nations should remain ethnically and religiously cohesive while embodying moral universality.

"Equality and justice in love, and compassion on all living beings, has been inculcated by the divine founder of christianity, to be alone the laws of states and nations."[62]

Adolf Hitler professed as much in a policy statement on the Enabling Act to the Reichstag on March 23, 1933:

"Similarly, the Reich Government, which regards Christianity as the unshakable foundation of the ethics and morality of the Volk, places great value on friendly relations with the Vatican and attempts to develop them."[63]

Arndt was a deeply religious man, a fact that is highly relevant when attempting to understand the sentiment toward religion among the thinkers who were indirectly responsible for the development of National Socialism. This religious element, often overlooked, adds a crucial layer to Arndt's worldview. Understanding these positions allows for a more accurate unraveling of personal sentiment from the true philosophy of National Socialism, allowing for a clear and impartial observation.

"My faith stands firm that without God nothing happens, and I have had signs that this was prepared for me by divine wisdom."[64]

While Ernst Moritz Arndt did not articulate a racial philosophy grounded in biology in any way comparable to that of National Socialism, he nonetheless occupies a foundational yet transitional place in the ideological development that would later culminate in it. His conception of the nation as a sacred, organic, and enduring entity, rooted in a shared blood, language, culture, and divine mission, strongly anticipated the spiritual vocabulary of the völkisch movement, and by extension, National Socialist doctrine. Through his rejection of cosmopolitanism and his belief in an inherited national character, Arndt helped to lay the foundation for a vision of "Germanness" that clearly transcended political structures or geographic boundaries. His emotionally charged brand of Romantic nationalism diverged from the more systematic thinkers such as Fichte, yet in doing so, he helped shape the mythic and symbolic underpinnings of National Socialism, fortifying rational ideas with emotional resonance.

Arndt stands apart from the later National Socialist position in multiple areas, most notably in his deeply religious worldview, which is only partially shared by National Socialism, and his relative avoidance of biological determinism. He was not a National Socialist, nor was he a systematic ideologue, but his essentialist writings and emphasis on ancestry and degeneration proved to be a cultural forerunner. Arndt must be understood not as a direct architect of the National Socialist framework, but as a critical precursor who helped define the soil from which National Socialist ideology would later grow.

Endnotes

1. Alfred G. Pundt, *Arndt and the Nationalist Awakening in Germany* (New York and Chichester, West Sussex: Columbia University Press, 1935), 140-196.

2. Hans Kohn, "Arndt and the Character of German Nationalism," *The American Historical Review* 54, no. 4 (1949): 787-803.

3. J. Hertel, "'...dass diese Gefühle und Gedanken wieder Gefühle und Gedanken wecken...': Ernst Moritz Arndt, Na-

tionalist Writing, and the Aesthetics of Interest," *German Quarterly* 98 (2025): 209-26.

4. George L. Mosse, "Mass Politics and the Political Liturgy of Nationalism," in *Confronting the Nation: Jewish and Western Nationalism*, ed. George L. Mosse (Hanover, NH: Brandeis University Press, 1993), 38–54.

5. Alfred G. Pundt, *Arndt and the Nationalist Awakening in Germany* (New York and Chichester, West Sussex: Columbia University Press, 1935), 140–196.

6. Rohan D'Olier Butler, *The Roots of National Socialism, 1848–1933* (London: Faber & Faber, 1941).

7. Alfred G. Pundt, *Arndt and the Nationalist Awakening in Germany* (New York and Chichester, West Sussex: Columbia University Press, 1935), 140–196.

8. Hans Kohn, "Arndt and the Character of German Nationalism," *The American Historical Review* 54, no. 4 (1949): 787–803.

9. Ernst Moritz Arndt, "The German Fatherland" (1813), *German History in Documents and Images*, https://germanhistorydocs.org/en/from-vormaerz-to-prussian-dominance-1815-1866/ghdi:document-237.

10. Hans Kohn, "Arndt and the Character of German Nationalism," *The American Historical Review* 54, no. 4 (1949): 787–803.

11. Adolf Hitler, *Mein Kampf*, (London: Hurst and Blackett

Ltd., 1939), 244.

12. Ernst Moritz Arndt, *Spirit of the Times*, trans. Rev. P. W. (London: W. M. Thiselton, 1808), 15.

13. Guy Tourlamain, *Völkisch Writers and National Socialism: A Study of Right-Wing Political Culture in Germany, 1890–1960* (Oxford: Peter Lang, 2014).

14. Peter Staudenmaier, "Fascist Ecology: The 'Green Wing' of the Nazi Party and Its Historical Antecedents," *Capitalism Nature Socialism* 3, no. 2 (1992).

15. Schutzstaffel, *SS Race Theory and Mate Selection Guidelines*, trans. from the original SS publication *Glauben und Kämpfen* (*Faith and Struggle*) (Berlin: SS-Hauptamt, c. 1936), 5.

16. Ernst Moritz Arndt, *Spirit of the Times*, trans. Rev. P. W. (London: W. M. Thiselton, 1808), 30.

17. Ernst Moritz Arndt, *The Life and Adventures of Ernst Moritz Arndt: The Singer of the German Fatherland*, comp. from the German, with a preface by John Robert Seeley (London: Seeley, Jackson, and Halliday, 1879), 139.

18. Joseph Goebbels, *Der Nazi-Sozi* (Munich: Franz Eher Nachfolger, 1932).

19. Ernst Moritz Arndt, *Spirit of the Times*, trans. Rev. P. W. (London: W. M. Thiselton, 1808), 40.

20. Ernst Moritz Arndt, *Spirit of the Times*, trans. Rev. P. W.

(London: W. M. Thiselton, 1808), 50.

21. Schutzstaffel, *SS Race Theory and Mate Selection Guidelines*, trans. from the original SS publication *Glauben und Kämpfen (Faith and Struggle)* (Berlin: SS-Hauptamt, c. 1936), 15.

22. Ernst Moritz Arndt, *Spirit of the Times*, trans. Rev. P. W. (London: W. M. Thiselton, 1808), 52.

23. Ernst Moritz Arndt, *Spirit of the Times*, trans. Rev. P. W. (London: W. M. Thiselton, 1808), 52.

24. Ernst Moritz Arndt, *Spirit of the Times*, trans. Rev. P. W. (London: W. M. Thiselton, 1808), 54.

25. Rudolf Jung, *National Socialism: Its Foundations, Development, and Goals*, 2nd fully revised ed. (Munich: Deutscher Volksverlag, Dr. E. Boepple, 1922), 67.

26. Ernst Moritz Arndt, *Spirit of the Times*, trans. Rev. P. W. (London: W. M. Thiselton, 1808), 54.

27. Rudolf Jung, *National Socialism: Its Foundations, Development, and Goals*, 2nd fully revised ed. (Munich: Deutscher Volksverlag, Dr. E. Boepple, 1922), 5.

28. Ernst Moritz Arndt, "Excerpts from *Germania and Europe* (1803)," trans. Thomas Dunlap, *German History in Documents and Images*, May 18, 2025.

29. Heinz A. Heinz, *Germany's Hitler* (London: Hurst & Blackett Ltd., 1934).

30. Ernst Moritz Arndt, *The Life and Adventures of Ernst Moritz Arndt: The Singer of the German Fatherland*, comp. from the German, with a preface by John Robert Seeley (London: Seeley, Jackson, and Halliday, 1879), 301.

31. Ernst Moritz Arndt, *The Life and Adventures of Ernst Moritz Arndt: The Singer of the German Fatherland*, comp. from the German, with a preface by John Robert Seeley (London: Seeley, Jackson, and Halliday, 1879), 301.

32. Ernst Moritz Arndt, *The Life and Adventures of Ernst Moritz Arndt: The Singer of the German Fatherland*, comp. from the German, with a preface by John Robert Seeley (London: Seeley, Jackson, and Halliday, 1879), 105.

33. Ernst Moritz Arndt, *The Life and Adventures of Ernst Moritz Arndt: The Singer of the German Fatherland*, comp. from the German, with a preface by John Robert Seeley (London: Seeley, Jackson, and Halliday, 1879), 115.

34. Ernst Moritz Arndt, "Excerpts from *Germania and Europe* (1803)," trans. Thomas Dunlap, *German History in Documents and Images*, May 18, 2025.

35. Fritz Brennecke, *The Nazi Primer: Official Handbook for Schooling the Hitler Youth*, 37.

36. Ernst Moritz Arndt, *Spirit of the Times*, trans. Rev. P. W. (London: W. M. Thiselton, 1808), 13.

37. Ernst Moritz Arndt, *Spirit of the Times*, trans. Rev. P. W. (London: W. M. Thiselton, 1808), 23.

38. Ernst Moritz Arndt, *Spirit of the Times*, trans. Rev. P. W. (London: W. M. Thiselton, 1808), 24.

39. Ernst Moritz Arndt, *Spirit of the Times*, trans. Rev. P. W. (London: W. M. Thiselton, 1808), 32.

40. Ernst Moritz Arndt, *Spirit of the Times*, trans. Rev. P. W. (London: W. M. Thiselton, 1808), 8.

41. Ernst Moritz Arndt, *Spirit of the Times*, trans. Rev. P. W. (London: W. M. Thiselton, 1808), 14.

42. Ernst Moritz Arndt, *Spirit of the Times*, trans. Rev. P. W. (London: W. M. Thiselton, 1808), 34.

43. Ernst Moritz Arndt, *Spirit of the Times*, trans. Rev. P. W. (London: W. M. Thiselton, 1808), 74.

44. Ernst Moritz Arndt, *The Life and Adventures of Ernst Moritz Arndt: The Singer of the German Fatherland*, comp. from the German, with a preface by John Robert Seeley (London: Seeley, Jackson, and Halliday, 1879), 356.

45. Anton Holzner, *The Eternal Front* (Hitler's Priest), trans. Ironmarch.org, from *Der Ewige Front* (Munich: Franz Eher Nachf., 1940), 15.

46. Ernst Moritz Arndt, *Spirit of the Times*, trans. Rev. P. W. (London: W. M. Thiselton, 1808), 50.

47. Ernst Moritz Arndt, *Spirit of the Times*, trans. Rev. P. W. (London: W. M. Thiselton, 1808), 51.

48. Ernst Moritz Arndt, *Spirit of the Times*, trans. Rev. P. W.

(London: W. M. Thiselton, 1808), 16.

49. Schutzstaffel, *SS Race Theory and Mate Selection Guidelines*, trans. from the original SS publication *Glauben und Kämpfen* (*Faith and Struggle*) (Berlin: SS-Hauptamt, c. 1936), 4.

50. Ernst Moritz Arndt, *Spirit of the Times*, trans. Rev. P. W. (London: W. M. Thiselton, 1808), 3.

51. Ernst Moritz Arndt, *Spirit of the Times*, trans. Rev. P. W. (London: W. M. Thiselton, 1808), 9.

52. Ernst Moritz Arndt, "Excerpts from *Germania and Europe* (1803)," trans. Thomas Dunlap, *German History in Documents and Images*, May 18, 2025.

53. Adolf Hitler, *Speech at the Party Congress of the Gau*, June 17, 1934.

54. Ernst Moritz Arndt, "Excerpts from *Germania and Europe* (1803)," trans. Thomas Dunlap, *German History in Documents and Images*, May 18, 2025.

55. Ernst Moritz Arndt, *Spirit of the Times*, trans. Rev. P. W. (London: W. M. Thiselton, 1808), 79.

56. Ernst Moritz Arndt, *Spirit of the Times*, trans. Rev. P. W. (London: W. M. Thiselton, 1808), 14.

57. Ernst Moritz Arndt, *The Life and Adventures of Ernst Moritz Arndt: The Singer of the German Fatherland*, comp. from the German, with a preface by John Robert Seeley

(London: Seeley, Jackson, and Halliday, 1879), 105.

58. Ernst Moritz Arndt, *The Life and Adventures of Ernst Moritz Arndt: The Singer of the German Fatherland*, comp. from the German, with a preface by John Robert Seeley (London: Seeley, Jackson, and Halliday, 1879), 384.

59. Heinz A. Heinz, *Germany's Hitler* (London: Hurst & Blackett Ltd., 1934).

60. Ernst Moritz Arndt, *The Life and Adventures of Ernst Moritz Arndt: The Singer of the German Fatherland*, comp. from the German, with a preface by John Robert Seeley (London: Seeley, Jackson, and Halliday, 1879), 232.

61. Joseph Goebbels, *Der Nazi-Sozi* (Munich: Franz Eher Nachfolger, 1932).

62. Ernst Moritz Arndt, *Spirit of the Times*, trans. Rev. P. W. (London: W. M. Thiselton, 1808), 49.

63. Adolf Hitler, *Speech to the Reichstag in Berlin*, March 23, 1933.

64. Ernst Moritz Arndt, *The Life and Adventures of Ernst Moritz Arndt: The Singer of the German Fatherland*, comp. from the German, with a preface by John Robert Seeley (London: Seeley, Jackson, and Halliday, 1879), 411.

Chapter 3
Johann Gottfried Herder

Johann Gottfried Herder (1744–1803) is a central figure to examine while tracing the genealogy of National Socialism, as his writings function as a bridge between Enlightenment rationalism and the cultural particularism of Romanticism. As some historians have noted, the ideological concepts that form the logical skeleton of National Socialism, such as Volk, organic nationhood, and the national spirit, were not invented by the NSDAP, but rather crystallized from earlier thought, with Herder holding an important position in its lineage.[1] These ideas, which Herder articulated, would later be consolidated into more rigid political doctrines. He was born in the town of Mohrungen in the Kingdom of Prussia to a modest and religious family, with his father being a teacher and cantor in a Christian church, thereby instilling an intimate familiarity with religious tradition along with a strong sense of duty, which Herder would later apply to the Volk. As Carlton J. Hayes notes, it was more Herder than Rousseau that defined a people as a determinate unit grounded in shared culture, rather than legal contract, drafting the foundations for modern nationalist philosophy.[2]

Herder's formal education began at the Pietist Collegium Fridericianum in Königsberg and continued at the University of Königsberg, where he studied theology, philosophy, and literature, eventually becoming a student of Immanuel Kant. Despite Kant's significant influence on Herder's worldview, particularly in regard to moral law, Herder nonetheless crafted his own philosophical orientation through the initial rejection of the rationalism and universalist abstraction inherent to the Kantian system. Herder would take up the lead from thinkers such as Jean-Jacques Rousseau and Johann Georg Hamann, coming to see the spirit of a people in its language, customs, and collective memory, rather than the abstract ideals of Enlightenment thought. Scholars emphasize that Herder's true break from this Enlightenment universalism stems directly from his adamant refusal to accept humanity as its own abstract category, instead insisting that the national unities remain in an irreducible form.[3]

Herder's sensitivity to cultural uniqueness emerged with his travels through Europe, particularly France and Italy, along with his time spent preaching, sparking a growing conviction that all nations develop differently according to their own internal principles. He initially emphasized geography, climate, history, and language as the shaping elements of national character, but his later writings increasingly recognized the role of biological inheritance as the primary element in shaping the essence of the people. Through his landmark work *Ideas for the Philosophy of the History of Mankind* (1784–1791), Herder laid out a sprawling collection of interconnected concepts, much of which challenged the Enlightenment notion of a singularly held universal reason. Herder's intellectual legacy derives from this diffuse body of writings, reflecting an organizing method of inquiry instead of a closed philosophical system, such as what can be observed with Fichte.[4] Instead, he emphasized an individual and unique national spirit (Volksgeist), arguing that the development of a nation should be carried out organically, according to the specific conditions and attributes of the nation. Scholars, like Fred Blakely, identify this organic conception of nationhood as one of Herder's most significant contributions, noting his frequent reference to the nation as a natural organism, complete with a common national spirit, a framework that would later be absorbed into National Socialist thought.[5]

When tracing National Socialist thought, Herder's worldview can be found occupying an ambivalent but overall indispensable place, especially when it comes to the development and protection of the cultural nation. Language, folklore, and myth were heightened and bound by Herder into a singular idea, developing the concept of the Volksgeist, which can be seen as crucial in both German Romanticism and the later völkisch movement, building up to the development of National Socialism. By departing from Enlightenment universalism, Herder instead sought to instill cultural authenticity within the lines of the organic and particular national character. In order to more fully understand the development of National Socialism, the concepts presented by Herder, along with the ideological bridge that he offered from Enlightenment thought to Romantic nationalism, must be examined. It has been asserted that the transfiguration of the concept of Volk itself was Herder's most consequential contribution, which became a primary focal point for nineteenth-century nationalism.[6]

In his aforementioned and foundational work titled *Ideas for the Philosophy of the History of Mankind*, Herder recognized the importance of the environment in the development of the individual, and thus also the nation. The suggested interdependence between human development and geography was later reflected in the Romantic belief of an organic and generative relationship between people and place. This is one of the primary sections of the previously mentioned ideological bridge which Herder developed, where the abstract reasoning of Enlightenment theories was rejected in favor of recognition for the specific contextual, geographical, and environmental conditions present for the nation.

This single ideological deviation caused a relatively significant separation of thought at the point of national conception itself, effectively challenging the idea of a single, universal path of human development. Herder's specific brand of cultural particularism comes bound to a quasi-deterministic worldview that shifted over time toward racial determinism, but was not strictly racial in nature to the extent that would be adopted by later thinkers. In this way, geography is not merely incidental to a nation, but rather foundational in many ways throughout its development, a concept that gave rise to the forms of blood and soil nationalism in the nineteenth and twentieth centuries, which bound land and race into a singular entity. Herder built upon the rejection of abstract universalism, articulating one of the earliest and most coherent philosophical defenses for the nation existing as an existential necessity instead of a simple political construct.[7]

"It is the same with the bay separating France and Spain, with the channel between France and England, with the very shape of Britain, Italy, and ancient Greece. Could we alter the outline of these countries, remove a strait here or fill in a waterway there; then the formation and devastation of the world, the fate of whole peoples and continents would for centuries take a divergent path."[8]

In the National Socialist publication titled *Ich Kampfe,* which was given to all new party enrollees from 1942 to1944, the very same element of rootedness that Herder offered to the Romantic movement can be seen in full display:

"The national community had to be determined by blood and bound to the native soil. All differences of political, social or religious doctrine that hitherto had dispersed nations in all directions had to be bridged. Any small- minded impulse of self interest in individuals or groups had to be drowned out by the command that dictated that all Germans must act in a united manner."[9]

The soil-bound nation is certainly not the main element of the previous quote, as racial unity clearly holds that position; however, it nonetheless exemplifies the ideological residue inherited from pre-National Socialist movements, such as the völkisch movement. Due to National Socialism's full assimilation of racial sciences into the heart of the worldview, external elements such as the alteration of landforms as suggested by Herder, take a clear backseat to biological composition, despite the ideological remnants that are ever-present.

Despite attributing significantly more weight to environmental factors than National Socialism later would, Herder still recognized the deterministic aspects of biology, attributing an organic field of growth to all organisms through their innate capabilities. He believed that the nature of an organism not only delineates the particular and organic field of growth, but also its limits, offering an element of biological realism that was relatively neglected under Enlightenment thought. Below, the assertion of a fixed condition which varies based on composition can be seen, departing from the Enlightenment and universalist worldview toward what clearly foreshadows the völkisch ideology that would follow.

"The tree develops what it can develop, and makes itself master of all that it may possess. It puts forth buds and germs, bears fruit and sows young trees; but it never budges from the spot where Nature has placed it, and it cannot acquire a single power [Kraft] with which it was not endowed.

It is, I think, especially humbling to man that with the sweet impulses that he calls love, and in which he thinks he exercises so much free will, he obeys the laws of Nature almost as blindly as a plant."[10]

In *Die Bestimmung des Menschen,* Fichte asserted almost exactly what Herder did at least fifteen years prior, through an overlapping metaphor relating to the particular organic growth of a tree according to its own composition. Through this, Fichte continues Herder's concept, introducing the individual's ability to stray from what nature has prescribed, giving rise to an ethical value being attributed to the adherence of organic nature. Herder argued that the obedience to nature is instinctive and almost inevitable, not requiring the conscious moral striving or universal reason as suggested by Fichte and Kant. When viewed in this comparative light, Herder's disregard for individually imposed ethical action, as determined through reason and communal obligation, leaves a rather large separation from the individual duty expected by National Socialism.

"Bestow consciousness on a tree, and let it grow, spread out its branches, and bring forth leaves and buds, blossoms and fruits, after its kind, without hindrance or obstruction: it will perceive no limitation to its existence in being only a tree, a tree of this particular species, and this particular individual of the species; it will feel itself perfectly free, because, in all those manifestations, it will do nothing but what its nature requires; and it will desire to do nothing else, because it can only desire what that nature requires."[11]

Below, Herder makes his anti-Enlightenment stance as apparent as possible through the deconstruction of the liberal notion of rational agency, suggesting that an individual's nature is more so a product of circumstance and natural compulsion. He posited that despite the reason and will of man, he is ultimately bound to the invisible natural laws of his kind, regardless of whether such is accepted by him or not.

"We are summoned into the world without our consent, and no one is asked what sex he will be, from which parents he will issue, whether he will live on poor or rich soil, by what accident, internal or external, he will at last meet his end. In all this man must follow higher laws, about which he is no more informed than the plant; indeed, which he obeys, guided by his strongest instincts, almost against his will."[12]

Examples taken from botany were frequently used as metaphors by Herder to demonstrate multiple points, one of which was the persistence of inherited traits within foreign environments. He noted that plants retain their native behavioral patterns even after decades abroad, challenging the Enlightenment notion that external factors alone have the capability to fully reshape the natural state of something. This analogy was used to demonstrate the limitations of environmental conditions on shaping human development, setting the stage for cultural and national particularism, while foreshadowing the soil-bound sentiments that would become popularized through the völkisch movement.

To Herder, each organism, including man, contains within itself the blueprints of development which only operate under these fixed inner laws, as demonstrated through his numerous botanical metaphors. Despite highlighting natural characteristics and behavior that resists environmental influence while positively correlating to its specific kind of organism, Herder's model was not based in the same racial recognition that National Socialism came to adopt. This perfectly illustrates the ideological shift from pre-National Socialist thought, centering around an environmental-cultural framework with heavy influence coming from geographic particularism, toward the biologically enforced destiny driven by eternal racial traits. The same principles of cultural continuity and development that Herder established with his soil-bound thinking carried into National Socialism, but were reengineered with racial absolutism.

"When plants from the southern regions of the globe are brought to Europe, they mature later in the first year, because they are awaiting the sun of their own clime, then the following summer somewhat sooner, because they have already become habituated to these new skies. In the artificial warmth of the greenhouse, each still observes the seasons of its native country, even if it has been fifty years in Europe. Plants from the Cape blossom in the winter, when it is summer in their homeland. The Marvel of Peru blossoms at night, presumably (says Linnaeus) because it is then day in America. Thus each sticks to the time, even to the hour of the day, when it opens and closes. "These things," says the botanical philosopher, "seem to indicate that something more is requisite to their growth than heat and water"; and to be sure, we likewise have to consider, in respect of the organic diversity of mankind and their adaptation to foreign climates something more, something other than heat and cold, particularly when we are speaking of another hemisphere."[13]

The development of National Socialism away from geographic determinism cannot be overstated, as the philosophy of National Socialism would be entirely incoherent or subject to ideological drift over time without such a racial anchor. National Socialism is bound to biological-racial science, allowing for a clear delineation of the nation in a way that prevents the introduction of ideological shortcomings common to nationalist worldviews. It is extremely common to find nationalism imbued with romantic notions of a historical spirit, giving rise to the predictable difficulty associated with quantifying or qualifying such in a way that allows for a clear demarcation of national boundaries. Herder's insistence on the plurality of nationhood was largely motivated by his explicitly recognized fear of despotism, which he believed would be sure to follow a large, centralized, and universal state.[14]

It is not uncommon to come across seemingly patriotic or geographically focused sentiment within historical National Socialist literature which appears to contradict the notion that National Socialist philosophy rests solely on racial principles. This is the previously mentioned ideological residue left over from Romantic and völkisch thought, coupled with misguided, but albeit natural, public sentiment following the First World War and significant internal strife. This logically must be the case, as the nation itself is entirely defined in racial terms under National Socialism, along with culture being understood to be a byproduct of racial composition, leading to a racially based philosophy demonstrated best through the acceptance of racially aligned foreign born individuals into the nation. National Socialism's racial foundation serves as a correction to the weak points in earlier national theories, offering an immutable foundation of national identity. This core racial principle is the National Socialist bulwark against the aforementioned ideological drift, offering an unparalleled defense against foreign subversion and genetic deterioration while simultaneously dictating clear requirements for membership within the nation.

Herder argued in favor of teleological organicism, where all species are formed through divine nature to fulfill a specific purpose, with all of their senses, body structure, and soul dedicated to such. Instead of viewing organisms as arbitrarily designed, he posited that form follows function and that the function reflects the essence of the species. This clearly separates Herder from the mechanistic nature of Enlightenment anthropological thought, toward a biologically focused worldview, where inner nature is unalterable. In this way, the soul is not presented as universal in nature, but rather specific to the species, further shaped by physical constraints and the demands of survival in a particular context.

"As the formative artist found that proportion of the quadruped to be best in which these creatures learned to exercise certain senses and powers [Kräfte] in combination and to unite them in a single form of thought and sensation: so she altered the conformation of each species according to its destination and mode of life, creating from these same parts and limbs a peculiar harmony of the whole and thus also a peculiar soul that is organically distinct from that of other species."[15]

Herder connected his perspectives on aesthetics, biology, and the metaphysical into an anti-mechanistic worldview, demonstrating the connection of form and inner essence through concepts that prefigured both Romantic essentialism, as well as the physiological determinism of the nineteenth century. This can be seen below where he idealizes the Greek profile, attributing intelligence and other attributes to the forward-inclined crown, which he contrasted with the reduced reasoning capabilities and brutish instinct of those whose physical structures were more animalistic. This must not be disregarded as surface level physiognomic speculation, because it holds a much deeper teleological argument where organisms are designed from the inside out in such a way as to allow for each feature to serve a higher function toward the realization of its particular innate potential.

"Why does the crown of the Greek head incline forward so pleasingly? Because this provides the amplest room for a brain that shall be free, while also revealing handsome and healthy frontal sinuses, and therefore encloses a temple of pure and youthfully beautiful thoughts. The occiput, by contrast, is small: for the animal cerebellum should not predominate. So it is with the other parts of the face; as sense organs they indicate the finest proportionality of the sensuous powers [sinnliche Kräfte] of the brain, every departure from which is brutish. I am certain that, in respect of the symmetry of these parts, we shall one day have such a beautiful science as physiognomy alone, being merely conjectural, can hardly deliver. The inner is the basis of the outer, because everything was formed by organic forces from within to without, and every creature is so whole and complete a form, as if Nature had created nothing else."[16]

Herder contrasted the Roman spirit with that of the Greeks, highlighting the enduring nature of the spirit of a people, even claiming that "the Roman senate never died." This is not literal, but rather a symbolic illustration of the living historical essence that is passed down, known as the Volksgeist. By Herder's estimation, the Roman Volksgeist originated with Romulus, the legendary founder of Rome, thus rooting spirit within the historical myths of the people, further demonstrating a separation from the pure racial determinism that sits as the ideological focus of National Socialism. Herder's conceptualization of national continuity being formed through the combination of the people's innate nature and their historical memory can be seen in the National Socialist publications with the concepts of pure bloodlines and the eternal racial spirit of the nation.

"The Roman spirit is distinct from that of the Greeks, too, including even Sparta, resting as it does on a tougher nature, on more ancient habit, and on principles more fixed. The Roman senate never died; its resolutions, its maxims, and the Roman character inherited from Romulus, were eternal."[17]

Below, in the 1938 publication written by Dr. Erich Schinnerer titled *German Law and Legislation*, Herder's Volksgeist and the particularistic and comparatively quasi-deterministic aspects of it can be seen clearly in the formation of both the Volksgemeinschaft and the justification for authority that the state draws from the nation.

Contemporary scholars emphasize that Herder recognized political authority as legitimate only insofar as it was contingent upon the proper preservation of the organic life of the nation.[18] The term Volksgemeinschaft, when utilized by National Socialism, is a racial community consisting of a "homogenous national character" that is composed of the "inner spiritual, political and material necessities which have developed through a common historical experience". The way that Dr. Schinnerer worded this passage is more than reminiscent of Herder's Volksgeist, even calling upon the internal organic conception of morality and the scope of conduct that blossoms from it. This is a crucial ideological element because it provides not just authority to the state to govern, but also the guiding ethics for legal frameworks that correspond to the natural proclivities of the community it serves. Herder's political philosophy offers authority to the state only conditionally, recognizing the state as an element contingent on whether it preserves the nation's spirit or not.[19] Furthermore, this ideological line can also be traced from Herder to Fichte through the interaction between rational individuals, whose behavior is ultimately shaped by internal qualities, offering an additional and comparable line of ideological input into National Socialist philosophy.

"In order to understand what is the basis of the new legislation one must have a clear grasp of what the Germans mean today when they speak of the Community of the People, the Volksgemeinschaft. This idea of the people is based on the fact that their members have a homogenous national character. When great multitudes act together, conscious of their historical unity and determined to pursue the fulfillment of one mission as a national unit, then they are a political unit also. Of this political unit those who are its leaders form an integrant part. All the members form one corporation which is called the Volksgemeinschaft, literally, Folk Community. Now the laws that govern the Folk Community emerge from the inner spiritual, political and material necessities which have developed through a common historical experience. Therefore in the National Socialist sense law is not the expression of the State's authority, to which the people must submit as a passive and inert mass. In harmony with the concept of the Folk Community, law is part of the life of the people. The legislator draws out and gives organic expression to the sense of what is just and unjust, the feeling for what is good and what is evil, which is inherent in the soul of the people. Therefore the starting point of the National Socialist conception of law is the people, not the State. The task of the State is to see that the law is carried out."[20]

In *Ideas for the Philosophy of the History of Mankind*, Herder repeatedly asserts the belief that all people are endowed by nature with an internal blueprint that leads the individual toward a state of mental and physical equilibrium. Through education and other forms of personal development, he believed that an individual can grow into their unique natural form, allowing for the fullest sense of enjoyment possible. This does not occur through a conformity to a universal model, such as that proposed by Enlightenment thought, but rather through the realization of a people's particular essence. Despite recognizing racial attributes and highlighting a few of the physical and mental differences between the races, Herder's framework stops short of ranking racial groups by value, instead recognizing and respecting the unique culture, internal logic, and destiny of a people. The particularism presented by Herder anticipated the rejection of cosmopolitanism by the later völkisch movement and National Socialism, initially applied directly to cultural affairs, and further adapted to include more explicit racial premises that utilize the same logic.[21]

"Everything is born that can be born on earth, maintaining itself when, according to the laws of Nature, it reaches its state of equilibrium. Thus, every individual human being carries within himself, both in the shape of his body and in the faculties of his mind, the symmetry for which he was made and which he must himself bring to completion. This symmetry runs through every species and form of human existence, from the most morbid deformity, scarcely able to preserve itself in life, to the most beautiful figure of a Greek demi-god; from the passionate ardor of the Negro brain to the capacity for the most beautiful wisdom. Through faults and errors, through education, necessity and practice every mortal seeks this symmetry of his forces, because in such alone lies the most complete enjoyment of his existence. But only a happy few achieve it in the purest and most beautiful manner."[22]

National Socialism similarly recognizes the unique needs and proclivities of a people, but offers a much more direct element of causation: race. Dr. Walter Groß, who headed the NSDAP's Racial Policy Office, recognized the same natural laws that define a nation and the Volksgeist which it carries, just as Herder asserted over a century prior. This is an illuminating comparison given how close it conforms to the national particularism that was proposed by Herder, where politics, religious practice, culture, and more spring from the unique attributes of the particular group. While racial policy and terminology under the NSDAP were in a constant state of flux following scientific advancement, the National Socialist perspective on race faced no need for continual update because it is founded in the eternal racial laws and logic that is naturally recognizable to the European. It must be noted that National Socialism recognizes the biological implications of racial composition in a much more direct way than Herder, despite Herder's frequent quasi-biologically deterministic statements.

"The races are different because their blood is different, as the proverb says, not because civilization is further advanced in one place than it is in another. We have to accept that, just as we have to accept any natural law on this earth. That means that any attempt to establish international culture, government, or religion is fundamentally wrong and hopeless to attempt, since it ignores the great racial laws that the Creator himself set as finding laws for humanity. This knowledge provides the ultimate and deepest justification for our ethnic striving toward our own nature and uniqueness in politics, economics, culture, and perhaps also religion.

Since peoples differ racially, each must follow its own nature, keeping it pure from physical or intellectual corruption."[23]

Herder walked the line between cultural relativism and early racial categorization with his proto-anthropological observations of foreign races and their associated characteristics. He observed both the physical and temperamental nature of the African as brutish and thoughtless, essentially illustrating a savage driven by sexual and otherwise instinctive motivations. These patterns of behavior were understood by Herder to be the internal core of the physical shell, just as it is for the Greeks and all else when viewed through the teleological lens, which essentially guaranteed this sort of physiognomical study from its conception.

"They are, depending on the region in which they live, more or less black in color and have curly, wooly hair; now and then we encounter the thick lips, flat nose, and white teeth; and it is remarkable how the Negro temperament once again coincides with this form. The same rude and healthy strength, thoughtless disposition [Sinn], and garrulous sensuality that we perceived among the Blacks of the mainland are exhibited by the Negrillos of the islands, but everywhere according to their climate and mode of life."[24]

If the physical traits and temperament of the African are a result of environmental conditions as Herder once asserted, then logic would hold that over time when exposed to a new environment, they would develop away from what was previously standard. Dr. Groß would later speak on this same concept, predictably rejecting any universalist attempts to form a singular world state, culture, and race, which would thereby destroy all of the unique nations and Volksgeist. This demonstrates a clear ideological intensification from the shallow racial concepts of Herder to the racial absolutist position of National Socialism.

"In fact, in the past people taught and believed that the differences between peoples and races in this world were really only accidental, caused by the climate or history or level of culture. The Negro was black because the hot sun in Africa crinkled his hair and darkened his skin. Had he been born somewhere along the North Sea coast with its grayness and lack of sun, he perhaps would have had light skin and blond hair, just like our fishermen in Friesland.

You can understand that these former views had very important political and worldview consequences. If the differences between the world's peoples and races are only the result of external conditions, one can overcome them. Advancing civilization would gradually eliminate social, cultural, and geographic differences. Formerly, people imagined that the differences between Europeans and Negroes could be eliminated by establishing schools, by civilizing Africa, by educating Negroes at European universities, thereby eventually ending the differences that still seem to exist today. People attempted to do this from every angle. They came to the logical conclusion that humanity could be brought to the same intellectual level, which would open the way for a single world state, united in governmental, political, and economic matters. The efforts of the Internationale were no more than the result of this fundamental idea."[25]

Below, Herder seemingly undercuts his earlier focus on environmental and cultural factors through the assertion that racial traits are fixed and heritable, contrasting his usual environmental determinism. It is clear that Herder, at least in some instances, recognized the importance of maintaining racial purity in order to safeguard the raw genetic material required to conform to the Volksgeist. This marks a subtle but nonetheless meaningful shift in Herder's thought, where an emphasis was placed on an eternal and immutable racial essence that stands paramount to upbringing or environment, foreshadowing the racial essentialism of the nineteenth and twentieth centuries.

"For this very reason the Negro figure is transmitted by inheritance and can only be reconverted genetically. Put the Moor in Europe, and he remains what he is; but let him marry a white woman and a single act of generation will bring about such change as the blanching climate would not have accomplished in centuries."[26]

This is continued by Herder with more examples that display differing temperaments across racial lines, suggesting that the emotional expression and general disposition of a people are shaped by their biological composition. While this statement avoided any direct construction of racial hierarchies, it justified the continuation or implementation of racial segregation in order to maintain the continuity of culture and to prevent unwanted miscegenation that would destroy the unique Volksgeist that was present in the previously unmixed generations. Herder framed these differences and the need for separation in a positive, romanticized way despite appearing harsh by modern standards, nonetheless diverging in as significant a way as seemingly possible from Enlightenment universalism.

"The European has no inkling of the fiery passions and fancies that glow in the Negro's breast, and the Indian has no notion of the restless desires that chase the European from one end of the earth to the other.

The savage, who cannot show his affections in an extravagant manner, tends rather to be quiet and composed in this regard; conversely, where the flame of benevolence scatters bright sparks, there it also soon blazes out and is extinguished."[27]

According to Herder, the world is not characteristically homogenous in such a way that universal standards can be applied equally while allowing for all to remain within their natural domain. Instead, it is suggested that each group should be demarcated from others based on their characteristics, so that diversity may be upheld and none would be forced to act contrary to their nature. Similar to how no animal is out of place in its rightful environment, so too do people belong in theirs, both physically and culturally. As previously discussed, Herder shifted more toward biological determinism with ideological maturation, which was not a very far leap from his initial teleological perspective, but all the same paved the way for the National Socialist rejection of ethnocentrism. Just as Herder recognized that a specific Volksgeist springs directly from its particular segment of humanity, so too does National Socialism, with both focusing philosophy heavily around the protection and continuation of this unique spirit.

"What do the caiman and the humming-bird, the condor and the pipa have in common? Each is organized for its element, each lives and moves in its element. No point in creation is without enjoyment, without organ, without inhabitant: every creature therefore has its own world, a new world."[28]

It is through Herder's recognition of the individual's role in the greater community that he concluded that an individual's biology could alter the entire course of a society through gradual genetic degradation. In this way, nature has bound a people's fate to not just physical constitution, but also climate and habit. This focus on biological determinism underscores the contingent nature of development, but only plays a partial role in Herder's overall outlook on the formation and maintenance of the Volksgeist. He asserted that at the core of the nation lies the infallible and eternal natural laws that offer perfection according to the particular nation's natural inclinations. This is both a deeply teleological and pluralistic worldview, which allows nations to be shaped organically through different but equally valid ranges of conduct.

"These clash in wild confusion until, following infallible laws of Nature, the opposing rules limit one another and a kind of balance and harmony of motion obtains. In this way, the nations modify themselves according to time, place, and their internal character; each carries within itself the symmetry of its perfection, incommensurable with that of others."[29]

For Herder, the love of one's own people and native lifestyle is not based on objective superiority, but rather on emotional and existential bonds. He argued that things such as customs, families, and national interest are cherished despite not necessarily being the most refined or enlightened because they are nonetheless one's own.

"Every man loves his country, his manners, his language, his wife, his children, not because they are the best in the world, but because, as time has proven, they are his and in them he loves himself and his labors. Thus every man grows accustomed even to the worst food, the harshest way of life, the crudest manners of the rawest climate, and ultimately finds in these comforts and repose. Even birds of passage nest where they were born, and the bleakest country often has the most attractive ties for those peoples who are acclimatized."[30]

In 1934, Dr. Walter Groß, while speaking at a women's meeting at the Gau party rally in Cologne mirrored this exact relativist sentiment in a way consistent with the established National Socialist position:

"The others may not be better or worse, but they are different than we are, and because they are different than we are, there is a kind of wall between us that is part of the laws of life. That is the core of National Socialism's racial thinking. Our goal is not to insult others, to say: "What a great guy I am!" Rather, we hold to the humble recognition that each healthy piece of life has its corner of the world, and its special tasks. This is just as true of humans as it is of plants and animals in all their multiplicity. We know that one type is no more valuable than another. But we also know that each variety of life has a right to existence only as long as it keeps itself pure and strong." [31]

Neither Herder nor National Socialism wish for any organism to be forced to conform to the natural expectations of a different organism, nor do either seek to form relative hierarchies. While clearly supporting cultural particularism, Herder simultaneously offers a universal principle: that all people have the right to regard their place in the world as their home. Not only is it asserted that a people cannot be judged according to the standards of another, but it is also asserted that all people have an equal claim to their natural existence, regardless of how it may contrast with that in a foreign land. Scholars emphasize that equality for Herder did not imply mutual intelligibility, as he held that no people could truly penetrate the world of another without first dissolving the boundaries that made national culture important to begin with.[32]

"Were we therefore to ask: " Where is man's homeland [Vaterland]? " Where is the center of the world? " then everywhere, whether near the ice-bound North Pole or directly beneath the burning noonday sun, we would receive the same answer: " Here, where you are standing! " Wherever men can live, and they can live almost anywhere, there men do in fact live."[33]

Herder was developing his conception of the nation and its unique character over a decade before he wrote *Ideas for the Philosophy of the History of Mankind*, which can be seen in his 1772 publication *Essay on the Origin of Language*. These earlier publications carry less biological determinism than would be seen later on but maintain an equivalent level of teleological inquiry, which logically leads to some degree of biological determinism. When teleology is applied to human biology, racial differences cease to become descriptive and instead take on a prescriptive role, leading toward the logic that every group has its own inherent destiny within the natural order.

Below, Herder asserted that empathy and a collectively shared sentiment are not learned, but rather natural laws that were implanted by nature in such a way that would bind those of the same kind into a singular entity. It is through this "language of feeling" that the metaphysical foundation of the Volksgeist emerges as a shared spirit inherent to the particular nature from which it blossoms. The identification of the nation's attributes and unique characteristics allow for a more comprehensive examination of the bounds to which the nation must adhere in order to live harmoniously within the innate cultural-emotional code of the nation. This conception provides a philosophical justification for national particularism that would later merge with other thoughts concerning national sovereignty and racial science to form the National Socialist position on national continuity.

"It was, as it were, the last motherly touch of the formative hand of nature that it gave to all, to take out into the world, the law, "Feel not for yourself alone. But rather: your feeling resound!" And since this last creative touch was, for all of one species, of one kind, this law became a blessing: "The sound of your feeling be of one kind to your species and be thus perceived by all in compassion as by one!" Do not now touch this weak, this sentient being. However lonesome

THE GENEALOGY OF NATIONAL SOCIALISM   151

and alone it may seem to be, however exposed to every hostile storm of the universe, yet is it not alone: It stands allied with all nature! Strung with delicate chords; but nature hid sounds in these chords which, when called forth and encouraged, can arouse other beings of equally delicate build, can communicate, as though along an invisible chain, to a distant heart a spark that makes it feel for this unseen being. These sighs, these sounds are language. There is, then, a language of feeling which is—underived—a law of nature."[34]

Herder maintained that language manifests inwardly and organically springs from the unique Volksgeist of the people, tying the expression of a people to the formation of their particular perspective. The remnants of this concept carried over into the rhetoric of the NSDAP in a contradictory manner that was more in line with popular Romantic sentiment than the continuation of National Socialist logic. Adolf Hitler said the following in a speech in Thuringia on January 18, 1927:

"Our national ideal is identical with our social ideal. We are National Socialists, that is to say what we understand by the word nation is not one class, nor one economic group; the nation is for us the collective term for all people who speak our language and possess our blood."[35]

This statement contradicts the National Socialist worldview because of the additional language qualifier that was included. Years after this quote, when the NSDAP came to power, ethnic Germans from all over the world were called back to their homeland, no matter if they spoke German or not. They were of course required to learn German to assimilate into the country, but this, along with the relative abandonment of linguistic rhetoric demonstrates the shedding of illogical Romantic notions, in favor of a solely racial position. This is because the nation is bound by race, not language. Similar to Herder, National

Socialism also understands language to be an organic expression of the nation's spirit. Unlike Herder, National Socialism focuses heavily on biological and racial determinism, recognizing that perspective, characteristics, culture and language come from genetic constitution, making language an element of secondary importance.

To many, the assertion that Adolf Hitler could be incorrect on National Socialist doctrine is preposterous, a position formed through either ignorance, incorrectly believing that Adolf Hitler was the grand engineer of National Socialism, or through a specific brand of hero worship, believing him to be infallible on the matter. One must only read Fichte or Rudolf Jung, who directly attributes his worldview to Fichte, to recognize that the philosophical components of National Socialism had been developed before Hitler's involvement. This is not to say that Adolf Hitler is irrelevant to the discussion of the implementation of National Socialism, but he is absolutely not the primary philosophical contributor, nor sole definer of such.

Herder's conception of the Volksgeist was imbued with resilience and an enduring national essence that is capable of surviving the cyclical process of decay and renewal, allowing for persistence through external collapse in the same way proposed by National Socialism, though the latter being much more directly contingent on racial hygiene.

"As soon as a Nature full of mutable things is set going [Gang], there must also be a going under [Untergang]; or rather, an apparent going under, an alternation of shapes and forms. But this never affects inner Nature, which, high above all ruins, always rises like a phoenix from the ashes and blooms with youthful forces. The formation of our mansion and all the substances that it could produce must prepare us for the frailty and vicissitudes of all human history. With every closer inspection we recognize this more clearly."[36]

Below, Herder can be seen admiring the civic structure of ancient Greek republics, specifically elements that would later form the Volksgemeinschaft under National Socialism, and of course by ideological association, the National Socialist conception of "socialism." The Volksgemeinschaft can be simply defined as a unified national community in which individual interests are subordinated to the nation's well-being. This public-spiritedness and emphasis on cultural cohesion can be seen in abundance throughout National Socialist literature, where the private adherence to national expectations amounts to a moral obligation. This is yet another area where Herder and National Socialism stand in direct contrast to Enlightenment liberalism, directly rejecting the prioritization of absolute individual autonomy.

"As in the Greek republics, everything was undertaken on behalf of the people or of the city, nothing that related to the tutelary deities or the glory of their name was too costly, while individual citizens, including even the notables, were satisfied with modest houses. This public-spiritedness, at least in appearance doing everything for the good of the whole, was the very soul of the Greek states, which doubtless Winckelmann also had in mind when he celebrated the liberty of the Greek republics as the golden age of art."[37]

Herder believed that an individual could only truly realize their full potential as a part of the greater community, where individual duty arises naturally from within, not via an external imposition. It was for this reason that at times Herder appeared more willing to concede some moral and educational functions to the governing state while it serves communal interest rather than abstract political authority.[38] This concept should not sound foreign, as it is the proto-communitarian ethic that would later influence Johann Gottlieb Fichte, who would inherit this Herdarian foundation and further refine it into an ethical system grounded in duty. Fichte echoed Herder's communal ethic, but introduced a level of Kantian moral idealism, truly demonstrating the large and multifaceted impact that Kant had in the development of National Socialism, even if a significant portion was the subject of rejection. The fusion between personal identity, individual responsibility and national continuity remained intact within National Socialist philosophy, leading to what could be labeled a quasi-communitarian worldview.

"For each individual, therefore, the common good becomes his own interest: for anyone who must endure the evils of the whole has the right and the duty to keep these evils from himself and to mitigate their effect on his fellows."[39]

There is no shortage of examples within primary National Socialist literature that demonstrate this national priority and individual subservience, such as that found within the twenty-fourth point in *The Program of the National Socialist German Worker's Party*. This can be seen clearly, especially in the light of the philosophies that have been thus examined, as existing at the core of the National Socialist ethical compass. Once this framework of individual ethical obligation toward the greater good is combined with the establishment of the nation as a racial element, the resulting perspective, once stripped of all potentially obfuscating terminology, can be defined as the unification and collectivization of racial interest and effort.

"We are convinced that the healing process of our nation can only be continued on the basis of the principle that public welfare has priority over individual welfare."[40]

For Herder, language was much more than a means of communication, as he understood it to originate in internal rational processes, where even those afflicted with the inability to speak nonetheless have an internalized language. In this way, a particular language can be seen as the vocal manifestation of the Volksgeist.

"The point here is that it is not an organization of the mouth that made language, for even one who is mute for life, if he is human and if he reflects, has language lying in his soul. The point here is that it is not a scream of emotion, for not a breathing machine but a reflective being invented language. Not a principle of imitation in the soul, for what there is of imitation of nature is merely a means to an end, the one end that is here to be explained. Least of all is it agreement, an arbitrary convention of society."[41]

The language of a people is thus determined by Herder to emerge through teleological means, crafted through the internal logical processes of the masses over time. These linguistic expressions are organically intertwined with the Volksgeist, according to Herder, where they both mirror the development and growth of one another. Linguistic sounds are shaped into this symbolic expression only after a reciprocal process with the natural order has taken place, situating language as a multi-variable dependent entity that connects the soul with the outside world.

"The latter go into his logic as the former into his vocabulary. Reason and language together took a timid step and nature came to meet them halfway—through the power of hearing. Nature did not merely ring out the characteristic mark, it rang it in, deep into the soul. There was a sound, the soul grasped for it, and there it had a ringing word."[42]

The quote below highlights the logical and doctrinal contradiction found in the 1927 Adolf Hitler speech that was previously mentioned, where the boundaries of the nation were drawn according to both racial and linguistic metrics. It is quite possible that this was said in error during an early speech or possibly that Adolf Hitler was still partial, or responding, toward völkisch and Romantic ideas that would have been much more recognizable than the newer biological racial sciences. In 1936 within the pages of Dieter Schwarz's publication in defense of National Socialism, titled *Attacks Against the National Socialist Worldview*, it is made clear that land, language and tradition are not bound to the race idea itself. National Socialism recognizes language, culture and tradition as originating from race, and how could it be otherwise? If it is recognized that race is tied to genetic composition, and that genetic composition creates predictable characteristics, then it must also be recognized that the races have predictably different characteristics, something that is typically understood to be a given in modern science. If these characteristics extend into disposition, intelligence and proclivities, then the previous assertion must be extended to say that predictably similar levels of external perception can be found originating in race. This is the logical process National Socialism takes to arrive at the conclusion that language and culture are important, but ultimately of secondary importance to race.

"Among those who attack or misconstrue the race idea, a further group can be distinguished by the similarity of their arguments. Their thesis is: race is indeed important for a folk, a state and its history, but in the final analysis the important thing is the land or the language or the self-imposed discipline or the tradition etc."[43]

For Herder, language was much more than just a tool for communication; it was a crucial part of his worldview, in which the Volksgeist and language form a living organ that determines culture and religious faith. He believed that an authentic spiritual life should grow naturally from the people, rather than be preserved from foreign forms or imposed by foreign forces. This is a similar position to the one Fichte would later adopt as well, focusing on the development of a religion through national purification and time. National Socialism agrees with the two in that a religion which is to be practiced by the nation must not be harmful to the whole, including foreign elements that erode organic spiritual standing.

"As Christianity operates chiefly by means of its doctrines, so much depends on the language in which it is taught and on the degree of culture already attained by that language—from which its orthodoxies take their cue. With a civilized [gebildeten] or universal language, then, Christianity not only propagates itself, but also acquires a peculiar culture and dignity. But if, as a sacred dialect of divine origin, it falls behind other living languages, or is confined to the narrow and secluded precincts of a rude ancestral tongue, as if banished to some crumbling, desolate castle; then it has no choice but to remain there, wretched and miserable, as either an impoverished tyrant or unwitting prisoner."[44]

Herder walks the line between ethnocentrism and the rejection of such multiple times, such as below where it is asserted that European culture and rank is elevated "above other peoples." The context in which he determines European cultural superiority or "rank" is unclear but would nonetheless require internal standards that are crafted by Herder's European mind to be used as the reference point for external comparison. He accepted the assertion that Europeans are superior in these ways, but on multiple occasions also rejected the notion that such could be determined at all, as there was simply no comparison to be made. This is eerily similar to the rhetoric that would later be used by the NSDAP where ethnocentrism was typically rejected, but on occasion, statements to the contrary were made. Regarding strictly National Socialism, the consensus is clear in the adoption of Herder's anti-ethnocentrist position which is only logical following the recognition of the nation as a unique entity that houses a particular Volksgeist. This is the case because under National Socialism, success is not measured through external metrics or capitalistic standards, but rather through an internal standard that only arises from the unique attributes of the nation, making all else totally incomparable.

"How, then, did Europe attain to its culture and to the rank that elevates it above other peoples? It was impelled by place, time, need, the conjunction of circumstances, the course of events; but above all else it obtained this rank as a result of its many common endeavors, its own manufactures."[45]

It could be reasonably argued that these contradictions arise from egotistical flare-ups, where the love for one's own people boils over in illogical, but all too human, ways. Herder believed that no amount of education could change the Indian's nature and allow for the acceptance or true integration into the nature of the European. This is extremely relevant to the philosophical development of National Socialism, as the exclusive and persistent Volksgeist is clearly recognized as incapable of transmitting itself into that which is foreign.

"At that the Indian does not follow the teachings and practices of every foreigner is evidently due to the institution of the Brahmins having already possessed his soul and filled his life so completely as to leave no room for anything else. Hence so many rites and festivals, so many deities and myths, so many holy places and meritorious works, so that from infancy the Indian's whole imagination is occupied and he is reminded of what he is in almost every moment of his life. Compared to this absolute mastery of the soul, the effect of all European institutions has been only superficial; and for as long as there are Indians, this will ever be the case."[46]

This is precisely why I asserted the following in my 2025 publication *National Socialism: A Comprehensive Examination*:

"The National Socialist Weltanschauung is crafted to fit perfectly atop of the natural requirements set in stone by racial law. These foundational racial laws vary from race to race which undoubtedly affects the connection point with the new Weltanschauung, causing either disharmony or the unnatural acceptance of a foreign state of being. Outside races should not look towards National Socialism as a solution, and likewise Europeans should absolutely not be pushing a European Weltanschauung on foreign peoples as they must find a system of governance and societal organization that allows for their national character to live free from the enslavement by foreign ideals."[47]

Herder rejected colonialism on moral grounds, defending the right of Africans to live as they please in their native lands, just as all else. This is not simply an emotional response fueled by empathy, but rather a continuation of thought through his teleological lens, asserting that people belong to their environments and form a unity with them in a particular way. When viewed in the context of the national particularism later developed within National Socialism, Herder's thoughts here represent an important philosophical precursor to later völkisch ideals. The same logic led Herder to condemn foreign religious systems, praising Luther for his restoration of German spirituality in the face of Roman Catholic universalism.[48]

"And what right do you ogres have even to approach the land of these unfortunates, much less snatch them from it by theft, fraud, and force? For thousands of years, this part of the world has been theirs, as they belong to it; their ancestors purchased it at the greatest cost to themselves: the price they paid was their Negro figure and complexion."[49]

While Herder never directly weighed the needs of his community and the extent to which they are morally or ethically justified in imposing on others for their own survival, in *The Program of the National Socialist German Worker's Party*, this can be seen plainly. While the program itself is not strictly National Socialist doctrine, doctrinal spirit and intention can nonetheless be pulled from points that address circumstantial concerns. Simply put, National Socialism knows no limit in the preservation and continuation of the nation, including colonization of foreign lands if necessary for survival. This should not be taken to mean that National Socialism is inherently colonialistic, as it only becomes so under conditions of necessity.

"We demand land and colonies so that we can provide food for our people and bring our overpopulation under control."[50]

Below, Herder reveals a culturally antisemitic position, even referring to Jews as "parasitic" in nature, existing to feed off of the "juices" of European nations. While dismissing the idea that Jews brought with them literal disease into Europe, he adds that what they brought with them was much worse, amounting to "moral leprosy" carried by a people alien to the European cultural and moral order. This moral leprosy took the shape of ethical corruption, where the negative traits of the European were being exacerbated by the Jew's role in commerce, finance, and governmental administration, accelerating European civilizational decay. Despite this, Herder acknowledged the Jews for their "indispensability," a concession that complicates his message, although not enough to distort the moral framing he provided previously. He partially dismissed the egregious behavior of the Jew through the attribution of their community action to cycles rooted in cultural pathology caused by widespread mistreatment.

"The Jews we consider here only as the parasitic plant that has attached itself to almost all the European nations, extracting more or less of their juices. After the fall of ancient Rome, there were still relatively few of them in Europe; but, owing to the persecutions of the Arabs, they fled here in great numbers and dispersed themselves over each nation. That they brought leprosy with them is unlikely; but worse was the moral leprosy they have spread: in every barbarous age they have been the vile instruments of usury, as bankers, brokers, and imperial servants, and thus stood to profit by confirming the Europeans in their rude and prideful ignorance of commerce. They were often treated with cruelty, and what they had gained by greed and deceit, or by industry, prudence, and method, was tyrannically extorted from them; but as they were habituated to such treatment, and had come to expect it, so they were led to commit ever-greater frauds and extortions. Nevertheless, they were indispensable: and to this day remain so in many countries."[51]

Closely following the previous quote, Herder recognized the Jews as a religious and cultural entity, not a racially foreign one, even suggesting integration is not just possible but guaranteed. National Socialism, by contrast, recognizes the Jews as a racially foreign group that are incapable of joining the nation, as they lack the biological prerequisite for a shared perspective with the European. While Herder's organicist worldview did add to the mounting list of antisemitic voices that would later influence völkisch antisemitism in the nineteenth and twentieth centuries, he absolutely did not hold the same position as National Socialism on the matter.

"There will come a time in Europe when no man will ask another whether he be Christian or Jew: for the Jews, too, will live according to European laws and contribute to the welfare of the state. Only a barbarous constitution has hitherto prevented them from doing so or rendered their abilities harmful."[52]

Despite much of Herder's earlier work being vehemently opposed to ethnocentrism, at least in proclamation, he clearly weighed racial groups in comparison to one another to a rather significant extent. Groups with European racial compositions were understood by Herder to be the builders of civilizations that are beneficial to the world, standing in sharp contrast to how he viewed the Negroes,

Tungus, Eskimos, etc. He recognized these racial groups that failed to produce civilization and culture to a level similar to the European as inert groups that are, and will remain, unproductive and historically irrelevant, as they are incapable of connecting with the European perspective. This is a continuation of the logic he was previously developing regarding the connection between physiognomy and individual attributes, as the sum of individual characteristics observably shifts the trends of the community toward the average. This is the point where Herder's deterministic and essentialist framework begins to solidify into what would later feed into völkisch ideology, where the language of cultural influences is grounded in natural processes.

"It was also one and the same principle of Nature that gave precisely the well-formed nations the most salutary influence over others; it bestowed on them that nimbleness and elasticity of spirit that is as much an appurtenance of their bodily frame as it is of their beneficial effect on other nations. The Tungus and Eskimos forever sit huddled in their caves and neither in weal nor woe concern themselves with distant peoples. The Negro has invented nothing for the benefit of the European; it has never once entered his mind to shower blessings or make war on Europe. From the regions of finely formed peoples we have derived our religion, our arts, our sciences; indeed, the whole fabric of our culture and humanity, however much of it we possess."[53]

In this final quote from *Ideas for the Philosophy of the History of Mankind*, Herder recognizes Europe as an heir of cultural vitality, as a singular unified intellectual group. This is an important point to be made, especially when considered in the context of the Volksgeist. It is directly asserted here that Herder understood Europeans to maintain a supranational Volksgeist, that connects all European nations, allowing for a unified perspective. This paved the way for a logical application of völkisch pan-Europeanism and National Socialist racial geopolitics, through the recognition of a racially bound spirit, not an ethnically bound one.

"The whole of Europe is one learned realm, having acquired, partly by internal emulation, partly by the auxiliary means for which it has scoured the world in modern times, an ideal figure that only the scholar comprehends and the statesman exploits to his advantage."[54]

In a speech given to the Reichstag on March 7, 1936, Adolf Hitler both suggested conformity to this concept, along with a deepening of this multi-ethnic interaction of cultures and spirit within Europe. He begins with acknowledging German duty toward "European culture and civilization", in a way that indicates that this obligation is shared amongst all racially European groups. From there, it is asserted that all of the "nations" within Europe offer their own unique attributes, which clearly fall in line with the aforementioned supranational Volksgeist that Hitler confirmed at the very start of the speech. In this way, the promotion of a specific group's culture and spirit is also the promotion of this supranational Volksgeist, to which all are expected to contribute. This is critical in understanding the interplay between European groups under National Socialism, especially when it comes to the formulation of appropriate political and social ties within the European race. Clearly, to both Herder and National Socialism, the overarching perspective of the European is that of a European nature, which certainly does not discount the cultural particularities of specific groups, but does offer additional evidence in confirmation that the National Socialist Weltanschauung is not strictly limited to those of German descent.

"One day I will be able to demand from history confirmation of the fact that at no time in the course of my struggle on behalf of the German Volk did I forget the duties I myself and all of us are obligated to assume toward maintaining European culture and civilization.

However, it is a prerequisite for the existence of this continent, which ultimately owes its uniqueness to the diversity of its cultures, that it is unthinkable without the presence of free and independent national states.

Each European people may be convinced that it has made the greatest contribution to our Western culture. On the whole, however, we would not wish to do without any of what the separate peoples have given, and thus we do not wish to argue over the value of their respective contributions. Rather, we must recognize that the greatest achievements in the most diverse areas of human culture doubtless stem from the rivalry between individual European accomplishments.

Therefore, although we are willing to cooperate in this European world of culture as a free and equal member, we are just as stubbornly determined to remain what we are."[55]

Johann Gottfried Herder stands as a critical figure in the early genealogy of National Socialist philosophy, functioning as the intellectual vehicle through which Enlightenment rationalism began to diverge toward Romantic particularism. The conception of the Volksgeist, emphasis on national uniqueness, and teleology lent themselves readily to later racial theorists who would further develop his ideas. In this way, Herder serves less as a direct precursor, especially when compared to a thinker such as Fichte, and more as a philosophical wellspring, whose philosophical waters would be redirected and deepen toward a more consistent, systematic, and logically developed structure under National Socialism.

Endnotes

1. Fred Blakey, "National Socialism," *Southern Quarterly* 6, no. 4 (1968): 438.

2. Carlton J. H. Hayes, "Contributions of Herder to the Doc-

trine of Nationalism," *The American Historical Review* 32, no. 4 (July 1927): 719-736.

3. Carlton J. H. Hayes, "Contributions of Herder to the Doctrine of Nationalism," *The American Historical Review* 32, no. 4 (July 1927): 719-736.

4. Carlton J. H. Hayes, "Contributions of Herder to the Doctrine of Nationalism," *The American Historical Review* 32, no. 4 (July 1927): 719-736.

5. Fred Blakey, "National Socialism," *Southern Quarterly* 6, no. 4 (1968): 438.

6. Carlton J. H. Hayes, "Contributions of Herder to the Doctrine of Nationalism," *The American Historical Review* 32, no. 4 (July 1927): 719-736.

7. Richard White, "Herder: On the Ethics of Nationalism," *Humanitas* 18, nos. 1-2 (2005): 166-81.

8. Johann Gottfried Herder, *Ideas for the Philosophy of the History of Mankind*, trans. and ed. Gregory Moore (Princeton, NJ: Princeton University Press, 2007), 26.

9. Nationalsozialistische Deutsche Arbeiterpartei, *Ich Kämpfe (I Fight): The Responsibilities of Party Comrades*, trans. Rad Cowdery, 9.

10. Johann Gottfried Herder, *Ideas for the Philosophy of the History of Mankind*, trans. and ed. Gregory Moore (Princeton, NJ: Princeton University Press, 2007), 35.

11. Johann Gottlieb Fichte, *The Vocation of Man*, trans. William Smith, with introduction by E. Ritchie (Chicago: The Open Court Publishing Company, 1931), 19.

12. Johann Gottfried Herder, *Ideas for the Philosophy of the History of Mankind*, trans. and ed. Gregory Moore (Princeton, NJ: Princeton University Press, 2007), 34.

13. Johann Gottfried Herder, *Ideas for the Philosophy of the History of Mankind*, trans. and ed. Gregory Moore (Princeton, NJ: Princeton University Press, 2007), 37.

14. Eggel, Dominic, Andre Liebich, and Deborah Mancini-Griffoli. "Was Herder a Nationalist?" *The Review of Politics* 69, no. 1 (2007): 48-78.

15. Johann Gottfried Herder, *Ideas for the Philosophy of the History of Mankind*, trans. and ed. Gregory Moore (Princeton, NJ: Princeton University Press, 2007), 67.

16. Johann Gottfried Herder, *Ideas for the Philosophy of the History of Mankind*, trans. and ed. Gregory Moore (Princeton, NJ: Princeton University Press, 2007), 82.

17. Johann Gottfried Herder, *Ideas for the Philosophy of the History of Mankind*, trans. and ed. Gregory Moore (Princeton, NJ: Princeton University Press, 2007), 396.

18. Eggel, Dominic, Andre Liebich, and Deborah Mancini-Griffoli. "Was Herder a Nationalist?" *The Review of Politics* 69, no. 1 (2007): 48-78.

19. Eggel, Dominic, Andre Liebich, and Deborah Mancini-Grif-

foli. "Was Herder a Nationalist?" *The Review of Politics* 69, no. 1 (2007): 48-78.

20. Erich Schinnerer, *German Law and Legislation* (Berlin: Junker und Dünnhaupt Verlag, 1938), 2.

21. Aret Karademir, "Heidegger and Nazism: On the Relation between German Conservatism, Heidegger, and the National Socialist Ideology," The Philosophical Forum 44, no. 2 (2013).

22. Johann Gottfried Herder, *Ideas for the Philosophy of the History of Mankind*, trans. and ed. Gregory Moore (Princeton, NJ: Princeton University Press, 2007), 437.

23. Walter Groß, *Rasse. Eine Rundfunkrede* (Berlin: Rassenpolitisches Amt der NSDAP, 1934).

24. Johann Gottfried Herder, *Ideas for the Philosophy of the History of Mankind*, trans. and ed. Gregory Moore (Princeton, NJ: Princeton University Press, 2007), 154.

25. Walter Groß, *Rasse. Eine Rundfunkrede* (Berlin: Rassenpolitisches Amt der NSDAP, 1934).

26. Johann Gottfried Herder, *Ideas for the Philosophy of the History of Mankind*, trans. and ed. Gregory Moore (Princeton, NJ: Princeton University Press, 2007), 183.

27. Johann Gottfried Herder, *Ideas for the Philosophy of the History of Mankind*, trans. and ed. Gregory Moore (Princeton, NJ: Princeton University Press, 2007), 222.

28. Johann Gottfried Herder, *Ideas for the Philosophy of the History of Mankind*, trans. and ed. Gregory Moore (Princeton, NJ: Princeton University Press, 2007), 54.

29. Johann Gottfried Herder, *Ideas for the Philosophy of the History of Mankind*, trans. and ed. Gregory Moore (Princeton, NJ: Princeton University Press, 2007), 437.

30. Johann Gottfried Herder, *Ideas for the Philosophy of the History of Mankind*, trans. and ed. Gregory Moore (Princeton, NJ: Princeton University Press, 2007), 17.

31. Dr. Walter Groß, *Nationalsozialistische Rassenpolitik: Eine Rede an die deutschen Frauen* (Dessau: C. Dünnhaupt, 1934).

32. Carlton J. H. Hayes, "Contributions of Herder to the Doctrine of Nationalism," *The American Historical Review* 32, no. 4 (July 1927): 719-736.

33. Johann Gottfried Herder, *Ideas for the Philosophy of the History of Mankind*, trans. and ed. Gregory Moore (Princeton, NJ: Princeton University Press, 2007), 17.

34. Johann Gottfried Herder, *Essay on the Origin of Language*, trans. John H. Moran and Alexander Gode, intro. Alexander Gode (Chicago: University of Chicago Press, 1986), 66.

35. Adolf Hitler, speech in Schleiz, Thuringia, January 18, 1927.

36. Johann Gottfried Herder, *Ideas for the Philosophy of the History of Mankind*, trans. and ed. Gregory Moore (Princeton, NJ: Princeton University Press, 2007), 16.

37. Johann Gottfried Herder, *Ideas for the Philosophy of the History of Mankind*, trans. and ed. Gregory Moore (Princeton, NJ: Princeton University Press, 2007), 360.

38. Eggel, Dominic, Andre Liebich, and Deborah Mancini-Griffoli. "Was Herder a Nationalist?" *The Review of Politics* 69, no. 1 (2007): 48-78.

39. Johann Gottfried Herder, *Ideas for the Philosophy of the History of Mankind*, trans. and ed. Gregory Moore (Princeton, NJ: Princeton University Press, 2007), 450.

40. Nationalsozialistische Deutsche Arbeiterpartei, *Ich Kämpfe (I Fight): The Responsibilities of Party Comrades*, trans. Rad Cowdery, 20.

41. Johann Gottfried Herder, *Essay on the Origin of Language*, trans. John H. Moran and Alexander Gode, intro. Alexander Gode (Chicago: University of Chicago Press, 1986), 86.

42. Johann Gottfried Herder, *Essay on the Origin of Language*, trans. John H. Moran and Alexander Gode, intro. Alexander Gode (Chicago: University of Chicago Press, 1986), 93.

43. Dieter Schwarz, *Attacks against the National-Socialist Worldview*, trans. from the SS newspaper *Das Schwarze Korps* (Berlin–Munich: Central Publishing House of the NSDAP, Franz Eher Nachf. GmbH, 1936).

44. Johann Gottfried Herder, *Ideas for the Philosophy of the History of Mankind*, trans. and ed. Gregory Moore (Princeton, NJ: Princeton University Press, 2007), 495.

45. Johann Gottfried Herder, *Ideas for the Philosophy of the History of Mankind*, trans. and ed. Gregory Moore (Princeton, NJ: Princeton University Press, 2007), 610.

46. Johann Gottfried Herder, *Ideas for the Philosophy of the History of Mankind*, trans. and ed. Gregory Moore (Princeton, NJ: Princeton University Press, 2007), 304.

47. Jake Leone, *National Socialism: A Comprehensive Examination* (2025), 89.

48. Carlton J. H. Hayes, "Contributions of Herder to the Doctrine of Nationalism," *The American Historical Review* 32, no. 4 (July 1927): 719-736.

49. Johann Gottfried Herder, *Ideas for the Philosophy of the History of Mankind*, trans. and ed. Gregory Moore (Princeton, NJ: Princeton University Press, 2007), 172.

50. Nationalsozialistische Deutsche Arbeiterpartei, *Ich Kämpfe (I Fight): The Responsibilities of Party Comrades*, trans. Rad Cowdery, 38.

51. Johann Gottfried Herder, *Ideas for the Philosophy of the History of Mankind*, trans. and ed. Gregory Moore (Princeton, NJ: Princeton University Press, 2007), 474.

52. Johann Gottfried Herder, *Ideas for the Philosophy of the History of Mankind*, trans. and ed. Gregory Moore (Princeton, NJ: Princeton University Press, 2007), 475.

53. Johann Gottfried Herder, *Ideas for the Philosophy of the History of Mankind*, trans. and ed. Gregory Moore (Princeton,

NJ: Princeton University Press, 2007), 147.

54. Johann Gottfried Herder, *Ideas for the Philosophy of the History of Mankind*, trans. and ed. Gregory Moore (Princeton, NJ: Princeton University Press, 2007), 309.

55. Adolf Hitler, speech to the Reichstag, Berlin, March 7, 1936.

Chapter 4
Friedrich List

Friedrich List was born on August 6, 1789, in Reutlingen, a Free Imperial City in Württemberg, toward the end of the Holy Roman Empire. Growing up in a middle-class family, List's formative years were shaped by the Napoleonic era and its far-reaching effects on the already fragmented German states. Entering the civil service of Württemberg at a young age, List quickly became frustrated with bureaucratic inefficiencies and seemingly unnecessary obstacles to national cohesion.

By 1817, List had become a professor of political economy at the University of Tübingen, despite lacking a formal degree. His unorthodox economic views and strong nationalistic leanings provoked the conservative state authorities, eventually leading to criminal charges against him, forcing him to flee to Switzerland to avoid prosecution. Struggling to maintain his livelihood there, he eventually surrendered to the authorities. After a short period in prison, he was exiled to the United States in 1825, where he initially attempted farming unsuccessfully. He later worked for a German-language newspaper in Pennsylvania and engaged in other ventures, most of which failed. Nonetheless, these experiences exposed him to the rapid industrialization of the United States and the protectionist economic system fostered by Alexander Hamilton and Henry Clay.

These observations proved transformative for List. He concluded that free trade policies primarily benefit the dominant industrial powers, and that protective tariffs and state-guided economic development are necessary to secure the sovereignty of emerging nations against outside industrial and economic dominance.

List eventually returned to Germany, dedicating himself to writing and politics, advocating for the creation of the Zollverein, a proposed German customs union, which he saw to be the first step toward economic and political unification. In advancing the Zollverein, List increasingly recognized that economic development did not harmonize all social interests automatically, leading to his assertion that political institutions must actively structure the economy to serve national interest.[1] His magnum opus, *Das nationale System der politischen Ökonomie* (*The National System of Political Economy*), published in 1841, offered a counterpoint to Adam Smith's classical liberalism. In it, List argued for the development of a historically and nationally grounded economic model that prioritized national power, productive capacity, and cultural continuity over abstract universalist principles. Some scholars have further suggested that the national economy as envisioned by List emerged from imperial contexts, where colonial and imperial models functioned as templates that were later reconfigured for implementation in a more modern context.[2]

In 1846, at the age of fifty-seven, List died by suicide, disillusioned with the public reception of his work and unaware of the long-term influence his ideas would have on German economic policy and the philosophical undercurrents of the völkisch movement. Additionally, his work laid a significant portion of the intellectual foundations that would later be drawn upon by National Socialism, particularly regarding economic sovereignty, protectionism, and national regeneration.

Friedrich List's contribution to German intellectual and political thought transcends conventional economic theory. He posited the nation as an organic economic community, characterized by an inseparable culture, history, and collective will. By embedding the economic health and development of a nation within the broader framework of national regeneration, List articulated a vision in which economic strategy was inseparable from the nation's morality, historical trajectory, and long-term continuity. Despite not requiring the same extent or specific form of collectivism that was later formalized under National Socialism, List clearly rejected laissez-faire liberalism and cosmopolitanism for the philosophical and pragmatic reasons that would later underpin National Socialist economic thought.

This becomes apparent in List's critique of Adam Smith and Smith's cosmopolitan individualism. List argued that the nation should have priority over individual self-interest, and that economic policies to the contrary undermine the historical and moral development of the people. He further emphasized that the nation should be focused on the development of long-term productive growth, rather than short-term profit. With the addition of List's cultural particularism, along with his views on state and economic sovereignty, the connection to later National Socialist economic theory becomes readily apparent.

The core metaphysical and political vision behind List's nationalism rests on his conception of the nation as an element which cannot be reduced down to a mere collection of individuals or extended in a universalistic sense to include all of humanity. List understood the nation as a concrete formation that stands as the mediator between the individual and the entirety of mankind. Similar to Johann Gottlieb Fichte and Johann Gottfried Herder, he rejected the Enlightenment premise that society is built from isolated, rational individuals. For

List, the nation evolves into a moral and legal entity, complete with internal coherence that exists beyond the influence of a select few thinkers. In an 1827 letter, List writes:

"A nation is the medium between individuals and mankind; a separate society of individuals, who, possessing common government, common laws, rights, institutions, interests, common history, and glory, common defence and security of their rights, riches, and lives, constitute one body, free and independent, following only the dictates of its interest, as regards other independent bodies, and possessing power to regulate the interests of the individuals, constituting that body, in order to create the greatest quantity of common welfare in the interior and the greatest quantity of security as regards other nations."[3]

A crucial element of the above statement is List's subordination of the individual to the interests of the nation, directly challenging liberal conceptions of individualism. Under this arrangement, the state cannot be passive, as might be feasible in an individualistic society, but must take an active role where it functions as the architect of collective wellbeing. Furthermore, List's acknowledgment of "other independent bodies", presupposes national sovereignty and interaction with other autonomous states, offering a realist approach to international economic relations. Universal harmony is thus not sought; rather, the aim is national flourishing and long-term strategic security, a position that anticipates later National Socialist economic thought, particularly regarding the primacy of collective national interest.

The previous quotation also clarifies List's conception of the nation. While he did not conceive of the nation in explicitly racial terms as found in National Socialism, he did present it as an entity with temporal depth and continuity, in which historical inheritance and a cumulative identity are passed on to subsequent generations for continuation. Through the rejection of a utilitarian view of the nation, and the embrace of a romantic-historicist position, akin to that of Ernst Moritz Arndt and Johann Gottlieb Fichte, the nation is recognized as a vessel for cultural transmission and a shared destiny.

In a Reichstag speech on January 30th, 1937, Adolf Hitler articulated a parallel conception of the nation under National Socialism:

"Fundamentally, our National Socialist program replaces the liberal concept of the individual and the Marxist concept of general humanity with the concept of a blood-bound and soil-bound people."[4]

The National Socialist description of the nation is noticeably more succinct than that of Friedrich List. Many of the additional descriptors that List mentions, such as common interests, government, and history, still apply to the National Socialist definition inasmuch as these attributes derive from a shared genetic origin. In this way, National Socialism presents a more exclusionary national model than List, but one that is nonetheless structurally consistent with his intentions for the economic nation.

In *The National System of Political Economy*, List claimed that the nation holds a metaphysical position between the individual and the rest of humanity, existing not merely as a spatial entity, but also as an existential and moral one. Within this framework, he believed that the individual is not capable of meaningful interaction with the outside world, as the nation carries the collective's identity, and with that, a sense of belonging expressed through language, literature, customs, and legal structure. The way in which List frames the nation echoes Herder's Volksgeist, while incorporating more explicit political and economic implications, making the national spirit not just a cultural entity, but also one with unique territorial, judicial processes, and sovereignty.

"Between each individual and entire humanity, however, stands the nation, with its special language and literature, with its peculiar origin and history, with its special manners and customs, laws and institutions, with the claims of all these for existence, independence, perfection, and continuance for the future, and with its separate territory; a society which, united by a thousand ties of mind and of interests, combines itself into one independent whole, which recognises the law of right for and within itself, and in its united character is still opposed to other societies of a similar kind in their national liberty, and consequently can only under the existing conditions of the world maintain self-existence and independence by its own power and resources."[5]

The "thousand ties of mind and of interests" that List identifies as proof the organic unity of the nation are not of a contractual or artificial nature as understood by liberal thought, but rather an inherited cohesion transmitted through time. List emphasized the internal moral autonomy inherent to the nation, granting it independent moral standing, in which the collective "recognises the law of right for and within itself". This also aligns with Herder's adamant rejection of externally applied national laws and standards, asserting that the traditions and consciousness of the nation hold distinct attributes and necessities, the discontinuation of which would result in national subjugation.

This approaches the core of List's geopolitical outlook: nations compete, and the universalistic harmony preached by some directly infringe on the individual nation's capacity to maintain the intangible integrity of its national character. Despite rejecting the notion that liberal free trade could guarantee peace, List recognized the interdependence of national economies to an extent, even proposing the formation of a world trade congress as a political mechanism to regulate international economic relations.[6] However, he asserted that in order for a nation to maintain its unique attributes, it must commit to a doctrine of national self-sufficiency rooted in power politics, through which it can guarantee its own independence by "its own power and resources." The principle that the survival and growth of a people cannot be entrusted to goodwill or abstract moral theories, but instead depends upon strength and internal development, foreshadows doctrines of national realism that later appeared in both the völkisch movement and National Socialist philosophy.

In *Germany Speaks*, Joachim Ribbentrop echoed these same concepts of sovereignty, which is a crucial element of National Socialism in all respects, including economics:

"Just as we believe that world peace can only be assured by the existence of free, sovereign and happy States, so do we also hold that world economy can only prosper on a basis of healthy national economies."[7]

Below, List critiques classical economics, particularly focused on the abstract universalism which claims to apply equally to all individuals in all places. This, List argues, is nonsensical because the cosmopolitan school ignores "the principle of nationality," failing to account for the differing national paths of development, cultural components, and overarching political interests that define the economic trajectory of the nation. The second defect that List identified in liberal economics is the "dead materialism" that is pervasive throughout, which neglects the "mental and political" dimensions of economic and national development, resulting in a spiritually and politically impoverished nation. For List, the objective was not wealth generation per se, but instead the development of productive power, which may not show short term profit, but in cases such as national education, technological innovation, and public spirit, could offer the nation a greater chance of thriving more in the future than if the focus was on short-term and highly individualistic objectives. Through the formalization of productive power, List distinguished three forms of capital: natural, material, and mental. Of these, List regarded mental capital, encompassing education, skill, enterprise, state institutions, discipline, and military organization, as the most important strategic and defensive force of the nation, allowing for the transformation of raw resources into national strength and independence.[8] Through this distinction, List was able to explicitly separate wealth itself from the causes of wealth, which rest heavily on the nation's mental capital.[9] These critiques align closely with Fichte's nationalism and Arndt's moral collectivism, and anticipate the anti-individualist ethos of National Socialism, in which the Volk is conceived as an organic unity and the state exists to harmonize the individual with the national whole.

"The system of the school suffers, as we have already shown in the preceding chapters, from three main defects: firstly, from boundless cosmopolitanism, which neither recognises the principle of nationality, nor takes into consideration the satisfaction of its interests; secondly, from a dead materialism, which everywhere regards chiefly the mere exchangeable value of things without taking into consideration the mental and political, the present and the future interests, and the productive powers of the nation; thirdly, from a disorganising particularism and individualism, which, ignoring the nature and character of social labour and the operation of the union of powers in their higher consequences, considers private industry only as it would develop itself under a state of free interchange with society (i.e. with the whole human race) were that race not divided into separate national societies."[10]

The rejection of cosmopolitanism and internationalism by National Socialism does not need to be reiterated, as it has already been well established; however, it is important to note that the National

Socialist rejection of foreign influence stems from deeper philosophical origins than is commonly asserted. This rejection originates in a carefully constructed philosophical position that does not inherently fear the foreign, but rather seeks to protect and maintain that which is naturally recognizable and formative to the nation and the individual. Through Fichte's moral system, Herder's particularistic Volksgeist, List's practical national economy, and other contributions, National Socialism synthesized earlier fragmented concepts that emphasized internal national priority over external interests, creating a more coherent framework than any of these predecessors achieved individually.

Attacking the liberal myth of social harmony through unregulated self-interest, List denied the notion that private vice could always equal public virtue through the exercise of practical irony. Those who are most active in pursuing their own self interest, such as criminals, clearly do not contribute to the development of the common good, demonstrating a fatal flaw in the idea that such a hands-off approach, even when coupled with personal incentive, would result in the most ideal outcome for the nation. This critique carries both economic and ethical implications: the pursuit of individual gain is not inherently socially beneficial.

"Or does the individual merely by understanding his own interests best, and by striving to further them, if left to his own devices, always further the interests of the community. We ask those who occupy the benches of justice, whether they do not frequently have to send individuals to the tread-mill on account of their excess of inventive power, and of their all too great industry. Robbers, thieves, smugglers, and cheats know their own local and personal circumstances and conditions extremely well, and pay the most active attention to their business; but it by no means follows therefrom, that society is in the best condition where such individuals are least restrained in the exercise of their private industry."[11]

The involvement of ethical standards focused on the wellbeing of the collective was a prominent theme throughout Gottfried Feder's works, and thus most of the economic literature of National Socialism. That same ethical involvement and coordinated internal growth were echoed in Feder's publication titled *The German State on a National Socialist Foundation*:

"In short therefore the economic policy of National Socialism will work towards removing a basically false concentration of economics on profitability and for that reason to restore to honor the only right and reasonable task of national economics: the fulfilment of demand.

This does not in any way exclude income and profit for the trader, factory owner and the honest businessmen; on the contrary, in no way should difficulties be created for the justified striving for earnings so long as this striving is contained within the scope of the public interests."[12]

Profit under National Socialism is permitted, provided that it is gained and managed ethically and directed toward productive ends. This theme of individual subordination to the interests of the nation and the national economy was heavily emphasized by both List and National Socialism, each seeking "lasting national prosperity." List proposes a collectivist economic ethic, in which the individual is obligated, both materially and behaviorally, to contribute to a shared national goal, echoing the moral duty that Fichte previously suggested the individual impose upon themselves. This convergence may have arisen from philosophical circumstances in which the rejection of Enlightenment ideals led to a natural antithesis: a non-universalistic approach that recognizes the foundations of human existence to transcend the individual into the national. While List doesn't directly cite

Fichte, it is possible that this alignment was more than a philosophical coincidence, given their intellectual milieu, geographic proximity, and temporal overlap, but no such direct evidence of influence exists.

Below, List references the coordinated and intergenerational effort that a unified people must employ in order to ensure their sovereignty and long-term national trajectory, both economically and socially. In this way, List held a teleological view of national economic development, in which the profit from such must serve a greater end beyond the short term material gain of the individual.

"We have proved historically that the unity of the nation forms the fundamental condition of lasting national prosperity; and we have shown that only where the interest of individuals has been subordinated to those of the nation, and where successive generations have striven for one and the same object, the nations have been brought to harmonious development of their productive powers, and how little private industry can prosper without the united efforts both of the individuals who are living at the time, and of successive generations directed to one common object."[13]

In an 1827 letter, Friedrich List directly rejected the commonly held notion that the nation is merely an administrative convenience, asserting instead that it is a substantive and sovereign actor, complete with real properties and will. This position aligns him with the Romantic tradition, in which the Volk and nation are understood to be an organic and spiritual organism, though he stops short of introducing explicit biological or racial themes, unlike many other Romantic thinkers of his time. The elevation of the nation into moral personhood through the attribution of "all the qualities of a rational being" anthropomorphizes the nation in a manner reminiscent of the Volksgeist, and clearly delineates the nation as a prevailing and autonomous entity.

"But the American nation can, as Mr. Cooper may learn from the title of many indictments. A being which elects presidents and representatives, which possesses a navy, land, and debts; which makes war and concludes peace; which has separate interests respecting other nations, and rights as well as obligations respecting its members, is not a mere grammatical contrivance; it is not a mere grammatical being; it has all the qualities of a rational being and real existence. It has body and real possessions; it has intelligence, and expresses its resolutions to the members by laws, and speaks with its enemy, —not the language of individuals, but at the mouth of cannon."[14]

List's focus on the protection of national sovereignty through force aligns closely with the National Socialist emphasis of military strength to accomplish the same ends:

But if you believe that you must be free, then you must learn to recognize that no one gives you freedom save only your own sword."[15]

List articulated his vision for a system that would empower national self-determination through pragmatic realism rather than subordinating national sovereignty to abstract notions of moral universalism. This not only reinforces what has already been extracted regarding national self-interest, but also provides ethical justification for the defense of such interests as national prioritization, even if it neglects the burdens of other nations. Kantian notions of perpetual peace and universal moral obligations were understood by List to be unrealistic and lead to the enslavement of the weaker nations to outside predatory elements. Due to this, List saw national survival as dependent on unity, reality, and strategic independence, providing philosophical infrastructure for the later völkisch movement and National Socialism, where this national self-interest becomes an existential racial imperative.

"A new people with a new form of government, and new ideas of general welfare and freedom has arisen. —This people has learned by a general and free discussion of every political matter, to distinguish the true from the false, visionary systems from clear perceptions, cosmopolitical from political principles, sayings from doings. This people cannot be accused of selfishness if it intends to rise by its own exertions to the highest degree of power and wealth without injuring other nations, but likewise without taking upon themselves the charge of promoting the welfare of mankind, because if it should not pursue that policy, its standing amongst the powerful nations of the earth and its whole system of society, would be lost."[16]

In 1827, List asserted national self-interest as a civilizational imperative, absolutely necessary given the circumstances of international existence and the associated external forces. He warned that "a nation would act unwisely" to place a higher priority on the welfare of the entire human race over its own, as the primary obligation of the state is not ethical universalism, but the survival of the nation. This is self-preservation, derived from the harsh realities of international power and global competition; a principle of natural law observable even at the individual level.

Within a community of self-interested parties, a singular egalitarian community member who disregards his own interests or survival to pursue the betterment of others will quickly find himself without the necessary provisions or security to sustain life. He has given these resources to the starving, and in doing so, has joined them in their former position at his own expense. At this point, some might say that it was a noble deed, until they are reminded that the starving man was the sole egalitarian within the community and now has nobody to help him from his self-appointed position, just as he had done for others. The world does not become better when the selfless and caring are surpassed by cunning vipers. This is why it becomes crucial to delineate the boundaries of the community, or in the wider sense, the nation, or else a group will quickly find themselves in a gradual slide toward selfless universalism at its own expense.

"In this present state of things, a nation would act unwisely to endeavour to promote the welfare of the whole human race at the expense of its particular strength;, welfare and independence. It is a dictate of the law of self-preservation to make its particular advancement in power and strength the first principles of its policy, and the more it is advanced in freedom, civilization and industry, in comparison with other nations, the more has it to fear by the loss of its independence, the stronger are its inducements to make all possible efforts to increase its political power by increasing its productive powers, and vice versa."[17]

In reality, there is no neutral space between strength and subjugation: nations either secure their independence through productive powers aimed at their own growth, or they decline and find themselves under the control of another that chose the former route. This concept aligns closely with the existential logic of National Socialism, where national survival becomes the ethical and moral absolute. Dr. Joseph Goebbels discussed this prioritization of national sovereignty and the associated "ethnic self defense" that exists at the heart of National Socialism in *Der Nazi-Sozi*:

"Then we will prove that National Socialism is more than a comfortable moral theology of bourgeois wealth and capitalist profit. A new spirit of nationalism will grow from the ruins, displaying the most radical form of ethnic self defense, a new socialism that will create the necessary foundation."[18]

List argued that nations must either continually advance or face inevitable decline, with economic stagnation serving as a clear sign of a civilizational death spiral. He linked the positive continuation of the nation with continual active acquisition of productive capacity and raw industrial power. This ever-growing industrial development was not intended by List to entail a ballooning imperial system, but rather a stable national economy focused on internal development and the acquisition of resources that provide for national sovereignty and self-defense. In List's view, nations that stagnate open themselves up to foreign domination and internal decay.

"To this very true observation he might have added—and because anyone strives only to retain without acquiring he must come to grief, for every nation which makes no forward progress sinks lower and lower, and must ultimately fall."[19]

Hitler expressed a remarkably similar idea in Zweites Buch (Hitler's Second Book):

"The great domestic task of the future lies in the elimination of these general symptoms of the decay of our people. This is the mission of the National Socialist movement. A new nation must arise from this work which overcomes even the worst evils of the present, the cleavage between the classes, for which the bourgeoisie and Marxism are equally guilty."[20]

List recognized the continuation of the nation throughout generations, which, if unified in thought and action, can join forces to build projects so enormous that they surpass the capacities of a single generation. Such undertakings require sacrifice and long-term vision, directly contrasting with the liberal economic view that valorizes short-term individual gain. Instead, List emphasized the role of each generation as a custodian of national interest, foreshadowing the later völkisch glorification of ancestral labor, and of course elements of National Socialism as well.

"Individual cities, monasteries, and corporations have erected works the total cost of which perhaps surpassed the value of their whole property at the time. They could only obtain the means for this by successive generations devoting their savings to one and the same great purpose.

Let us consider the canal and dyke system of Holland; it comprises the labours and savings of many generations. Only to a series of generations is it possible to complete systems of national transport or a complete system of fortifications and defensive works."[21]

Dr. Groß articulated the same concept of national inheritance in a 1934 speech, framing temporary national existence within a larger historical continuity of the nation. It must be noted that List's conception of the national construct was primarily historical and economic, whereas National Socialism emphasizes a biological, and thus racial, context. Despite these differences, the continuity of national interests remains a prevailing theme in both List's economic philosophy, as well as under National Socialist racial theory, highlighting a conceptual connection.

"We know well enough that each person lives a double life. The first is the one he lives between birth and death. We are to do as much as we can to make this life rich, to accomplish that which is good and beautiful, to use our strengths and gifts for others. That is the duty of the individual. But as a person you are something more: You are a member of the chain of life, a drop in the great bloodstream of your people."[22]

List's correspondence in 1827 provides further insight into the formation of the nation as an independent entity through his direct critique of cosmopolitanism, accusing Adam Smith and his followers of dealing only with impractical abstractions. He saw the neglect of the concrete realities of national existence as resulting in an unnecessarily susceptible nation, where things such as global conflict could reduce the standing of the people if not properly bound and shielded by the nation. His phrase "the fracture of the human race into nations" demonstrates his philosophical divergence from liberal internationalism. Unlike Smith's vision of a world composed of freely trading individuals, List emphasized that economic activity is always embedded in national contexts, which possess unique attributes, desires, necessities, and developmental trajectories. This is what List called the Nationalökonomie, which recognized the economy as a national tool to cultivate international power, protect sovereignty, and provide for the moral cohesion of the nation's citizens. Over time, this emphasis on the independent development of nationhood grew in philosophical depth, combining with emerging racial science to take on a more systematic, and more exclusive framework under National Socialism.

"This, sir, is the theory of Adam Smith, and of his disciple, Dr. Cooper. Regarding only the two extremities of the science, they are right. But their theory provides neither for peace nor for war; neither for particular countries nor for particular people; they do not at all recognise the fracture of the human race into nations."[23]

To List, the national economy was more than a system designed for the abstract generation of profit, and instead was conceived as a strategic instrument to position the nation in such a way that allows for self-sufficiency, sovereignty, and the development of state power. Through the rejection of universal economic goals and ideals in favor of purely national ones, the nation can establish a "world in itself," allowing for both international trade and a degree of individual liberty, but only insofar as individual actions do not threaten the sovereignty, security, or productive capacity of the nation. Despite the overarching restraint on individual action, List did not advocate for arbitrary restrictions; rather, he insisted that restrictions should be imposed only "as the welfare of the people permits," directly linking economic policy with national well-being.

"National Economy teaches by what means a certain nation, in her particular situation, may direct and regulate the economy of individuals, and restrict the economy of mankind, either to prevent foreign restrictions and foreign power, or to increase the productive powers within herself—or in other words: How to create, in absence of a lawful state, within the whole globe of the earth, a world in itself, in order to grow in power and wealth to be one of the most powerful, wealthy and perfect nations of the earth, without restricting the economy of individuals and the economy of mankind more than the welfare of the people permits."[24]

Extremely similar rhetoric can be seen in the 1942 publication *Ich Kampfe*, where laissez-faire economics were disregarded in favor of a deliberative, moral, and future-oriented economic policy that integrates statecraft and national interest into a unified doctrine. If one does not recognize the differences between List's conception of the nation and the National Socialist understanding, it may be difficult to separate the two economic models, and rightfully so.

"We are convinced that the healing process of our nation can only be continued on the basis of the principle that public welfare has priority over individual welfare."[25]

In the quotation below, List differentiated the individual economy, political economy, and cosmopolitan economy, tying back to his critique of Smith's "invisible hand," which conflated what is beneficial to the individual with what is beneficial to the entirety of the nation. Just as a merchant may profit at the expense of the nation, so too can individual countries, or unions of such, benefit at the expense of others. In this way, List applies his critique of Smith's economic ideals at every level of organization, extending to the cosmopolitan model of global collaboration. Importantly, this perspective also accounts for temporal planning, where actions that are predicted to result in long-term national gain are considered despite the short-term burden that may be placed on individuals.

"Further: Conditions, events, & c. may be profitable in individual economy for some persons, and injurious to the community; or, on the contrary, they may be injurious to individuals, and prove highly beneficial to the community: Individual economy is not political economy.

So-measures, principles can be beneficial to mankind, if followed by all nations, and yet prove injurious to some particular countries, and vice versa. Political economy is not cosmopolitical economy. 1. Every nation has its particular economy."[26]

The particularist approach that List takes in his pursuit of economic development, grounded in national self-interest and adaptive planning, mirrors the particularistic Volksgeist as presented by Herder, as well as Fichte's moral particularism.

"It must be remembered that I intended here not to exhaust those matters, but only to allege as much of them as was necessary to prove, that every nation must follow its 'particular course in developing its productive powers."[27]

To List, the limitation of private exertion was not a denial of freedom, but a necessary measure to secure the general welfare and meet the collective needs of the nation. In asserting this, he did not shy away from the potentially burdensome consequences of his proposition for individuals who stray from the accepted course of conduct. This stands in stark contrast to liberalism's heavy focus on individual rights, instead rooting the legitimacy of policy in its impact on the nation's sovereignty, development, and collective survival.

"A nation provides for the social wants of the majority of its members, as far as the individuals cannot satisfy these wants by their private exertions; it provides not only for the present, but for future generations; not only for peace, but for War; its views arc extended not only over the whole space of land it possesses, but over the whole globe. An individual, in promoting his own interest, may injure the public interest; a nation in promoting the general welfare, may check the interest of a part of its members."[28]

Many of the economic concepts that Fichte presented, specifically in his 1800 publication *The Closed Commercial State*, were further elaborated in List's more comprehensive economic model, never abandoning the inward national focus which Fichte originally emphasized. The prioritization of national interest and the fulfillment of public need within the boundaries of the nation predates List's contributions to the economic foundations of National Socialism, but it does not diminish his role as a leading intellectual influence. Much of the criticism that List received was debated in terms of economic outcomes rather than the greater philosophical framework upon which his proposed economic concepts rested. Fichte anticipated this tension through his philosophical excavation of freedom and the voluntary application of limitation upon the self, as explored in depth within Fichte's respective chapter.

"The fulfilment of demand is the task of the national economy – not profitability, which is today almost solely decisive in the production of goods. With this fundamental attitude of National Socialism, we enter in definite opposition to the basic economic ideas of the capitalist state."[29]

In List's magnum opus, *The National System of Political Economy*, a brilliant metaphor is offered to depict national economic independence: likening a strictly agricultural nation to a one-armed individual relying on a foreign prosthetic. Through this analogy, he highlighted the functional incompleteness, dependency, and resulting vulnerability of a nation that lacks its own domestic manufacturing base. Additionally, List argued that commerce is not inherently productive, but rather serves as a conduit between already productive economic sectors. To maintain a stable supply of goods, List emphasized that a nation must be as domestically capable as possible to avoid damaging supply chain interruptions or losing national sovereignty to outside money powers. This internal development toward economic completeness forms the core of List's economic thesis, a principle that parallels Fichte's earlier insights.

"A nation which only carries on agriculture, is an individual who in his material production lacks one arm. Commerce is merely the medium of exchange between the agricultural and the manufacturing power, and between their separate branches. A nation which exchanges agricultural products for foreign manufactured goods is an individual with one arm, which is supported by a foreign arm. This support may be useful to it, but not so useful as if it possessed two arms itself, and this because its activity is dependent on the caprice of the foreigner. In possession of a manufacturing power of its own, it can produce as much provisions and raw materials as the home manufacturers can consume; but if dependent upon foreign manufacturers, it can merely produce as much surplus as foreign nations do not care to produce for themselves, and which they are obliged to buy from another country."[30]

This focus on developing domestic production became the cornerstone of the NSDAP's economic strategy under the Four Year Plan. Ultimately, National Socialism prioritizes the rejection of foreign influence in order to secure national sovereignty, whether in culture, religion, or economics, making the focus on self-sufficiency a logical continuation of the ideas articulated by Fichte, List, and other national economists.

"First, the securing of supplies of raw materials for industry. All measures serving this aim are included in the Four-Years-Plan the aim of which is to make Germany as independent as possible of imports by increasing domestic production.

Second, an increase in domestic agricultural production with the aim of making Germany, as far as possible, self-sufficient in the field of foodstuffs."[31]

List also challenged the conflation made by liberal economists, who asserted that "free trade" was a moral good on par with religious and civil liberties. He argued that because international economic activity could affect national sovereignty and collective survival, it cannot be allowed to freely operate without limitations guided by national interest. At the very heart of List's argument is the idea that protective policies do not restrict freedom, but instead create the conditions that allow for greater freedom through the avoidance of foreign servitude. Moreover, while List's conception of the nation was not strictly racially exclusive, it nonetheless contained existential and civilizational elements within his national particularism, which National Socialism later incorporated.

"Freedom of trade is spoken of in the same terms as religious freedom and municipal freedom. Hence the friends and advocates of freedom feel themselves especially bound to defend freedom in all its forms. And thus the term 'free trade' has become popular without drawing the necessary distinction between freedom of internal trade within the State and freedom of trade between separate nations, notwithstanding that these two in their nature and operation are as distinct as the heaven is from the earth... Indeed, it is even possible that the greatest freedom of international trade may result in national servitude, as we hope hereafter to show from the case of Poland."[32]

These existential concerns are echoed throughout National Socialist literature. *Ich Kampfe* described the National Socialist revolution in Germany as an "existential fight" to defend the native from the inorganic and foreign. National Socialist ideologues repeatedly emphasized the racial, cultural, and linguistic threats to the nation, advocating for unified sacrifice in order to preserve these elements.

"The revolution however, was not started here. It only came to an end in this way. It was the existential fight of a nation that with its traditional way of life and antiquated views, was close to collapse."[33]

List recognized that material wealth was subordinate to higher developmental goals aimed at long-term national improvement. This emphasis on sacrifice and the subordination of short-term profit to national objectives is echoed in later National Socialist philosophy. Like Fichte, List imbued a moral quality into the process of national development, heightening proper economic activity as a means to achieve moral regeneration and long-term national survival.

"The nation must sacrifice and give up a measure of material property in order to gain culture, skill, and powers of united production; it must sacrifice some present advantages in order to insure to itself future ones."[34]

Below, Friedrich List's strategic protectionist framework foreshadows later National Socialist economic planning, particularly the prioritization of critical industries through state-led industrial coordination. List argued that critical industries which are essential to national survival deserve state protection, since their collapse or foreign domination would lead to an erosion of national sovereignty. With the development and consolidation of industries representing the "first necessaries of life," comes the growth of subsidiary industries around them, which List believed did not require the same protection. This hierarchical model of protectionism anticipated and directly influenced the NSDAP's Four-Year Plan, where the laissez-faire liberalist model was discarded in favor of a centralized strategic vision, as suggested by List a century earlier.

"Only the most important branches require special protection, for the working of which much outlay of capital in building and management, much machinery, and therefore much technical knowledge, skill, and experience, and many workmen are required, and whose products belong to the category of the first necessaries of life, and consequently are of the greatest importance as regards their total value as well as regards national independence (as, for example, cotton, woollen and linen manufactories, &c.). If these main branches are suitably protected and developed, all other less important branches of manufacture will rise up around them under a less degree of protection."[35]

In an 1827 letter, List elaborates a concept that is mostly implicit throughout his work: the economy exists to serve the nation and provide for its continuity above all else. This surpasses mere economic reasoning, crossing over into the territory of moral and patriotic imperatives.

"It requires a mind of perfect independence to acknowledge that for so long a time we gave full credit to an erroneous system, particularly if that system is advocated by private interests."[36]

This principle aligns precisely with National Socialist economic policy, which explicitly reserves the right to redirect profit-seeking enterprises once they begin to stray from the best interests of the nation, as determined by the state. Both the economic model of List and the nearly overlapping National Socialist model permit profitable domestic enterprise outside of critical industries, provided that such enterprises do not harm the nation or compromise national continuity. While some critics consider this to be restrictive, it is arguably a moderate limitation, particularly when compared to laissez-faire capitalism, which risks subordinating national interest to private profit.

"This means that the State is not concerned with economic conditions as long as they do not conflict with the welfare of the nation. The principle of private initiative has been maintained. However, where it seem necessary to bring business into line with the welfare of the nation, the State will not hesitate to intervene and direct business into the desired channels."[37]

Unsurprisingly, List situated European morality and Christianity as central elements in the regeneration of inferior nations that are incapable of self-maintenance. He framed these elements as civilizational tools that offered a sort of governance to the savage, rather than a true conversion to a European way of life or European spirituality. This is clear evidence of List's Eurocentric civilizational hierarchy, in which Europe stands as the standard of conduct and civilization, reinforced by national particularism and rejection of foreign standards..

"In this utter chaos of countries and peoples there exists no single nationality which is either worthy or capable of maintenance and regeneration. Hence the entire dissolution of the Asiatic nationalities appears to be inevitable, and a regeneration of Asia only possible by means of an infusion of European vital power, by the general introduction of the Christian religion and of European moral laws and order, by European immigration, and the introduction of European systems of government."[38]

Friedrich List's philosophical and economic thought constitutes a critical intellectual precursor to the development of National Socialist philosophy, particularly regarding statecraft, economic nationalism, and national moral imperatives. Primarily, List emphasized the subordination of the individual and economic interests to the nation, pursuing sovereignty through self-sufficiency and a domestic economic focus. His ideas are nationally particularistic, given his national vision of a "world in itself," echoing the moral and cultural particularism found in the philosophies of Fichte and Herder. List's framework, in which protective policies and state intervention are both justifiable and necessary to ensure the continued survival of the nation, became the most central pillar of National Socialist economic theory. This National Socialist prioritization of public welfare over private interests can be seen in the Four-Year Plan and other initiatives, including industrial protection measures and coordinated economic planning efforts, which ensured the effective application of this concept.

In conclusion, List's economic philosophy combining strategic statecraft, national moral imperatives, and particularist economic planning, formed an intellectually coherent trajectory from early nineteenth-century German nationalism to the more philosophically developed National Socialism. The emphasis that List placed on self-sufficiency, national development, and moral economics situates him as a key contributor to the conceptual underpinnings of National Socialism. Rudolf Jung, the primary synthesizer of National Socialism, explicitly acknowledged this twice in his book *Der nationale Sozialismus*, originally published in 1922, leaving little doubt that List's ideas were directly drawn on throughout the creation of the National Socialist philosophy.

"We are accused of not having a doctrinal system such as that possessed by Marxism. But is that necessary? What our forebears forged and created, what Fichte, Friedrich List, and Adolf Wagner taught, was nothing other than National Socialism."[39]

Endnotes

1. David Levi-Faur, "Friedrich List and the Political Economy

of the Nation-State," *Review of International Political Economy* 4, no. 1 (1997): 154-178.

2. Onur Ulas Ince, "Friedrich List and the Imperial Origins of the National Economy," *New Political Economy* 21, no. 4 (2016): 380-400.

3. Friedrich List, *Outlines of American Political Economy, in a Series of Letters Addressed to Charles J. Ingersoll, Esq.* (Philadelphia: Samuel Parker, 1827), 9.

4. Adolf Hitler, "Reichstag Speech: Four Years of National Socialism," January 30, 1937, in *In His Own Words: The Essential Speeches of Adolf Hitler*, trans. and comp. C. J. Miller (Antelope Hill Publishing, 2022).

5. Friedrich List, *The National System of Political Economy*, trans. Sampson S. Lloyd (1841; repr., Indianapolis: Liberty Fund, 2010), 132.

6. David Levi-Faur, "Economic Nationalism: From Friedrich List to Robert Reich," *Review of International Studies* 23, no. 3 (1997): 359-370.

7. Joahim von Ribbentrop, *Germany Speaks: By 21 Leading Members of Party and State*, pref. by Joachim von Ribbentrop (London: T. Butterworth Ltd., 1938), 361.

8. David Levi-Faur, "Friedrich List and the Political Economy of the Nation-State," *Review of International Political Economy* 4, no. 1 (1997): 154-178.

9. David Levi-Faur, "Economic Nationalism: From Friedrich

List to Robert Reich," *Review of International Studies* 23, no. 3 (1997): 359-370.

10. Friedrich List, *The National System of Political Economy*, trans. Sampson S. Lloyd (1841; repr., Indianapolis: Liberty Fund, 2010), 132.

11. Friedrich List, *The National System of Political Economy*, trans. Sampson S. Lloyd (1841; repr., Indianapolis: Liberty Fund, 2010), 126.

12. Feder, Gottfried. *Der deutsche Staat auf nationaler und sozialer Grundlage*. (Munich: Verlag Franz Eher Nachfolger, 1923), 74.

13. Friedrich List, *The National System of Political Economy*, trans. Sampson S. Lloyd (1841; repr., Indianapolis: Liberty Fund, 2010), 125.

14. Friedrich List, *Outlines of American Political Economy, in a Series of Letters Addressed to Charles J. Ingersoll, Esq.* (Philadelphia: Samuel Parker, 1827), 29.

15. Adolf Hitler, speech in Munich, April 27, 1923.

16. Friedrich List, *Outlines of American Political Economy, in a Series of Letters Addressed to Charles J. Ingersoll, Esq.* (Philadelphia: Samuel Parker, 1827), 17.

17. Friedrich List, *Outlines of American Political Economy, in a Series of Letters Addressed to Charles J. Ingersoll, Esq.* (Philadelphia: Samuel Parker, 1827), 30.

18. Joseph Goebbels, *Der Nazi-Sozi* (Landpost Press, 1992), 9.

19. Friedrich List, *The National System of Political Economy*, trans. Sampson S. Lloyd (1841; repr., Indianapolis: Liberty Fund, 2010), 29.

20. Adolf Hitler, *Hitler's Second Book: German Foreign Policy: The Full Text of the Unpublished 1928 Book*, trans., intro., and annot. Arthur Kemp (London: Ostara Publications), 127.

21. Friedrich List, *The National System of Political Economy*, trans. Sampson S. Lloyd (1841; repr., Indianapolis: Liberty Fund, 2010), 209.

22. Walter Groß, *Nationalsozialistische Rassenpolitik: Eine Rede an die deutschen Frauen* (Dessau: C. Dünnhaupt, 1934).

23. Friedrich List, *Outlines of American Political Economy, in a Series of Letters Addressed to Charles J. Ingersoll, Esq.* (Philadelphia: Samuel Parker, 1827), 9.

24. Friedrich List, *Outlines of American Political Economy, in a Series of Letters Addressed to Charles J. Ingersoll, Esq.* (Philadelphia: Samuel Parker, 1827), 8.

25. Nationalsozialistische Deutsche Arbeiterpartei, *Ich Kämpfe (I Fight): The Responsibilities of Party Comrades*, trans. Rad Cowdery, 20.

26. Friedrich List, *Outlines of American Political Economy, in a Series of Letters Addressed to Charles J. Ingersoll, Esq.* (Philadelphia: Samuel Parker, 1827), 24.

27. Friedrich List, *Outlines of American Political Economy, in a Series of Letters Addressed to Charles J. Ingersoll, Esq.* (Philadelphia: Samuel Parker, 1827), 27.

28. Friedrich List, *Outlines of American Political Economy, in a Series of Letters Addressed to Charles J. Ingersoll, Esq.* (Philadelphia: Samuel Parker, 1827), 28.

29. Feder, Gottfried. *Der deutsche Staat auf nationaler und sozialer Grundlage.* (Munich: Verlag Franz Eher Nachfolger, 1923), 15.

30. Friedrich List, *The National System of Political Economy*, trans. Sampson S. Lloyd (1841; repr., Indianapolis: Liberty Fund, 2010), 123.

31. Wilhelm Bauer, *German Economic Policy* (Berlin: Terramare Office, 1939), 4.

32. Friedrich List, *The National System of Political Economy*, trans. Sampson S. Lloyd (1841; repr., Indianapolis: Liberty Fund, 2010), 31.

33. Nationalsozialistische Deutsche Arbeiterpartei, *Ich Kämpfe (I Fight): The Responsibilities of Party Comrades*, trans. Rad Cowdery, 40.

34. Friedrich List, *The National System of Political Economy*, trans. Sampson S. Lloyd (1841; repr., Indianapolis: Liberty Fund, 2010), 112.

35. Friedrich List, *The National System of Political Economy*, trans. Sampson S. Lloyd (1841; repr., Indianapolis: Liberty

Fund, 2010), 135.

36. Friedrich List, *Outlines of American Political Economy, in a Series of Letters Addressed to Charles J. Ingersoll, Esq.* (Philadelphia: Samuel Parker, 1827), 6.

37. Wilhelm Bauer, *German Economic Policy* (Berlin: Terramare Office, 1939), 3.

38. Friedrich List, *The National System of Political Economy*, trans. Sampson S. Lloyd (1841; repr., Indianapolis: Liberty Fund, 2010), 282.

39. Rudolf Jung, *National Socialism: Its Foundations, Development, and Goals*, 2nd fully revised ed. (Munich: Deutscher Volksverlag, Dr. E. Boepple, 1922), 54.

Chapter 5
Richard Wagner

Richard Wagner was born in Leipzig on May 22, 1813, into modest circumstances. His biological father was a police clerk who died when Richard was only a few months old, leaving his mother, a baker's daughter, to remarry an actor and playwright by the name of Ludwig Geyer. Wagner's stepfather introduced him to the arts at an early age, sparking a career that would make him one of the most influential figures in the development of nineteenth-century European culture, with his philosophy and political thought resonating well beyond opera houses and dim libraries.

Despite frequent moves and financial instability, Wagner excelled in both academics and musical studies, eventually studying the classics in Dresden and later Leipzig. There, he began composing small pieces of music while cultivating a fascination with German literature and mythology.

Wagner's early operas, such as *Die Feen* (1834) and *Das Liebesverbot* (1836), blended German Romanticism with operatic tradition, but achieved little success, leaving him with financial struggles and limited opportunities. Due to this, he moved from one European city to another, ultimately returning to Dresden to compose *Rienzi* (1842),

Der fliegende Holländer (1843), and *Tannhäuser* (1845), securing his place in Germany's opera scene.

Wagner's participation in the 1848 Dresden uprising and his association with revolutionary nationalists such as Mikhail Bakunin forced him into exile in Switzerland. This period of political radicalism marked the beginning of his lifelong effort to link art and cultural renewal with national destiny. During his time in Switzerland, Wagner wrote some of his most important theoretical works, including *Art and Revolution* (1849) and *The Artwork of the Future* (1849), which advanced his concept of the "Gesamtkunstwerk," a "total artwork" that unites music, poetry, and stage design into an organic whole.

Despite most of Wagner's writings dealing more directly with culture and aesthetics than with the political or philosophical, his more practically oriented work garnered significant attention. His infamous 1850 essay *Das Judenthum in der Musik (Jewishness in Music)* engaged directly with the politics of the day, in which he systematically articulated his critique of Jewish involvement within European culture. In other essays, such as *Religion and Art* (1880), Wagner focused on the role of art and other forms of cultural expression in the spiritual revival of modern society, suggesting that German myth and volkish traditions offered the cure to the internationally rooted illness. These writings positioned Wagner as a prophet of German cultural regeneration, synthesizing Romantic nationalism and mythic revivalism in such a way that would profoundly influence later völkisch movements and, subsequently, National Socialism. His cultural pessimism aligned him with racial theorists such as Arthur de Gobineau, who recognized the racial deterioration of the West to be forecasting its permanent decline.[1]

Wagner died in Venice on February 13, 1883, and was buried in Bayreuth, leaving behind a transformative legacy for both operatic tradition and the political ideologies of nineteenth-century Germany.

Wagner represents a crucial link within the genealogy of German thought, situated as the cultural and aesthetic counterpart to the earlier nationalist theorists such as Johann Gottfried Herder, Johann Gottlieb Fichte, Ernst Moritz Arndt, and Friedrich List. In addition to Fichte's conception of communal freedom, Arndt's demand for moral regeneration, and List's critique of liberal capitalism, Herder's Volksgeist and its associated emphasis on organic unity and national identity were all inherited by Wagner and subsequently embedded into an aesthetic framework that conjoined myth, art, and national morality. Despite these connections, only a limited portion of existing scholarship recognizes that the elements of contemporary National Socialism were already in existence during the nineteenth century.[2]

Wagner believed that this framework, consisting of art, religion, and the folk, offered a means of cultural renewal in the face of the morally oppressive state of modernity, resulting from industrialization, materialism, and cosmopolitanism. While many of his philosophical predecessors placed great emphasis on cultural particularism, Wagner undeniably tied his worldview to exclusionary racial discourse, which is particularly noticeable in his antisemitism. In this way, Wagner was a synthesizer of earlier traditions in his own right, one who managed to shift public debate away from philosophy and economics toward culture and art, thereby preparing the foundation for later appropriation by the völkisch movement and National Socialism. Despite the moderate amount of political and philosophical work that he left behind, he admittedly constrained himself for his and his wife's sake, as he recognized the dangers associated with open dissent in an era of severe ideological polarization.

"...therein I recognise the danger, in these times, of speaking out an independent thought, and such as does not fully bear the hallmark of one party or the other; and it did not need the entreaties of my wife, to win my promise never again to take a personal part in questions of the day."[3]

Nationalism was not a secondary matter within politics according to Wagner, but instead a decisive element in the moral and cultural destiny of a people. He asserted that the nation itself is the living embodiment of the folk, bound by shared culture and tradition. The proper arrangement and concentration of a people would thus provide a level of freedom, not in the form of liberal individualism, but in the greater freedom Wagner saw as originating from the ability to act organically as a unified body. The restoration of the folk-spirit was therefore prescribed in order to restore meaning to public life and form the foundation for the nation's truly recognizable expressions of art and culture.

In 1845, Wagner published *The Art-Work of the Future*, where he rooted the folk in primordial social units: the family, tribe, and nation. This organic vision of peoples emerging naturally from their kinship and commonalities echoes Herder's vision and appeared as a Romantic position, where the nation exists as more than a mere abstraction, amounting to a lived historical continuity.

"The Folk," was from the old inclusive term for all the units which made up the total of a commonality. In the beginning, it was the family and the tribe; next, the tribes united by like speech into a nation. Practically, by the Roman world-dominion which engulfed the nations, and theoretically, by the Christian religion which admitted of naught but men, i.e. no racial, but only Christian men the idea of " the People " has so far broadened out, or even evaporated, that we may either include in it mankind in general, or, upon the arbitrary political hypothesis, a certain, and generally the propertyless portion of the Commonwealth."[4]

Two historical ruptures were identified here by Wagner: first, the Roman Empire's absorption of nations in such a way that dissolved their individuality into the universality of the Empire, and second, Christianity's replacement of national identity with a purely spiritual conception of man. Both of these forces, he believed, were responsible for the separation of the people's natural spirit and its reformation into a way of life that lacked the ethnic, linguistic, and cultural grounding native to a people. The abstraction of a concrete folk to mankind in general or into a mere political category was also sharply detested within National Socialist literature, even making its way into the nineteenth point of the Program of the National Socialist German Workers' Party.

"19. We demand that Roman law, which served a materialistic world order, be replaced by German common law."[5]

Roman law, rooted in the past empire's legal traditions, had by the nineteenth century become the backbone of European civil law, including in Germany, thereby conflicting with German Common Law (Deutsches Gewohnheitsrecht). Much of German common law was unwritten, but closely tied to the German folk in a more organic way than the codified and universalized Roman system, which Wagner and later thinkers regarded as comparatively individualistic and materialistic. This point echoes not only the wording of Wagner, but also the intention behind it, referring less to technical law reform and more to a worldview itself and the rejection of alien systems in favor of a law that originates organically from the nation.

The connection between Wagner and National Socialist thought is illuminated by Rudolf Jung, the primary synthesizer of National Socialism, who referenced Richard Wagner directly as a major philosophical influence on the development of the new Weltanschauung. This influence can be clearly seen in his publications, where, besides directly naming Wanger, he draws heavily from the cultural and spiritual regeneration suggested by him. Below, Jung can be seen rejecting a church rooted in foreign tradition, instead seeking a representation of faith that is consistent with the spirit of the nation. This theme of national particularism in National Socialist philosophy cannot be overstated, as it plays a critical role in the grounding of the people and, as such, extends into every area of life, including religious practice and national morality.

Jung's position here on Christianity should not be confused as prohibitory, as he described a process of reform (the removal of the Old testament, reliance on the Vatican, and similar elements) to allow for the purification of Christianity into a form that could be naturally recognized by the nation, free of foreign influence and consistent with the nation's spirit.

"When we now speak of a German People's Church, we have in mind an amalgamation of the two churches spread out across German lands. This would have to involve a renunciation of Roman centralism, the internationalist spirit, and the Old Testament, those fundamentally Jewish entities, and would also have to be the work of German priests, priests who love their Volk and are imbued with its spirit. Those who believe that they cannot free themselves from the influence of Rome should bear in mind that the papacy was once rescued from filth and squalor in the early centuries of its history by the German kings."[6]

In Wagner's 1849 publication, *The Art-Work of the Future*, he assigned a moral charge to the people, with those who have properly joined the body of the masses acquiring legitimacy, authenticity, and righteousness. To Wagner, this volk-body was an exclusive entity, which became infiltrated by foreign entities in times of unrest, elements who looked toward the collective strength of the whole for protection without sharing in its spirit or destiny. This is an implicit critique of liberal tendencies to invoke intranational partisan division, effectively separating socio-economic classes and more in a way that Wagner saw as entirely unnecessary. The rhetorical question, "Who then is the People?" reflects the Romantic struggle for popular unity in contrast to the political fragmentation of the modern state, capturing Wagner's search for a moral and aesthetic unity that went beyond social class.

Herder and Fichte also identified the nation as an organic totality that could not be reduced to political representation because of the underlying unity that persists. For Herder, this concept was tied to the Volksgeist; for Fichte, it was a moral obligation to bind oneself to and and to assist in the preservation of the nation. Wagner synthesized both the Volksgeist and Fichte's inherent morality, along with Romantic myth, into a philosophical foundation that would later be drawn upon in subsequent nationalist movements, including under National Socialism.

"But beyond a frivolous, this term has also acquired an ineradicable moral meaning; and on account of this it is, that in times of stir and trouble all men are eager to number themselves among the People; each one gives out that he is careful for the People's weal, and no one will permit himself to be excluded from it. Therefore in these latter days also has the question frequently been broached, in the most diverse of senses: Who then is the People? In the sum total of the body politic, can a separate party, a particular fraction of the said body claim this name for itself alone? Rather, are we not all alike " the People, " from the beggar to the prince?"[7]

In a speech at the Hofbräuhaus-Festsaal in Munich 1920, Adolf Hitler, a man who deeply admired Wagner, echoed these sentiments, disregarding the importance of party politics in favor of a unified national objective. The rejection of political factions and socio-economic rifts was frequently touched on in similar terms throughout National Socialist literature, with the wellbeing of the nation taking precedence above all else.

"For us, being nationalists does not mean belonging to one party or another, but rather examining every action to see whether it benefits the whole people, and love for the whole people without exception."[8]

Additionally, Wagner defined the Folk as a collective bound by shared necessity, creating both an ethical and existential commitment toward the wellbeing of the whole. In this way, he rejected liberal individualism and instead continued developing the idea of organic unity, foreshadowing the völkisch movement and later National Socialism, where an individual's identity was filtered through their relation to the nation.

"The " Folk " is the epitome of all those men who feel a common and collective Want. To it belong, then, all of those who recognise their individual want as a collective want, or find it based thereon; ergo, all those who can hope for the stilling of their want in nothing but the stilling of a common want, and therefore spend their whole life's strength upon the stilling of their thus acknowledged common want."[9]

Otto Dietrich reflected Wagner's earlier synthesis in his theories on community and worldview, where he directly identified the individual's life as actualizing in full only through the proper interaction with the community.

"Man by definition therefore lives in community with others; his life actualizes itself only in the community. Community is a concept to which the whole history of humanity is subordinate; it is the form in which human life runs its course from cradle to grave, without which it would be unthinkable."[10]

National Socialism and Wagner both reject atomism, where the individual is seen as something unique or original in isolation, because such a view erodes the depth of the collective, dissolving it into mere imitation and interpersonal competition. To Wagner, individual self-dependence represented a parasitic element within the community; wherein every person lives at the expense of others under the guise of freedom. In this way, freedom and originality cannot be seen as authentic when they are divorced from the collective wellbeing, and instead represent selfish pretenses for possibly harmful action. Below, Wagner can also be seen attributing this atomized and selfish nature to the liberal ethos, where it comes to represent a reversal of Christian values. This inversion of values undermines the spirit of giving, replacing it with a self-centered mindset focused on personal gain, which Wagner condemns as corrosive in no uncertain terms. Fichte's vision of freedom as requiring self-limitation for the betterment of the nation are clearly echoed here by Wagner in 1849.

"This is the isolation of the single, in which each severed nullity shall rank as somewhat, but the great commonalty as naught; in which each unit struts as something special and "original," while the whole, forsooth, can then be nothing in particular and for ever a mere imitation. This is the self–dependence of the individual, where every unit lives upon the charges of his fellows, in order to be "free by help of God;" pretends to be what others are; and, briefly, follows the inversion of the teaching of Jesus Christ: "To take is more blessed than to give."[11]

Wagner thus articulated the community as being the source of a higher form of freedom that can only be achieved through the mutual recognition of others' wellbeing and the cultivation of affection toward the collective. Again, Fichte and the influence from his self-positing Ich can be clearly observed in Wagner's formulation of freedom and national duty, where reciprocal acknowledgment to the whole is crucial for the development of harmony. Wagner extends Fichte's philosophy further, grounding individual obligation not only in duty, but also in love, thereby further developing the Folk in accordance with a Romantic character. This forms the two sides of Wagner's conception of the Folk: one consisting of a material bond of necessity, which binds through shared struggle, and the other being love that binds through voluntary recognition and mutual affirmation.

"Their confines, therefore, are removed by this agreement; but only those that love each other can agree, and 'to love' means: to acknowledge the other, and at like time to know one's self. Thus Knowledge through Love is Freedom; and the freedom of man's faculties is All–faculty."[12]

A very important addition is offered after this formulation, where Wagner narrows the Folk to a select segment of the entire population. This true Folk exists as a higher community that remains present but unseen, surviving within the surrounding chaos and outlasting the exploitative elite. Membership in the folk thus requires both knowledge and participation, as one cannot simply label themselves a member of the folk without truly embodying its spirit. This notion reflects Herder's Volksgeist in that the spirit of the group can only be truly felt and connected to by those who are naturally attuned to it.

"However, neither you nor this rabble do we understand by the term, the Folk: only when neither Ye nor It shall exist any longer, can we conceive the presence of the Folk. Yet even now the Folk is living, wherever ye and the rabble are not; or rather, it is living in your twin midst, but ye wist not of it. Did ye know it, then were ye yourselves the

Folk; for no man can know the fulness of the Folk, without possessing a share therein."[13]

In terms of later continuity, Wagner's exclusive Volk anticipated the National Socialist conception of the Volksgemeinschaft, where not all of the people who live within the borders of the country were necessarily a part of the volk. In the context of National Socialism in particular, the Volksgemeinschaft represents the ideal of the organic racial community, where all internal divisions are overcome through collective sacrifice in favor of a unified nation. Additionally, in alignment with Herder's particularistic Volksgeist, Wagner's statement that "no man can know the fulness of the Folk without possessing a share therein" foreshadows the National Socialist position that the spirit of the nation can only be joined by those possessing the requisite racial characteristics, who then must join to the greater national objective, leaving citizenship to depart from the abstract toward the embodiment of belonging itself. This is precisely why the NSDAP restricted citizenship beyond the frequently recognized racial requirement, additionally conditioning it upon personal sacrifice and devotion through national service.

"There is work and food. People are happy again and have found new faith. And all are working in the same direction. The people make up a great community, tied together a million-fold by common blood, and faces its future with heads held high."[14]

In *The Art-Work of the Future*, Wagner distinguishes between two stages of human development: the general national and the unnational universal. The generic national stage is a natural and organic community, rooted in ancestry, language, and homeland. This innate connection to the collective unconsciously develops into a unified natural order, whereas the contrasting stage of unnatural universalism only offers a future devoid of national particularism, in favor of the abstraction of universal humanity. In close alignment with Romantic organicism and Herder's concept of the Volksgeist, Wagner placed great stress on shared ancestry and land, holding authentic national identity to be an inevitable product of these conditions.

"Two cardinal moments of his development lie clear before us in the history of Man: the generic national, and the unnational universal. If we still look forward to the Future for the completion of the second evolutionary step, yet in the Past we have the rounded–off conclusion of the first set clear as day before our eyes. To what a pitch man once so far as, governed by generic ancestry, by community of mother-–tongue, by similarity of climate, and the natural surroundings of a common fatherland, he yielded himself unconsciously to the influence of Nature to what a pitch man once was able to unfold himself beneath these directly moulding influences, we have certainly full reason to acknowledge with most heartfelt thanks."[15]

In the publication *Ich Kampfe*, the same rejection of the universal in favor of the naturally constructed national is seen clearly echoing Wagner's earlier formulation:

"It is not a universal world dominion of any religious, economical or political kind, but we see a structured universe; national systems marked off by races and an organic-dynamic structure in Europe based on biological resources and the political effectiveness of nations bound together in a biosphere determined by destiny."[16]

According to Wagner, this nation, complete with its own identity and spirit, does not rely on artificially constructed binary oppositions, such as aristocratic vs. democrat or Catholic vs. Protestant, but instead derives solely from its own internal nature. It then follows that the nation's political and cultural trajectory must align with the organic essence of the nation, not political factions or foreign influence. This rejection of partisan politics reflects a Romantic desire for the unification of the whole without the burden of artificial division. This disdain for national polarity would later be mirrored with the concept of the "Third Way" under National Socialism, where a nationally beneficial middle ground between liberal capitalism and socialist radicalism is established in such a way that the volk themselves become the decisive political subject, rather than a party of creed. Additionally, Fichte's focus on a nationally specific ethical mission is echoed by Wagner in this conception, as legitimacy is rooted in the spiritual essence of the German people themselves.

"We have also found it possible to discuss a relation so important, involving every section of society and undeniably developed by our history itself, without in any way employing the showy catchwords of a party, or the ideas that lie beneath them: we have appealed to neither aristocratic nor democratic, to neither liberal nor conservative, neither monarchical nor republican, to neither catholic nor protestant interests; but in each demand of ours we have relied on nothing but the character of the German Spirit, which we have already had occasion to define."[17]

A significant portion of Wagner's political and social commentary can be extracted from his cultural critiques. Throughout his work, a pattern emerges where the core cultural element is that which organically springs from within a people. He contrasted this blossoming "of a natural culture" with that which is imposed "from above" and cultivated by the elites or their sterile institutions. Furthermore, repeating the Romantic ideal of authenticity, foreign cultural elements disrupt the harmony of the culture that is recognizable to the Volk, leading to misunderstanding and disingenuous cultural growth.

"The only thing which, in the position thus assigned to her, our Modern Art should be able to effect and among honest folk, indeed, endeavours namely, the spreading abroad of culture, she cannot do;

and simply for the reason that, for Art to operate on Life, she must be herself the blossom of a natural culture, i.e., such an one as has grown up from below, for she can never hope to rain down culture from above. Therefore, taken at its best, our "cultured" art resembles an orator who should seek to address himself in a foreign tongue to a people which does not understand it: his highest flights of rhetoric can only lead to the most absurd misunderstandings and confusion."[18]

Völkisch and National Socialist ideology would later echo this assertion, as had many prior Romantic and nationalist thinkers before, arguing that artificial cosmopolitanism should be discarded in favor of a natural and understandable way of life and culture for the German people. The National Socialist position on cosmopolitanism and cultural particularism has already been well established thus far, but remains a critical element for understanding the inner logic of the worldview. Simply put, National Socialism rests on the principle of biological determinism that gives birth to the cultural particularism forming its ethical and philosophical base. Adherence to the natural arrangement of society and culture was presented as the fulfilment of the inborn spirit, thus reducing the circumstance to either the blossoming of native spirit, or its decay and eradication. National Socialism identifies this dynamic directly and seeks to offer true freedom through the personal and societal adherence to proper, organic growth.

Wagner shaped his theory of organic culture in explicitly exclusionary terms:

"During the whole period that music, as a separate art possessed a really organised necessity for existence, right down to the time of Mozart and Beethoven, we find no trace of any Jewish composer; for it was impossible that an element so foreign to that life should form part of its living organism."[19]

This quotation above, taken from Wagner's 1850 essay *Judaism in Music*, presents national culture as a living organism in which foreign elements, such as Judaism, could not integrate. There is little question regarding Wagner's racially exclusive stance, as he explicitly framed Germanness as the sole locus of authentic art for the German people from a racialized perspective, excluding even those who had been born and raised within German borders. Much of Wagner's critique of Jews originated in what he perceived as their cultural and spiritual incompatibility with Germans, along with the practical concerns, as is the case with their domination of finance for example. Wagner goes as far as to assert that the Jew possesses more freedom than the German, controlling the average citizen through money and market power.

"In the present state of things the Jew is more than free, for he dominates; and, as long as money continues the power before which all our doings and strivings are as naught, he will continue to do so."[20]

While neither Wagner nor later National Socialist literature was free of the type of antisemitism that deals with intangible qualities, such as the spirit or destiny, the vast majority of rhetoric from both focused on the tangible and negative impacts of Jewish involvement at the time. In 1920, Adolf Hitler openly claimed that the NSDAP did not hate the existence of the Jews themselves, but rather their involvement in Germany and its affairs. Delivered in a sarcastic manner, in which Hitler offered the rest of the world the Jews who were residing in Germany, he directly laid out the priorities of the nation. The primary priority of Germany was the German people, and all was expected to be done to benefit them.

"Here, too, we know perfectly well that systematic knowledge can only be the groundwork, but that behind this knowledge must come the organization which will one day put it into action, and in this action, the removal of the Jews from our people, we will remain adamant. Not because we begrudge them their existence—we congratulate the whole rest of the world on their visit—but because the existence of our own people is a thousand times more important to us than that of a foreign race."[21]

As previously mentioned, Wagner did attribute some of his antisemitic vision to what he described as intangible elements, such as visual self-evidence and aesthetic repulsion, amounting to a physiological reaction and subsequent rejection. This incongruity served as evidence to Wagner that the Jew is an alien element that is not capable of harmonization within the host society. To him, this rejection surpassed social construction, into the realm of spiritual ontology, surfacing later in a very similar way within the völkisch movement and under National Socialism.

"The Jew who, as we all know, claims to have a God all to himself, arrests our attention in ordinary life firstly by his exterior appearance. It matters not to which particular European nationality he may belong, the Jew's appearance strikes us as something so unpleasantly incongruous that, involuntarily, we wish to have nothing in common with him."[22]

To Wagner, even the complete mastery of German, or another European language, would not assist the Jew in overcoming his Jewish identity, meaning that he would remain permanently alien to a European nation. These linguistic markers were treated as signs of an immutable racial essence, shifting popular antisemitism from religion and behavior toward nature itself, thereby introducing a permanence to one's racial identity.

"The Jew converses in the tongue of the people amongst whom he dwells from age to age, but he does this invariably after the manner of a foreigner."[23]

In addition to the tangible Jewish involvement in finance and their immutably alien spirit, Wagner also recognized a moral and emotional incapacity to assimilate. Jews, Wagner asserted, are unable to share genuine feeling or altruistic passion, only understanding performance, measured through metrics of self-interest. In this way, the Jew became a moral alien as well which is constitutionally incapable of sincerity, empathy, or self-sacrifice, which are the same virtues that Wagner idealized in the homogenous German Volk. This perspective instilled a philosophy of moral and racial essentialism that would influence many National Socialist ideologues, including Rudolf Jung himself.

"Never does the Jew become aroused in merely sentimental expression with us. If ever he becomes excited at all it is on behalf of some special and selfish interest."[24]

In *The Little ABC of National Socialism*, Dr. Joseph Goebbels answered the question "Why is the NSDAP anti-Jewish?" The very first point mentioned concerns the alien morality of the Jew, followed by what Dr. Goebbels asserted to be an inherently destructive nature that negatively impacted the German population, and then finally the financial and speculative markets where the Jew thrive at the nation's expense. These elements all align with Wagner's earlier antisemetic philosophy, where the tangible and intangible were woven together to create a more comprehensive and moralized ideological stance than the strictly practical or the purely intangible.

It is evident that National Socialist philosophy, and its antisemitic components which are not inherent to its existence, are not based on blind hatred, but rather a response to the inversion of German tradition by an outside element. National Socialist philosophy is perfectly capable of retaining its coherency in the absence of Jews, and in fact seeks to do so, thus making antisemitism obsolete within a homogenous nation that is not being impacted from internal or external Jewry. In this way, antisemitism falls under the broader category of National Socialism's rejection of the foreign, likely only becoming such a popularly noted aspect of the philosophy due to the commonly held perception of historical events and the circumstances that fueled them.

"Because the Jew is a corrosive foreign body in the German people; because he poisoned German folk-morality through his mendacious "cultural institutes"; because he tears down instead of building up; because he is the father of the concept of class warfare through which he tears the German people into two parts in order to be able to control them all the more brutally; because he is the creator and bearer of international stock-market-capitalism, the main enemy of German liberty."[25]

While the objective of this book is to exhaustively track the primary philosophical progression of National Socialism, at times more depth of concept is needed to pick up on the vocabulary and logic trends of the earlier thinkers so as to contrast them with what appears in National Socialist literature. Many of these ideas exist outside the realm of eternal racial nature, such as with the financial industries which both Wagner and the NSDAP saw as dominated by Jewish influence. Wagner's emphasis on the unproductive capital that he believed the Jew to be benefiting from was directly echoed in the very heart of National Socialist economics, with the speculative and unproductive being rooted out in favor of strictly productive labor where one adds to the process of development in some tangible way.

"The turn taken by our social development has resulted in money becoming more and more frankly exalted to the level of nobility. In consequence of this the Jew, whose money has not been acquired by personal labour but merely by his one and only trade of usury, is no longer excluded from the enjoyment of title."[26]

In *Art and Revolution*, Wagner further rejected industrial capitalism and the alienated wage labor that originates when production is organized for exchange value. This arrangement reduces the individual to mechanical toil, which Wagner saw as economic slavery, forming a proto-social vision where the economy exists to serve the Volk rather than profit.

"But if he bargains away the product of his toil, all that remains to him is its mere money–worth; and thus his energy can never rise above the character of The busy strokes of a machine; in his eyes it is but weariness, and bitter, sorrowful toil. The latter is the lot of the Slave of Industry; and our modern factories afford us the sad picture of the deepest degradation of man, constant labour, killing both body and soul, without joy or love, often almost without aim."[27]

The National Socialist rejection of for-profit ventures that place priority over the wellbeing of the nation is well supported thus far and hardly needs any additional evidence, as it forms an overwhelming consensus. In *The Art-Work of the Future*, Wagner again approaches a proto-socialist moral economy where he critiques the capitalist system that results in the worker being drained of their energy to further enrich the interests and comfort of the elite. He recognized a lack of reciprocity between the classes, fitting neatly within the broader Romantic anti-capitalist movement, anticipating much of the later völkisch and National Socialist rhetoric that saw this imbalance as corrosive to the nation.

"Thus the luxury of the rich is built upon the penury of the poor; and it is the very want of the poorer classes that hurls unceasingly fresh fodder to the luxury of the rich; while the poor man, from very need of food for his life-forces, thus offers up his own life-strength unto the rich."[28]

Wagner's work frequently contains declarations of Romantic naturalism, where he asserts mankind's unity with its "inner natural necessity," also known as its inherent nature, to be the purest expression of authentic being. This contrasts with foreign institutions which offer artificial and inorganic constructs that alienate man from his proper life-forces. Much of this position is conveyed through his commentary on art, with the comparatively occasional societal commentary included, the emphasis remaining on grounding within the organic instead of the mechanical or bureaucratic.

"Man will never be that which he can and should be, until his Life is a true mirror of Nature, a conscious following of the only real Necessity, the inner natural necessity, and is no longer held in subjugation to an outer artificial counterfeit, which is thus not necessary, but an arbitrary power. Then first will Man become a living man; whereas till now he carries on a mere existence, dictated by the maxims of this or that Religion, Nationality, or State."[29]

As discussed in prior chapters, National Socialist philosophy also places a heavy emphasis on harmonizing with the natural order against artificial constructs, inheriting Wagner's dichotomy between nature as a positive expression or organic community and artifice, resulting from cosmopolitanism and other foreign worldviews.

"The more such a view coincides with the natural laws of organic life, the more useful its conscious application will be for the life of a people."[30]

In Wagner's Romantic philosophy, nature surpasses the purely physical realm into that of the moral and aesthetic, providing the prescription for humanity not to seek transcendence from nature, but to mirror it in daily life and art. In a manner that echoes Aristotelian essentialism, Wagner asserted that individual fulfilment ultimately lies in the realization of one's own potential according to one's natural design. This concept prefigured the völkisch, as well as the National Socialist ideal of the people's organic totality, where the nation's unique essence is fulfilled through individual service to the natural community.

"Like to this blissful harmony of Nature, will she endure and ever show her fruitfulness, as the purest and most perfect satisfaction of the truest, noblest need of perfected mankind; i.e. of men who are all that which of their essence they can be, and therefore should and shall be."[31]

In addition to the plethora of primary National Socialist examples that point toward the search for an underlying natural order, the eternal aspect of said nature is also frequently referenced. Wagner offered a mystical logic containing these two elements, the natural and the eternal order, directly anticipating the aforementioned moral and metaphysical framework of National Socialism. Under National Socialist philosophy, the characteristics of the nation are carried by the volk and expressed in a largely predetermined manner tied directly to the nation's racial constitution. While this single statement cannot fully outline the entirety of National Socialist philosophy, as no single sentence could, it does convey a direct congruence with Wagner's worldview, particularly the synthesis of nature, destiny, and morality.

"National Socialism recognizes the divine origin and meaning of life. Its worldview strives for the complete overcoming of materialism in the German people and a renewal that leads to a return to the eternal in man and the divine powers as revealed in the values of race and people."[32]

This rejection of materialism was also expressed by Wagner as a national priority, warning that cultural decay would follow the degradation of national spirit. Wagner's philosophy sought to defend against the hollowing of the German ethos through the Romantic critique of pure utilitarianism; when life is lived for profit, culture dissociates from its natural roots and degenerates into a soulless form.

"Nevertheless we cannot put aside the fear that, if this immediate existence continues turning more and more away from an evolution of the duties of the spirit, those heaped-up treasures may some-day sink to valueless and useless chattels."[33]

Gottfried Feder spent a considerable amount of time dealing with what he referred to as Mammon, discussing the unethical individual drive for material excess in the face of national scarcity, thereby imposing ethical obligations upon economic involvement. In *Why We Fight*, it was directly asserted that a nation infected with materialism inherently faces an existential threat. While there are certainly pragmatic reasons for such an ethically bound economy, the suppression of its self-inflation also had spiritual implications for National Socialism, similar to what was described by Wagner, echoing his vocabulary and stance on the matter.

"A people that cannot master materialism carries the germ of death in itself!"[34]

Wagner further places the continuation of the volk through the implementation of self-defense to be an integral component to proper statecraft. All healthy people seek to continue their lives, and because humans must cooperate with one another to satisfy their biological imperatives, the community must too take on a collectively defensive role for its own survival as a non-individual organism. Of course, this concept of collective self defense for the continuation of the nation, even if it must come at the expense of other nations, sits at the heart of National Socialist philosophy. All matters are examined through the lens of racial continuation and protection, but the concept itself likely came from multiple earlier sources, with Wagner certainly being one, but not the sole contributor. This arrangement of priority appears

THE GENEALOGY OF NATIONAL SOCIALISM   225

as the most moral and ethical state expression despite what it may mean for others, and this becomes clear when the alternative is directly identified for what it is: the eradication of a nation for foreign interest.

"Self-preservation is still the real prime motor here, since the quiet, and thus the power, of one's own State appears securable in no other way than through the powerlessness of other States..."[35]

In *Art and Politics*, Wagner critiques the short-sightedness that is commonplace within political will, along with the tendency for leaders and the wider public to engage only with immediate necessity rather than with what would be more beneficial in the long term. This is proposed to be a symptom of an all-too-common human flaw: an instinctive and reactionary will that fails to grasp the enduring and collective. As a result, the people are guided through history by circumstance, which Wagner seeks to minimize in favor of foresight and deliberate will, allowing for more than temporary success and the establishment of true political order.

"So we recognise that nothing really happens but what has issued from this not far-seeing Will, from this Will that answers merely to the momentarily-experienced need; and thus we see that practical success, throughout all time, has attended only those politicians who took account of nothing but the momentary need, neglecting all remoter, general needs, all needs as yet unfelt to-day, and which therefore appeal so little to the mass of mankind that it is impossible to count on its assistance in their ministration."[36]

The rejection of moral relativism and short-termism is heavily present in National Socialist philosophy and can be seen within state economic planning as well as nearly all other spheres, as the continuation of the nation is directly bound to its long-term development. Grounded in the eternal laws of life, National Socialism positions itself to correct the decaying pragmatism that Wagner had previously described.

"National Socialism is thus a folkish worldview. Everything, every comrade of the people, every family, and clan, every public institution - party, Wehrmacht, state, administration, economy, art, and science, must serve the prosperity of the people and their eternal struggle." [37]

Wagner saw a king as embodying the organic totality of the nation, acting as the synthesis of the culture, will, and destiny of the Volk. Wagner asserted that this monarchical ideal provides stability through the natural embodiment of leadership grounded in the nation's spirit and character, in a way that constitutions and laws fail. These ideas align with Romantic organicism, where the state is understood to be a living organism, with the king acting as the body's conscious head. In addition to Romantic organicism, Wagner aligns with the Fichtean and Hegelian moral conceptions of the state and their rejection of liberal-democratic values. To Wagner, parliamentary governmental systems only fragmented the will of the Volk, whereas the monarch, if properly attuned to the people, possessed the ability to fully unify the moral and cultural life of the nation. This concept was not unique to Wagner, but it nonetheless anticipates the Führerprinzip, or leader principle, that would later emerge on the NSDAP. Wagner increasingly envisions a redemptive figure who would restore unity and vitality to the German people, amounting to a heroic archetype, which has been argued by some to have unintentionally primed thought for Adolf Hitler's rise to power.[38]

The Führerprinzip is often presented as a unique aspect of National Socialism, or as a new innovation that Hitler himself philosophically contributed to National Socialism, but clearly neither of these claims withstand scrutiny. Wagner's Romantic monarchism provides a metaphysical and aesthetic precedent for later leadership who derived power from the organic necessity of the Volk itself.

"It therefore is established as the most essential principle of the State; and as in it resides the warrant of stability, so in the person of the King the State attains its true ideal."[39]

Such a central ruler, if working in tandem with the organic order, also possesses a greater ability to remain flexible in state administration, and as the entire purpose of law is to defend the enduring essence of the people, this can be best carried out through the adaptation to shifting circumstances. For Wagner, a nation's laws should not remain perfectly static, but rather function as a living framework that adjusts to the needs of the moment without undermining its foundational structure.

"General laws in provision of this possibility, whilst they allow of minor alterations, thus aim alike at maintenance of stability;and that law which, reckoned for the possibility of constant remedy of pressing needs, contains withal the strongest warrant of stability, must therefore be the most perfect law of State."[40]

The concept of eternal laws is also persistent throughout National Socialist literature and forms the internal core of the worldview that anchors the nation to its organic existence in precisely the way described by Wagner above. National Socialism recognizes both the natural laws that all biological life forms face and the racially particularistic laws that each race must face individually, most commonly referencing the eternal racial laws of the nation.

"We are piously convinced that in accordance with the eternal laws of this earth we must stand by every deed, every word and every thought."[41]

Like Fichte and many others, Wagner held that freedom did not exist for an autonomous individual as liberal ideals assert, but rather as a product of communal unity. For Wagner, true freedom is not self-dependent, as nothing in nature truly is, and instead draws meaning from its relationship to that which is outside of the self, redefining freedom as interdependent. This aligns closely with Fichte's conception of freedom, wherein the individual is morally compelled toward duty to the whole. This same conception and framework of freedom was adopted by the Völkisch movement and later again under National Socialism, as discussed in Fichte's respective chapter.

"It is a sorry misconception of Freedom that of the being who would fain be free in loneliness. The impulse to loose one's self from commonalty, to be free and independent for individual self alone, can only lead to the direct antithesis of the state so arbitrarily striven after: namely to utmost lack of self–dependence. Nothing in Nature is self–dependent excepting that which has the conditionments of its self–standing not merely in itself; but also outside of itself: for the inner are first possible by virtue of the outer."[42]

The question regarding religion and National Socialism is frequently discussed, with a wide array of assertions being made leading to nearly every possible conclusion one could imagine. Understanding the religious perspectives of National Socialism's philosophical predecessors may not directly confirm the position of National Socialism, as no single philosopher who predated the synthesis of National Socialism fully aligned with the entirety of the worldview, but it will certainly assist in clarifying its intellectual foundations. Wagner believed that religion is an organic creation originating in the collective soul of a people, amounting to an inseparable element, along with art, of the Volksgeist.

"The Art–work is the living presentation of Religion; but religions spring not from the artist's brain; their only origin is from the Folk."[43]

Wagner was not shy in condemning institutional Christianity, which he believed was grounded in a renunciation and contempt for life, in favor of an unattainable ideal that opposed true existence. This is a distinctly Romantic position against the otherworldliness common to Christianity, where life, nature, and the Volk's creative life serve as the truest source of meaning for a person and nation. He saw the modern Christian world as exemplifying hypocrisy through the continued exploitation of the masses, greed, and egoism, anticipating some of the later lines of völkisch critiques. In this way, Christianity stopped functioning as a living religion of the folk and instead degraded into a universalist system that undermines the natural connection between man and his natural life. This functions as one of the many intellectual bridges to the later reinterpretation of religion that heralded a natural and racially grounded faith.

"If history knows an actual Utopia, a truly unattainable ideal, it is that of Christendom; for it has clearly and plainly shown, and shows it still from day to day, that its dogmas are not realisable."[44]

Despite his critique of Christianity, Wagner believed that religion transcends the moral and spiritual limitations of the state, allowing for a greater depth of human existence than what political structures could otherwise provide. Wagner's moral hierarchy places the state in the position to address temporal matters, while religion attends to the eternal and internal matters of man. He did not outright reject the state, but rather subordinated it to the more deeply rooted moral order that lives within the soul of the volk. In this way, authentic religion grounds the actions of righteous rulers in spiritual truth, beyond simply law or power, anticipating the völkisch ideal in which the leader becomes both the head of the nation and the moral embodiment of its collective soul. The later development of this principle, culminating in the Führerprinzip, demonstrates not a new concept, but instead the political formalization of what Wagner had articulated around seventy-five years prior.

"To him more deeply and more inwardly than is possible to the State-citizen, as such, is it therefore given to feel that in Man there dwells an infinitely deeper, more capacious need than the State and its ideal can ever satisfy. Wherefore as it was Patriotism that raised the burgher to the highest height by him attainable, it is Religion alone that can bear the King to the stricter dignity of manhood (zur eigentlichen Menschenwürde)."[45]

Wagner directly acknowledged what he saw to be the universal scope of Christianity in *Art and Politics*, which was devoid of a specific ethnic character. A distinctly ethnocultural perspective on religion is subsequently introduced, in which the faith of a people must align with the inborn feeling of the volksgeist, overlapping with the inherent character of the nation. This is a crucial point for understanding Wagner's religious philosophy, as he moves beyond a mere critique of organized religious authority or church dogma into the realm of religious nationalism infused with racial logic.

"The Christian religion belongs to no specific national stock: the Christian dogma addresses purely-human nature. Only in so far as it has seized in all its purity this content common to all men, can a people call itself Christian in truth. However, a people can make nothing fully its own but what becomes possible for it to grasp with its inborn feeling, and to grasp in such a fashion that in the New it finds its own familiar self again."[46]

The argument on behalf of a religion attuned to the frequency of the nation was directly carried over into both völkisch and National Socialist interpretations of faith, which sought to align religious practice to the organic spirit and nature of the German people. Wagner provided a bridge from Romantic particularism to the concept of Positive Christianity, which aimed to remove all elements of Christianity that were not organically aligned with the eternal racial Volksgeist.

"We demand a freedom of religious confessions in this state, as long as they do not endanger the nation's existence or interfere with the moral sense of the German race. The NSDAP party argues for a positive Christianity, although it is not bound to any single confession."[47]

Below, Wagner expresses his belief that true religion is only ever able to emerge following the complete maturity of the state, which must first become self-sufficient with no need for the support of religious institutions. Under this evolved condition, religion is no longer required to sustain societal order, and thus is unshackled from its political function, allowing for the expression of said religion to become purely spiritual, stripped of its weighty institutional demands.

In this way, Wagner's religious conception of "true religion" only comes to fruition when all of the external supports fall away, marking a philosophical shift from the use of religion for civic ends toward religion becoming the conscience of the nation. This is an important nuance within Wagner's religious philosophy in that it details the way in which religion lives and evolves within the community, finding purity through state progression. This concept departs from the National Socialist framework as National Socialism does not seek to separate the spiritual from the political necessity in the same way that Wagner proposed, instead redefining faith in a national context rather than as individual and spiritual.

"Only in the wholly adult State, where these religions have paled before the full-fledged patriotic duty, and are sinking into inessential forms and ceremonies; only where "Fate" has shewn itself to be Political Necessity—could true Religion step into the world."[48]

The purpose of the state, according to Wagner, is to provide stability to the nation, offering moral justification for state authority. It is not through unceasing conquest that the state achieves its understood purpose, but through the creation of a stable framework that affords the appropriate space to the people for their own spiritual evolution. Once the basic "primal needs" of a society are met, the nation is then capable of engaging with a higher process of spiritual-moral development, making necessity the prerequisite for a culture to flourish. This partially aligns with National Socialist philosophy's focus on order, unity, and subordination to the state, which serves the organic and eternal laws of the nation. However, Wagner placed a greater emphasis on the aesthetic and moral, rather than the political or racial, as is the case with National Socialism. The prime driver of his worldview is not the continuation of the race, but the thriving of spirit, art, and culture, which he does ultimately link to race, as previously discussed, but not to the same extent as National Socialism.

"Stability is therefore the intrinsic tendency of the State. And rightly; for it constitutes withal the unconscious aim in every higher human effort to get beyond the primal need: namely to reach a freer evolution of spiritual attributes, which is always cramped so long as hindrances forestall the satisfaction of that first root-need."[49]

In a 1937 address to the National Socialist Women's League in Nuremberg, Adolf Hitler discussed the roles of men and women and the process to which they unified under National Socialism, with the objective being the continuation of the people. As emphasized in this publication, the continuation of the race is the primary objective of National Socialism to which all decisions of the state and individuals must be subordinated. It is only secondary to this that National Socialism seeks to assist in the development and growth of the racial byproducts, such as culture, which is a more biologically rooted, and less Romantic position than what Wagner had suggested earlier.

It can be seen that in almost, if not all, of these major philosophical predecessors to National Socialism, exists seeds of racialism that had not yet developed until the biological determinism of the twentieth century. Thus, none can truly be said to fully embody National Socialism before its creation, despite the possibly romantic or exaggerated claims of Rudolf Jung and later scholars.

"As soon as this solution is accepted, the problem itself is no longer so difficult. Then it is no longer a question of so-called equal rights, but more a question of respective duties. There is no longer a dispute about which of the two sexes is privileged; rather, the profound realization arises that these sexes together make up the people, and that the continuation of the people is only possible through their cooperation."[50]

In no uncertain terms did Wagner call for the creative destruction of the inorganic society to serve as the catalyst for cultural renewal, rejecting the conservative impulse to preserve the decaying structure. Revolution offers an opportunity for the people to return to their particular authentic state, following necessity and nature instead of artificial or foreign authority.

"But only Revolution, not slavish Restoration, can give us back that highest Art–work."[51]

Again, this demonstrates both continuity and divergence with National Socialism, as it too positions itself as revolutionary, seeking the total cultural and moral separation from liberal modernity, but does so through an emphasis on racial construct, not artistic creation, as previously discussed. This is not to say that the rebirth of culture is not sought by National Socialism, but rather that it is understood to be eternally connected to the racial construct of the people and thus nearly guaranteed to flourish within racially appropriate circumstances. Conversely, the death of the race would also entail the death of its culture, for it can only come from its respective race.

In *Germany Speaks*, Joachim Ribbentrop wrote to this effect:

"But who would wish to deny that National Socialism is the great revolutionary revival of the German people in all spheres of life."[52]

Wagner can be seen moving towards the same thread of racial essentialism that was inflated following the influx of nineteenth-century racial science and philosophy, shifting from his focus on the cultural and moral decay of Europe toward a link between blood and spirit. He suggested that a nation's cultural renewal cannot occur outside of the biological context to which they are organic, transforming cultural decay from the realm of morality to a shared moral-biological one. This example demonstrates an uncommon ideological bridge from Wagner to National Socialist thought where it had been lacking, and as previously examined, had been obfuscated through his intense focus on culture itself. While this line of reason may be brief, it serves as a pivotal link in the intellectual connection between earlier German Romanticism and the later biological racialism.

"As there a total regeneration was needed of the European Folk-blood, so here a rebirth of the Folk-spirit might be required."[53]

Wagner believed that patriotism, and the fuel that drives this willingness to subordinate personal interest for the collective good, was commonly a byproduct of a spirit that was fundamentally competitive and egoistic, rather than rooted in moral duty or pure national love. This could be understood through a quasi-pacifist lens where Wagner is highlighting the torment of some for the greatness of others, or through a nationalist lens, where he is calling for a return to pure nationalism through an inward focus.

"The patriot subordinates himself to his State in order to raise it above all other States, and thus, as it were, to find his personal sacrifice repaid with ample interest through the might and greatness of his fatherland. Injustice and violence toward other States and peoples have therefore been the true dynamic law of Patriotism throughout all time."[54]

Despite the popular claim that National Socialism is an inherently imperialistic worldview, it does not seek competition with external forces outside of that required to safeguard the nation. The ultimate objective is the continuation of the race, for the sake of the race, not in opposition to a foreign one, which is of the same nature as the pure nationalism that Wagner had previously discussed.

In sum, many of Wagner's ideas and themes were adopted throughout both völkisch and National Socialist thought, most notably his organic vision of the nation as a living unity rooted in a shared culture and inner necessity. The rejection of the foreign and cosmopolitan in favor of community, nature, and a moral economy became solidified into primary components of National Socialist thought, with others, such as a central leader acting as the embodiment of national will, being formalized into codified law and often mischaracterized as a unique innovation under the NSDAP. In what could have been an act of self-protection from public scrutiny, Wagner frequently emphasized the aesthetic-moral and redemptive themes of European society through art, myth, and spirituality, leaving racial characteristics comparatively subdued when compared to their prominence within National Socialist thought. Wagner came to embody many of the symbolic elements that were later absorbed into National Socialism, with his writings and music supplying additional myth fit for appropriation. Finally, Adolf Hitler and Rudolf Jung both emphasized Wagner's importance, with Hitler asserting that an understanding of Wagner was essential to grasping the character of National Socialism[55]

Endnotes

1. Frank B. Josserand, "Richard Wagner and German Nationalism," *The Southwestern Social Science Quarterly* 43, no. 3 (1962): 223-34.

2. Evalyn A. Clark, "Adolf Wagner: From National Economist to National Socialist," *Political Science Quarterly* 55, no. 3 (1940): 378-411.

3. Richard Wagner, *Art and Politics*, trans. William Ashton Ellis (Lincoln: University of Nebraska Press, 1995), 147.

4. Richard Wagner, *The Art-Work of the Future*, trans. William Ashton Ellis (London: Kegan Paul, Trench, Trübner & Co., 1895), 4.

5. Nationalsozialistische Deutsche Arbeiterpartei, *Ich Kämpfe (I Fight): The Responsibilities of Party Comrades*, trans. Rad Cowdery, 20.

6. Rudolf Jung, *National Socialism: Its Foundations, Development, and Goals*, 2nd fully revised ed. (Munich: Deutscher Volksverlag, Dr. E. Boepple, 1922), 77.

7. Richard Wagner, *The Art-Work of the Future*, trans. William Ashton Ellis (London: Kegan Paul, Trench, Trübner & Co., 1895), 4.

8. Adolf Hitler, speech at the Hofbräuhaus-Festsaal, Munich, August 13, 1920, in *In His Own Words: The Essential Speeches of Adolf Hitler*, trans., comp., and with commentary by C. J. Miller (Antelope Hill Publishing).

9. Richard Wagner, *The Art-Work of the Future*, trans. William Ashton Ellis (London: Kegan Paul, Trench, Trübner & Co., 1895), 4.

10. Otto Dietrich, *The Philosophical Foundations of National-Socialism: A Call to Arms of the German Mind*, lecture delivered at the University of Köln, 16 November 1934, trans. Hadding Scott (2015), 5.

11. Richard Wagner, *The Art-Work of the Future*, trans. William Ashton Ellis (London: Kegan Paul, Trench, Trübner & Co., 1895), 15.

12. Richard Wagner, *The Art-Work of the Future*, trans. William Ashton Ellis (London: Kegan Paul, Trench, Trübner & Co., 1895), 14.

13. Richard Wagner, *The Art-Work of the Future*, trans. William Ashton Ellis (London: Kegan Paul, Trench, Trübner & Co., 1895), 58.

14. Kurt Schrey, *You and Your People: An English Translation of Du und dein Volk* (Munich, 1936), trans., ed., and introd. by Nathan R. Lawrence (Munich: Deutscher Volksverlag for the Reichsleitung der NSDAP, Hauptamt für Erzieher, 1936).

15. Richard Wagner, *The Art-Work of the Future*, trans. William Ashton Ellis (London: Kegan Paul, Trench, Trübner & Co., 1895), 10.

16. Nationalsozialistische Deutsche Arbeiterpartei, *Ich Kämpfe (I Fight): The Responsibilities of Party Comrades*, trans. Rad

Cowdery, 33.

17. Richard Wagner, *Art and Politics*, trans. William Ashton Ellis (Lincoln: University of Nebraska Press, 1995), 123.

18. Richard Wagner, *The Art-Work of the Future*, trans. William Ashton Ellis (London: Kegan Paul, Trench, Trübner & Co., 1895), 48.

19. Richard Wagner, *Judaism in Music (Das Judenthum in der Musik): Being the Original Essay Together with the Later Supplement*, trans. and ed. Edwin Evans, Sr. (London: William Reeves, 1910), 45.

20. Richard Wagner, *Judaism in Music (Das Judenthum in der Musik): Being the Original Essay Together with the Later Supplement*, trans. and ed. Edwin Evans, Sr. (London: William Reeves, 1910), 4.

21. Adolf Hitler, speech at the Hofbräuhaus-Festsaal, Munich, August 13, 1920, in *In His Own Words: The Essential Speeches of Adolf Hitler*, trans., comp., and with commentary by C. J. Miller (Antelope Hill Publishing).

22. Richard Wagner, *Judaism in Music (Das Judenthum in der Musik): Being the Original Essay Together with the Later Supplement*, trans. and ed. Edwin Evans, Sr. (London: William Reeves, 1910), 9.

23. Richard Wagner, *Judaism in Music (Das Judenthum in der Musik): Being the Original Essay Together with the Later Supplement*, trans. and ed. Edwin Evans, Sr. (London: William Reeves, 1910), 11.

24. Richard Wagner, *Judaism in Music (Das Judenthum in der Musik): Being the Original Essay Together with the Later Supplement*, trans. and ed. Edwin Evans, Sr. (London: William Reeves, 1910), 14.

25. Joseph Goebbels, *The Little ABC of National Socialism* (Munich: Zentralverlag der NSDAP, Franz Eher Nachf., 1933).

26. Richard Wagner, *Judaism in Music (Das Judenthum in der Musik): Being the Original Essay Together with the Later Supplement*, trans. and ed. Edwin Evans, Sr. (London: William Reeves, 1910), 18.

27. Richard Wagner, *Art and Revolution*, trans. William Ashton Ellis (London: Kegan Paul, Trench, Trübner & Co., 1895), 12.

28. Richard Wagner, *The Art-Work of the Future*, trans. William Ashton Ellis (London: Kegan Paul, Trench, Trübner & Co., 1895), 6.

29. Richard Wagner, *The Art-Work of the Future*, trans. William Ashton Ellis (London: Kegan Paul, Trench, Trübner & Co., 1895), 2.

30. The Personnel Office of the Wehrmacht, *Why We Fight* (Berlin: Oberkommando der Wehrmacht, 1941), 113.

31. Richard Wagner, *The Art-Work of the Future*, trans. William Ashton Ellis (London: Kegan Paul, Trench, Trübner & Co., 1895), 7.

32. The Personnel Office of the Wehrmacht, *Why We Fight* (Berlin: Oberkommando der Wehrmacht, 1941), 167.

33. Richard Wagner, *Art and Politics*, trans. William Ashton Ellis (Lincoln: University of Nebraska Press, 1995), 67.

34. The Personnel Office of the Wehrmacht, *Why We Fight* (Berlin: Oberkommando der Wehrmacht, 1941), 107.

35. Richard Wagner, *Art and Politics*, trans. William Ashton Ellis (Lincoln: University of Nebraska Press, 1995), 16.

36. Richard Wagner, *Art and Politics*, trans. William Ashton Ellis (Lincoln: University of Nebraska Press, 1995), 10.

37. The Personnel Office of the Wehrmacht, *Why We Fight* (Berlin: Oberkommando der Wehrmacht, 1941), 117.

38. Z. M. Szaz, "The Ideological Precursors of National Socialism," *Western Political Quarterly* 16, no. 4 (1963): 924-945.

39. Richard Wagner, *Art and Politics*, trans. William Ashton Ellis (Lincoln: University of Nebraska Press, 1995), 12.

40. Richard Wagner, *Art and Politics*, trans. William Ashton Ellis (Lincoln: University of Nebraska Press, 1995), 12.

41. Heinrich Himmler, *Defender against Bolshevism*, trans. from *Die Schutzstaffel als antibolschewistische Kampforganisation* (Berlin: Reichsführung-SS, 1936), 19.

42. Richard Wagner, *The Art-Work of the Future*, trans. William Ashton Ellis (London: Kegan Paul, Trench, Trübner & Co., 1895), 14.

THE GENEALOGY OF NATIONAL SOCIALISM   241

43. Richard Wagner, *The Art-Work of the Future*, trans. William Ashton Ellis (London: Kegan Paul, Trench, Trübner & Co., 1895), 11.

44. Richard Wagner, *Art and Revolution*, trans. William Ashton Ellis (London: Kegan Paul, Trench, Trübner & Co., 1895), 17.

45. Richard Wagner, *Art and Politics*, trans. William Ashton Ellis (Lincoln: University of Nebraska Press, 1995), 23.

46. Richard Wagner, *Art and Politics*, trans. William Ashton Ellis (Lincoln: University of Nebraska Press, 1995), 155.

47. Nationalsozialistische Deutsche Arbeiterpartei, *Ich Kämpfe (I Fight): The Responsibilities of Party Comrades*, trans. Rad Cowdery, 38.

48. Richard Wagner, *Art and Politics*, trans. William Ashton Ellis (Lincoln: University of Nebraska Press, 1995), 23.

49. Richard Wagner, *Art and Politics*, trans. William Ashton Ellis (Lincoln: University of Nebraska Press, 1995), 11.

50. Adolf Hitler, "Address to the National Socialist Women's League," Reich Party Congress *"Rally of Labor,"* Nuremberg, September 10, 1937, in *In His Own Words: The Essential Speeches of Adolf Hitler*, trans., comp., and with commentary by C. J. Miller (Antelope Hill Publishing).

51. Richard Wagner, *Art and Revolution*, trans. William Ashton Ellis (London: Kegan Paul, Trench, Trübner & Co., 1895), 14.

52. Joahim von Ribbentrop, *Germany Speaks: By 21 Leading Members of Party and State*, pref. by Joachim von Ribbentrop (London: T. Butterworth Ltd., 1938), 120.

53. Richard Wagner, *Art and Politics*, trans. William Ashton Ellis (Lincoln: University of Nebraska Press, 1995), 40.

54. Richard Wagner, *Art and Politics*, trans. William Ashton Ellis (Lincoln: University of Nebraska Press, 1995), 16.

55. George Beiswanger, "Richard Wagner: Oracle of National Socialism," *The American Scholar* 11, no. 2 (1942): 228-42.

Chapter 6
Friedrich Wilhelm Joseph Schelling

Friedrich Wilhelm Joseph Schelling (1775-1854) was a philosopher who served as yet another bridge between Immanuel Kant's critical philosophy and the German idealism that would flourish throughout the early nineteenth century. The majority of Schelling's philosophy sought to reconcile nature and the spirit, a theme that sat at the core of many subsequent nationalist worldviews, including National Socialism. Schelling was an early disciple of Fichte and exerted an early intellectual influence on Hegel, firmly positioning himself within the genealogy of German Idealism itself.[1] Due to his relatively small impact on the overall development of National Socialist thought, he will be afforded a smaller chapter proportionate to his contribution, which can be mostly seen in his rejection of rigid forms of rationalism and his insistence on nature existing as a living, self-organizing entity complete with intelligence and purpose.

Schelling's early works, particularly *Ideas for a Philosophy of Nature* (1797) and *First Outline of a System of the Philosophy of Nature* (1799), posited that nature is ruled by eternal laws that work as self-legislating powers, unfolding according to interior drives rather than through external reaction. Many of these themes were echoed by thinkers such as Oswald Spengler and Alfred Rosenberg, who envisioned the nation as an organic lifeform that is bound to preordained natural and spiritual laws, though they reinterpreted these laws in a more material and racial sense that diverged from Schelling's metaphysical intention. Schelling eventually linked freedom to the eternal moral essence of the individual in his later work, *Philosophical Investigations into the Nature of Human Freedom* (1809), aligning with the Romantic search for a unity within the natural order.

Although Schelling did not directly engage with political philosophy, some of his concepts, especially involving the organic fulfillment of the self, the natural hierarchy that appears in nature, and the rejection of the universal, contributed to the Romantic conception of the Volksgeist. Despite rejecting the mechanistic materialism that characterized a significant aspect of Enlightenment rationality, his teleological and autonomous conception of nature offered a metaphysical framework that allowed for a deeper synthesis with later racial theory. In this way, his work exists more as a Romantic foundation from which the organic tendencies of later nationalism found root, rather than a direct ideological precursor to National Socialism.

Schelling's philosophy proved to be a pivotal point of transition for German Idealism, situated between Fichte's moral voluntarism and Hegel's dialectical rationalism. He decisively influenced Romanticism's shift toward organic metaphors of life, spirit, and nation, which would later be seen as providing central vocabulary to nineteenth and twentieth-century nationalists. National Socialist philosophy later took up the conception of eternal law, albeit in a different capacity to that of Schelling, but nonetheless with similar vocabulary and a recognizable philosophical structure. In Schelling's 1809 publication, *Philosophical Investigations into the Nature of Human Freedom*, freedom is presented as an eternal moral essence rooted in divine order. In this way, all people's deeds reveal the character of their eternal will. When directly compared to National Socialist thought, language referring to destiny and predestination can be frequently seen, with both united in the concept of eternal participation in the divine. The philosophical connection diverges sharply at this point, as National Socialism directly connects the eternal spirit and will with the biological composition of the nation itself, whereas Schelling conceives of a much more abstract metaphysical earthly whole.

"We too assert a predestination but in a completely different sense, namely in this: as man acts here so has he acted from eternity and already in the beginning of creation. His action does not become, just as he|himself does not become a moral being, but rather it is eternal by nature."[2]

As can be seen in the earlier presented examples of the National Socialist position on antisemitism, the hate that National Socialists expressed were rooted in a profound love for their community and the rejection of that which was damaging it. This connects with Schelling's metaphysical examination of polarity, where he concluded that evil and hatred are not independent principles, arising when divine love is resisted or misdirected. Hatred is thus not an autonomous power, but rather love tinged by self-will.

"The soul of all hate is love, and in the most violent wrath only the stillness of the most inner centrum, attacked and excited, shows itself."[3]

Schelling rejected the mechanistic worldview common with Enlightenment rationalism, describing nature as a self-legislating and self-organizing organism that produces not only its own sense of order, but also its purpose. It has been claimed that later National Socialist thinkers misappropriated this concept through its repositioning as a philosophical backing to biological determinism, a philosophically reductive interpretation. As ideas develop, it is only natural for aspects to be shed and new elements to be introduced to fortify the weaker points of previous thought, and this is a clear example of such. Schelling certainly contributed to the broader atmosphere of organic existence and fulfillment, but he was far from the only one to contribute in such a way and focused most of his studies away from the areas that truly powered National Socialist thought, which is why he has been afforded a slimmer chapter compared to the likes of Fichte or Wagner.

"Since Nature gives itself its sphere of activity, no foreign power can interfere with it; all of its laws are immanent, or Nature is its own legislator (autonomy of Nature)."[4]

Additionally, the idea that natural law cannot be interfered with contradicts a major focus of National Socialism: the resistance of foreign influence. It is because foreign influence and spirit are capable of altering the cultural and social dynamic of the nation that National Socialism seeks to resist its involvement. Schelling's autonomy of nature speaks to a universal order which is incapable of being externally corrupted, whereas National Socialism reinterprets this concept at the level of the national community. In *The Little ABC of National Socialism*, Joseph Goebbels describes the need for the nation to expel the culturally and racially foreign from the nation in order to restore wholeness to the nation's spirit.

"By the means of eliminating everything racially and culturally foreign from the body of the German Volk and leading the German people back to the original wellsprings of the German race, German spirit, and German culture."[5]

Similar to the later work of Oswald Spengler, Schelling emphasized the determinate development of natural stages, each corresponding to the character and nature of the subject. To him, nature progresses through structured stages, all containing a distinct character, teleologically moving towards the absolute. The individual stages are set in particular forms, with freedom belonging not to the individual, but to the total process itself. Therefore, it can be said that to Schelling, freedom is found in upholding the preordained characteristics of the configuration of natural law, connecting to National Socialist thought in a relatively abstract way, and outside of their focus on the material.

"Every stage of development has a peculiar character. At every stage of development, formative Nature is restricted to a determinate—sole possible—form; it is completely bound with respect to this form, and in the production of this form it will show no freedom at all."[6]

While Schelling does speak on eternal elements, he does so in a far more abstract way than its expression under National Socialist thought. For Schelling, the concept of eternity was in reference to the continuation of the creative process, amounting to continuous cycles of formation and dissolution, whereas National Socialism repositioned this metaphysical concept into one that is centered around the biological permanence of race. National Socialism adopts the position of eternal racial laws that stand unchanged throughout time, forming the philosophical-biological backbone of its exclusionary doctrine. It is through this backbone, absent in Schelling's philosophy, that the means of national continuation are sought and recognized as the primary national objective. It is for this reason that the contributions

Schelling provided in this regard were at most taken from the general organic metaphors he articulated, rather than his specific formulation. Many of the philosophers discussed previously, particularly Fichte and Arndt, would handle the concept of eternal organic law in a more directly proto-völkisch manner that fed into National Socialist thought.

The placement of the individual within the span of one's ancestors is highly reminiscent of later National Socialist rhetoric, speaking to the self-perpetutating process of life and death, all within the greater divine organism. Schelling recognized continuity to reflect the endless circulation of organic law, with life returning to spirit and spirit into life. Despite the parallel imagery, Schelling's vision of endless circulation was not carried forward as he initially intended into National Socialist thought, which narrowed the metaphysical focus into a biological and nationalistic one, examining racial continuity from a biological standpoint.

"The individual passes away, only the species remains, but Nature never ceases to be active. However, since Nature is infinitely active, and since this infinite activity must present itself by means of finite products, Nature must return into itself through an endless circulation."[7]

In no uncertain terms does National Socialism position the nation, and thus the race, as the ultimate moral unit, and in some ways it can be argued that it collapses spiritual depth into biological constraints. This is a crucial element to examine when attempting to understand the National Socialist position on religion, as the moral rooting of the nation is found in biological continuation, not in external spiritual authority or constraints. The entirety of National Socialist philosophy is dedicated to the support of the biological unit itself; which becomes the central moral focus of the nation: its continuation. This is precisely why National Socialist texts from leading figures such as Adolf Hitler, Joseph Goebbels, and Gottfried Feder, speak to the limitation of religious practice within the bounds of harm it may pose to the nation and its morality. This demonstrates both the scope of acceptable conduct, which is set by the state to serve the nation rather than the church, and the existence of a racially-bound moral order outside of established religion and its practice. All aspects of life, including the individual practice of faith, becomes subservient to national wellbeing and collective progress.

Hitler spoke to such in a 1939 speech, where he asserted, in a way aligned with the sentiments of the aforementioned thinkers, that National Socialism does not seek to control religious practices, but that religious practice is nonetheless confined to a certain extent.

"The National Socialist state has neither closed a church, nor prevented a service, nor has it ever had any influence on the form of a service. It has neither influenced the doctrine nor the confession of any denomination. In the National Socialist state, everyone can seek salvation in his own fashion. However, the National Socialist state will deal with priests who, instead of being servants of God, make it their mission to denigrate our present Reich, its institutions, or its leading minds, by making them realize that the destruction of this state by anyone will not be tolerated. As soon as a priest steps outside the bounds of the law, he will be held accountable to the law just like any other German citizen."[8]

Schelling presents organic life as absolute and immortal, due to its embodiment of the self-perpetuating vitality of the divine, making life itself an eternal manifestation of spirit. To him, death represents a spiritual return to the infinite, a reabsorption of the finite organic form into the eternal being, rather than an end. This concept opposes the mechanistic materialism of Enlightenment thought, instead emphasizing the transient nature of the individual within a larger, infinite process. This aspect of Schelling's philosophy again entered into the greater worldview that is National Socialism, applying the concept of the eternal wellspring of spirit within a biological context. National Socialism does look toward the complete system of existence, of which the nation is but a part, as providing laws for organic life, but recognizes the larger system to be maintained by separate, interacting, components. The disconnect between the philosophy of Schelling and National Socialism is clear at this point of biological deviation, which constitutes the primary system of interest and spirit for National Socialist thought, operating in parallel concepts to that of Schelling.

"As long as it is organic the product can never sink into indifference. If it is to support the universal striving toward indifference, then it must first sink to a product of a lower potency. As an organic product it cannot die, and when it does die it is really already no longer organic. Death is the return into universal indifference. Just for that reason the organic product is absolute, immortal. For it is an organic product at all, because indifference can never be reached by it. Only at the moment when it has ceased to be organic does the product resolve itself into the universal indifference."[9]

Schelling highlighted the nature of disease as a relative phenomenon, existing only when in relation to the organic whole, and arising as a true state of disease only when it begins to threaten the organism's continued existence. The very concept of disease thus presupposes a harmonic norm, through the identification of a deviation from equilibrium. The concept of a diseased body politic was adopted by National Socialist thought, albeit in the aforementioned racial-biological context, in a way that does not stand in blatant contradiction to Schelling's framework but nonetheless reduces his dialectical vision to a more rigid and narrow adaptation of its logic.

"The concept of disease is a completely relative concept, for first of all it has meaning only for the organic product of Nature; that is, in the concept of disease one thinks not only the concept of a deviation from some rule, order or proportion, but also that the deviation does not exist with the existence of the product as such; the latter determination really completes the concept of disease."[10]

In *First Outline of a System of the Philosophy of Nature,* Schelling articulated a core principle from his Naturphilosophie: that all organisms remain confined to their predetermined forms, and that healthy action is movement toward the continued reproduction of the determined form. Schelling's emphasis on limitation functioning as a positive and creative force reveals his belief that necessity itself is not the negation of freedom, but its greater realization. This metaphysical vision where life functions as the self-repeating embodiment of the divine order aligns with the central component of National Socialist thought, with the continuation of the nation being represented in similar vocabulary and philosophical structure. It must be noted once more that despite the similarities in metaphysical construction, Schelling was ultimately suggesting a spiritual law of continuity that stands apart from the concentrated biological focus toward racial preservation characteristic of National Socialism.

"Since each organism is limited to a determinate form, all of its activity must be directed toward the production and reproduction of this form. Therefore, the real reason why every organism reproduces only itself to infinity is to be sought in the original limitation of its formative drive, but not in some preformed seeds, for whose existence there is not a shadow of proof."[11]

Friedrich Schelling's philosophy, particularly his conception of nature as a self-legislating, organic whole animated by divine intelligence, marked a significant philosophical turning point away from the mechanistic materialism of Enlightenment thought toward a unity of life and spirit. His portrayal of eternal reproduction, renewal, and the harmony he envisioned between freedom and necessity resonated with later Romantic and nationalist imagery. Despite this, Schelling's contribution to National Socialist philosophy remains indirect and symbolic. The organic metaphors he constructed blended with biological determinism and racial science, further developing and transforming the spiritual continuity which he presented. In this sense, Schelling's organic metaphysics that were born from Romantic idealism, were conceptually inherited yet transformed by National Socialist thought, blending with the works of other thinkers to produce the distinct National Socialist worldview.

Endnotes

1. Arthur S. Dewing, "The Significance of Schelling's Theory of Knowledge," *The Philosophical Review* 19, no. 2 (March 1910): 154-167.

2. Friedrich Wilhelm Joseph Schelling, *Philosophical Investigations into the Essence of Human Freedom*, trans. Jeff Love and Johannes Schmidt (Albany: State University of New York Press, 2006), 52.

3. Friedrich Wilhelm Joseph Schelling, *Philosophical Investigations into the Essence of Human Freedom*, trans. Jeff Love and Johannes Schmidt (Albany: State University of New York Press, 2006), 64.

4. Friedrich Wilhelm Joseph Schelling, *First Outline of a System of the Philosophy of Nature*, trans. Keith R. Peterson (Albany: State University of New York Press, 2004), 17.

5. Joseph Goebbels, *The Little ABC of National Socialism* (1935).

6. Friedrich Wilhelm Joseph Schelling, *First Outline of a System of the Philosophy of Nature*, trans. Keith R. Peterson (Albany: State University of New York Press, 2004), 35.

7. Friedrich Wilhelm Joseph Schelling, *First Outline of a System of the Philosophy of Nature*, trans. Keith R. Peterson (Albany: State University of New York Press, 2004), 42.

8. Adolf Hitler, speech on church and state, Berlin, January 30th, 1939, in *In His Own Words: The Essential Speeches of Adolf Hitler*, trans., comp., and with commentary by C. J. Miller (Antelope Hill Publishing).

9. Friedrich Wilhelm Joseph Schelling, *First Outline of a System of the Philosophy of Nature*, trans. Keith R. Peterson (Albany: State University of New York Press, 2004), 68.

10. Friedrich Wilhelm Joseph Schelling, *First Outline of a System of the Philosophy of Nature*, trans. Keith R. Peterson (Albany: State University of New York Press, 2004), 159.

11. Friedrich Wilhelm Joseph Schelling, *First Outline of a System of the Philosophy of Nature*, trans. Keith R. Peterson (Albany: State University of New York Press, 2004), 47.

Chapter 7
The Völkisch Movement

The German Völkisch movement emerged in the late nineteenth century, taking the form of a reaction to widespread industrialization, cosmopolitanism, and Enlightenment rationalism. The perceived moral decline of Germany, alongside the mechanization of life, provoked many Germans to look toward national tradition and myth, along with the land and blood from which it springs. This search for national redemption that formed the Völkisch movement resulted in the formation of the living embodiment of the Romantic ideal that began with Herder's Volksgeist, Fichte's moral nationalism, and Arndt's national spirituality, among others.

Unlike much of the philosophy present at the time, the Völkisch movement was not constrained to theory, as it permeated the cultural, moral, and political lives of Germans, producing tangible effects. Despite the commonalities, it cannot be said that this movement was monolithic, nor that it carried over a consistent systematic philosophy as is the case with Fichte's work or National Socialism. Additionally, despite philosophers and academically involved thinkers offering concepts that would later be carried into practice, the Völkisch ideal did not flourish academically in the same way that it did in the popular imagination, where hiking clubs, youth leagues, folk societies, and more embodied the concept through the union of nature and nation.

The German Völkisch movement did not constitute the emergence of a new philosophy, but rather a shifting synthesis of ideas stemming from a century of German idealist, romantic, and nationalist thought. Many of these intellectual and emotional precursors overlap with National Socialist philosophy, but it is important to note that while they may be closely related temporally and spatially, and in many ways ideologically, they are not interchangeable expressions of the same concept. Herder's particularistic organic essence, the Volksgeist, was recognized as manifesting through the language, land, and traditions of the people, just as Fichte's concept of national renewal through collective moral duty heavily impacted Völkisch thought. From men such as Arndt and Jahn came a populist appeal to physical regeneration and purity, which merged with the particular and communal spirit to form this shared philosophical backbone. Completed through List's economic nationalism and rejection of cosmopolitan trade, Wagner's Romantic aesthetic and myth, and the contributions of many more thinkers, statesmen, and artists, this synthesis of thought can more clearly be understood. It is also for this reason why National Socialism stands as the logical continuation of such an undefined and open-ended social-intellectual movement, as it could only progress towards a systemized philosophy or digress away from such.

Philosophically, this movement was heavily rooted in the Herderian Volksgeist, which emphasized the spiritual and cultural particularism of a people, and was carried over from imagination into deliberate practice during this movement. Herder's construction of the Volksgeist, along with its later application has already been detailed in his respective chapter, but it must be emphasized that this new development of national particularism was rooted more directly in race than with its original conception, and as applied by the Völkisch movement surpassed the previous civic nationalistic concept that was primarily centered on legal citizenship. Instead, emphasis shifted toward language, faith, and blood. This transition from civic to ethnic nationalism marks a major milestone in the development of National Socialist philosophy, as a metaphysical pivot toward National Socialism's biological foundations, where the philosophy that drives the worldview functions to support the racial framework.

Beginning as a quest for cultural renewal, this movement quickly evolved into a loosely organized range of writers, artists, and activists who sought to rebuild German spirituality through popular myth and heritage. The vocabulary of rebirth awakened Germany and provoked a renewed interest in the sacred bond formed between the people, land, and their history. Collective redemption was sought through the resurrection of folk tradition, pagan symbology, and medieval legend, replacing liberal concepts with the ancestral self. In this way, the Völkisch movement was not merely a reactionary occurrence, but rather a deeper metaphysical shift that took up odds against national deracination, asserting its organic form as the healthy point of national reference. Simply put, to be "Völkisch" was to see redemption through the eternal and natural laws of life.

Due to the connection between the Völkisch movement's ideas and thinkers and that of National Socialism, it has remained a heavily contested subject in modern German historiography. While some have dismissed its driving thought as indistinguishable from National Socialism, modern historians have increasingly begun to recognize it as separate, but nonetheless a final point of fusion between its intellectual lineages that directly fed into National Socialism. It would be most accurate to describe this movement as the last major point of philosophical and ideological convergence because if it were to be the

THE GENEALOGY OF NATIONAL SOCIALISM   257

definitive final point of such it would be equivalent as no additional integration would have occurred, which is clearly not the case. Thus, it can be said that the Völkisch movement vaguely and sporadically synthesized a significant portion of the range of ideas that would lead to its final construction under National Socialism.

Before 1945, the Völkisch movement was discussed more in terms of the living embodiment of the ideals themselves rather than analyzed in academic terms or through the placement of National Socialism as the direct successor to the Völkisch worldview. The term is derived from the German word Volk, meaning "people," and was popularized by intellectuals who were seeking a moral and cultural renewal for Germany, but the movement itself functioned as a living organism that was less intellectualized and more experienced as living revelation.[1]

Through French involvement, both relating to Napoleon and to the French Revolution itself, the philosophical inheritance had been shaped and German thought had begun to recognize the political potential of national consciousness, as can be seen with Fichte's *Addresses to the German Nation*, where a national moral imperative is created. This coupled with the influence of early Romantics, like Schelling, Arndt, Jahn, and Görres, established an ideological dichotomy that defined Völkisch thought: the organic nation versus the mechanized, inorganic. This vocabulary drew from nineteenth-century philosophy and nationalistic debate that sought identity through language, culture, and history, and such can be seen in the reconciliation of religion, art, and all else into a singular moral unity.[2]

Thinkers such as Paul de Lagarde, Julius Langbehn, and Houston Stewart Chamberlain also played a role in shaping the vocabulary of the movement. In *Deutsche Schriften*, Lagarde directly rejected cosmopolitanism, and liberalism in favor of a Christianity purified by the nation.[3] Legarde's rejection of cosmopolitanism continued to ground truth in the national, not the universal, thus connecting religion and blood as inseparable elements. Similarly, Langbehn's *Rembrandt als Erzieher* contrasted the authentic spirit of Germany with that of the superficial urban decadence that he saw to be gripping the nation, further focusing public rhetoric on the aforementioned organic dichotomy.[4]

The racial depth of the movement primarily originates from Chamberlain's 1899 publication *Foundations of the Nineteenth Century*, which portrayed history as the product of the indomitable Aryan spirit.[5] Through his works, Chamberlain provided a scientific and logical justification for biological deterministic theory and its impact on cultural and civilizational development. This step from metaphysical notions of spirit to biological ones of blood functioned as a decisive step from Romantic organicism to the variety of racial determinism that is shared by both the Völkisch and National Socialist worldviews.[6]

From these works, came a blended moral theology and societal criticism into a program devoted to the salvation of the nation in body and spirit. This blend was later identified as crucial to the movement's development by historians who recognized it as a bridge between the criticism of culture and full-scale political radicalization.[7] These racial foundations that defined this earlier movement functioned as the core of National Socialist racial theory.

Throughout the Wilhelmine Empire (1888-1918), many historians and writers framed Völkisch thought as less of an ideology, and more of an expression of German patriotism. Even large journals like *Der Kunstwart* and *Heimat* encouraged such ideologies as a cure for the rampant materialism that followed Western Europe's period of industrialization.[8] Additionally, well-respected historians such as Heinrich von Treitschke interacted with the growing movement's ideas and framed nationalism as a central element to the fulfillment of Germany's historical mission.[9]

Unlike with National Socialism, the intellectual construct that resulted in the Völkisch movement was more based in romantic idealism than systematic doctrine, allowing for widespread adaptability across many disciplines such as politics, art, and religion. Flexibility in this way is not seen under National Socialism's rigid central framework that maintains a particular composition with no deviation permitted.[10]

Völkisch ideas reemerged in the Weimar Republic following Germany's loss in World War I, with thinkers like Arthur Moeller van den Bruck and Oswald Spengler re-envisioning the earlier romantic positions in the context of rebirth and civilization decline. Both men envisioned the fall of Germany to be the crucible through which the nation would be purified; a resurrection through national catastrophe.

Many of these ideas were synthesized into their nearly final form throughout the 1910's by Rudolf Jung, who took elements of Völkisch thought in order to produce the systematic philosophical doctrine that is National Socialism. Jung's 1922 publication, *Der Nationale Sozialismus*, transformed the loose cultural spirituality of the Völkisch movement into a complete philosophy, containing its own unique and interconnected worldview centered around eternal racial laws. Under the Third Reich, the state chose certain völkisch authors to be recognized as prophetic forebears of National Socialism, further tightening the diversity of the movement retrospectively. This may be one of the reasons for the over-conflation of the two by some scholars, along with the retrospective flattening of the multiplicity of thought that truly characterized Völkisch thought.

Uwe Puschner's *Die völkische Bewegung im wilhelminischen Kaiserreich* frames the movement as a nationale Gegenkultur, or counterculture, where publishers, religious reformers, and the public united under the quest for moral renewal and cultural reform. He further asserted the unique way in which Völkisch ideas circulated, surpassing class and regional boundaries, connecting middle-class intellectuals, farmers, clergy, and artists within a common language of renewal.[11] In *Die Völkischen in Deutschland*, Stefan Breuer mapped the pluralist extent of Völkisch thought, examining its range from mystical Christian influences to elements of racialism. Both of these historians emphasized the role of diverse thought in the Völkisch movement, contrasting the previously held perspectives by scholars that summed its entirety to be a singular, unified worldview.[12]

Breuer's research demonstrates how religious practice within the Völkisch movement existed along a wide spectrum that spanned from Protestant to Neopagan. The philosophical merger between faith and nation completed the process which began with Fichte's moral idealism and Wagner's aesthetic myth, imbuing the people with the divine, continuing only through collective national salvation. Through the analysis of religion as a cultural symbol in addition to a faith, the depth of the Völkisch search for rebirth can be seen beyond everyday political discourse. This has illuminated the way in which the language of religion, such as purity, redemption, and divine providence, was infused into the German nationalism of the time, creating a quasi-religious movement.

More modern research focuses on regional comparisons, demonstrating the way that Völkisch themes and language appeared in similar movements across Europe, and in doing so demystifies both the philosophy and the history of the movement. The heavy emphasis on nature, the obsession with national myth, and the rejection of cosmopolitanism parallel France's *Action Française*, England's Arts and Crafts movement, and Russia's Slavophile revival, suggesting that the German movement was one part of a larger European movement away from internationalism and liberal notions of "modernity." When taken together, a twenty-first-century study of the movement indicates that the Völkisch movement was multidimensional and constituted much more than simply a precursor to National Socialism.

Following Germany's loss of World War II in 1945 came a radical shift in how scholars interpreted the ideas that took hold throughout the Völkisch movement, leading to the eventual development of the Sonderweg thesis, which portrayed the Völkisch movement as contributing to Germany's spiritual deviation from liberal modernization. The thesis identified a tangible point of spiritual deviation, although the source was not centered around the rejection of liberalism alone but from Enlightenment rationalism itself as well.

Regarding postwar historiography, Fritz Stern and George L. Mosse led the way with in-depth examinations of leading Völkisch figures. Thinkers such as Lagarde and Langbehn were portrayed by Stern in his 1961 book *The Politics of Cultural Despair* as frustrated intellectuals who sought to transform modernity into moral absolutism.[13] In actuality, Lagarde's religiously infused nationalism and Langbehn's aesthetic moralism mark one of the last major milestones of the development of National Socialist philosophy before its direct emergence, with both emphasizing morality and unity above freedom and individuality.

In *The Crisis of German Ideology*, George L. Mosse analyzed the mystical elements of Völkisch nationalism and racial idealism as cultural and political forces, describing Völkisch ideology as a sort of secular religion.[14] This assertion does seem to be well grounded in this instance, as there was a prevailing influence of national metaphor and myth that had been animated through Romantic thought, which fused politics and spirituality to a certain extent. Historical examples of nations who have claimed providential guidance or the like are many, diminishing an often overused point in that the Völkisch movement and National Socialism were extreme due to this unification of spiritual destiny and nationhood. Furthermore, it can be asserted that National Socialism features a more moderate approach to theological ideas and their integration than some of the factions within the Völkisch movement, again speaking to the unification and precision of the National Socialist worldview, and the lack of such within the greater Völkisch movement.

Hans Kohn's *The Idea of Nationalism* primarily focused on contrasting Germany's racial and philosophical nationalism with the civic nationalist models of France and Britain.[15] Kohn made a point of noting the dangers associated with grounding a national identity in race rather than citizenship, which is commonly recognized as the negative moral turning point. The proposition of such is simply asserting the objective correctness of the liberal model, meaning that the Völkisch movement, and thus too its successor in racial theory, National Socialism, are inherently immoral because they are not liberal. This epidemic of "critical" historians transformed Völkisch studies from what was largely unbiased scholarship into a moral inquiry, connecting much of the scholarship to the NSDAP, regardless of their factual association, in order to impose moral judgment. This severely flattens the true ideological diversity that existed within the Völkisch movement.

The *Völkisch* movement reached its philosophical peak during the years surrounding the First World War and under the Weimar Republic. The concept that redemption could be found through an organic unity of people, land, and destiny, otherwise known as the Volksgemeinschaft, can be clearly seen as the logical continuation of

German idealist thought, not a concept distinct to the NSDAP, or even National Socialism. It must be noted that while this concept is not unique to National Socialism, the way in which it synthesizes it with biological determinism and then anchors the resulting product as the moral core of the nation, is certainly unique to National Socialism.

It was not until these concepts were fully synthesized in 1922 by Rudolf Jung, that a true systematic philosophical doctrine was born. Jung's *Der nationale Sozialismus* was the first complete program that defined National Socialism, its objectives, and its connections to earlier German thought, positioning him the true father of National Socialism. The *Völkisch* notion of national rebirth was thus reformed to be defined through action and will instead of merely faith. Later under the Third Reich, the state chose certain völkisch authors to be recognized as prophetic forebears of National Socialism, further tightening the diversity of the movement retrospectively.

Historiographically, it was not until the 1970s-1990s when the pluralist thesis emerged, placing a large emphasis on recognizing the diversity and discontinuities of the *Völkisch* movement and its ideas. Scholars like Roger Chickering, David Blackbourn, and Geoff Eley contend that the Völkisch movement was not a direct precursor to National Socialism, but instead one of the many reactions to industrialization and social change. This more tempered approach recognizes that nationalism, populism, and romanticism were not uncommon throughout all of Europe at the time, stripping the uniqueness from Germany's circumstances, returning Germany to its European context in which it more accurately should be situated. Despite this growing understanding of the diversity within the Völkisch movement, the sources and arguments dealing with the matter must contend with an imposing moral residue, resulting from both the actions of the past, and reactionary bias of the initial researchers.

The legacy of the *Völkisch* movement is not simply historical, but also philosophical, nearing the closure of the circle started by the early German Romantics, and finishing in National Socialist philosophy.

Endnotes

1. Stefan Breuer, *Die Völkischen in Deutschland: Kaiserreich und Weimarer Republik* (Darmstadt: Wissenschaftliche Buchgesellschaft, 2008).

2. Fritz Stern, *The Politics of Cultural Despair: A Study in the Rise of the Germanic Ideology* (Berkeley: University of California Press, 1961).

3. Paul de Lagarde, *Deutsche Schriften* (Göttingen: Dieterich, 1878-1881).

4. Julius Langbehn, *Rembrandt als Erzieher* (Leipzig: Hirschfeld, 1890).

5. Houston Stewart Chamberlain, *Die Grundlagen des neunzehnten Jahrhunderts* (Munich: F. Bruckmann, 1899).

6. George L. Mosse, *The Crisis of German Ideology: Intellectual Origins of the Third Reich* (New York: Grosset & Dunlap, 1964).

7. Fritz Stern, *The Politics of Cultural Despair: A Study in the Rise of the Germanic Ideology* (Berkeley: University of California Press, 1961).

8. Uwe Puschner, *Die völkische Bewegung im wilhelminischen Kaiserreich: Sprache, Rasse, Religion* (Darmstadt: Wissenschaftliche Buchgesellschaft, 2001).

9. Fritz Stern, *The Politics of Cultural Despair: A Study in the Rise of the Germanic Ideology* (Berkeley: University of California Press, 1961).

10. Stefan Breuer, *Die Völkischen in Deutschland: Kaiserreich und Weimarer Republik* (Darmstadt: Wissenschaftliche Buchgesellschaft, 2008).

11. Uwe Puschner, *Die völkische Bewegung im wilhelminischen Kaiserreich: Sprache, Rasse, Religion* (Darmstadt: Wissenschaftliche Buchgesellschaft, 2001).

12. Stefan Breuer, *Die Völkischen in Deutschland: Kaiserreich und Weimarer Republik* (Darmstadt: Wissenschaftliche Buchgesellschaft, 2008).

13. Fritz Stern, *The Politics of Cultural Despair: A Study in the Rise of the Germanic Ideology* (Berkeley: University of California Press, 1961).

14. George L. Mosse, *The Crisis of German Ideology: Intellectual Origins of the Third Reich* (New York: Grosset & Dunlap, 1964).

15. Hans Kohn, *The Idea of Nationalism: A Study in Its Origins and Background* (New York: Macmillan, 1944).

www.ingramcontent.com/pod-product-compliance
Lightning Source LLC
Chambersburg PA
CBHW060454030426
42337CB00015B/1591